Also Published By Transgress Press

Giving It Raw:
Nearly 30 Years with AIDS
Francisco Ibañez-Carrasco

Letters for My Sisters:
Transitional Wisdom in Retrospect
Edited by Andrea James and Deanne Thornton

Manning Up:
Transsexual Men on Finding Brotherhood, Family and Themselves
Edited by Zander Keig and Mitch Kellaway

Hung Jury:
Testimonies of Genital Surgery by Transsexual Men
Edited by Trystan Theosophus Cotten

Love, Always

Love, Always

Partners of Trans People on Intimacy, Challenge, and Resilience

Edited by
Jordon Johnson and Becky Garrison

First published 2015 by Transgress Press

Library of Congress Cataloguing in Publication Data
Love, Always: Partners of Trans People on Intimacy, Challenge and Resilience / Edited by Jordon Johnson and Becky Garrison

ISBN: 0986084409
ISBN: 9780986084409
Cover design by Seth Raines
Transgress Press, Oakland, California

Contents

CHALLENGES

Foreword

Diane Anderson-Minshall and Helen Boyd

We all have origin stories, those little fables—true or not—that help us make sense of who we are, where we came from, and where we fit in the world around us. They are the emotional vignettes we trot out when we fall in love, get married, have kids, lose someone dear, choose (or lose) a career and so much more.

For some people, coming out as trans*—or at least waking up to their own gender differences—helps reframe or illuminate their origin story, like pieces of a baffling puzzle long worked on that can finally be finished. So much of their life makes sense in this new light, so many things ultimately explained.

The irony is that the same origin story can be read in innumerable ways, depending on the needs of the storyteller. A child assigned female at birth who hated playing with dolls may later think that's because he is really a trans* man; another also assigned female at birth may later think that's because she is really a lesbian. And that's true for each of them; our origin stories are our own to shift, rethink, rescale, and reorganize like those puzzle pieces to explain our own lives to ourselves and to others.

The partners of trans* people are no different in this, except it is often our partner's shifting identity that influences, sometimes even reinforces, our own. When Diane's wife of 16 years came out as a trans* man, she steadfastly held on to the lesbian identity she claimed, later shifting to lesbian-identified bisexual to queer. When Helen's boyfriend first told her she "sometimes like to wear women's clothes" and later came out as trans*, Helen's identity shifted from heterosexual to queer het to just plain queer. Today, Helen has a wife of 13 years, Diane has a husband of 24 years, and neither of us is as dogmatic and unwavering in our own identity as we once were. And there's a beauty in that insecurity that is life changing, affirming, confusing and chaotic all at once.

That's what having a trans* partner can do for some, as many of the best pieces in this collection show. Whether they were with their partner before or after they came out as a trans* person, their identity may influence yours in ways you've never imagined, and suddenly you are perceived by the outside world at least as gay or straight, lesbian or bisexual, when those were never words you previously used to define yourself. Often, it leaves us somewhere in the middle, wanting to both grow into this wonderful new way of being and still clinging to the identity we've always claimed.

Connie North learns to rely on Gloria Anzaldúa 's theory of *borderlands*, the reality that "some part of us always bleeds beyond the boxes of our own making." She writes that she "craved an understanding from those around me that I still identified as queer—that I still fit into a queer community—despite our outer trappings when we entered a room together or the male pronouns I used when describing my partner to others. Partly out of necessity, I let go of the desire to control other people's assumptions as well as a fear of rejection. In short, I stopped expending so much energy trying to revise others' scripts of me."

Georgia Kolias admits that she was incredibly resistant to being seen as heterosexual. "It was ironic really, since nobody can tell I'm a lesbian when they look at me. But this had been a sore point for me over the years to feel so invisible. Willy was my tell, my queer identification card. When he became a man, I felt I would sink wholesale into obscurity, into a life that I hadn't chosen for myself."

We rhapsodize, pontificate, and debate whether our identity is tied up with our partner's, something the writers in this collection fall across the spectrum on. But at some point, like Connie and others in this book, most partners of trans* folks learn we must stop listening to others and find our own ways to navigate an identity that few understand. Sometimes we are an orientation all our own. It is, writes Lacey Losh, that: "so much silence remains about a wide swath of human variance and experience, and that silence often feels weightier than words spoken aloud."

In author Laura Harrington's essay, "Personal is Political," we feel her tug from every direction as she worries about her trans* husband, her young son for whom he is a role model, and for herself in one swift, choked breath: "I worry about the world my husband and son live in—the one that denies them insurance coverage for the necessary medical care they need, that tells us the story that "Boys Don't Cry," and that simply doesn't understand them—will destroy them. I see an opportunity to tell our story and to keep changing the world one personal interaction at a time. I want my husband and son to be safe, whole, and happy. I want the attraction I feel for my husband to be recognized, to have a name that doesn't hide behind *bisexual*, *heterosexual*, or even *queer*."

A name that isn't concealed behind a label, or a definition, one that lets us navigate our own feelings without the cultural baggage of history and popular culture may be harder to find. "If there's one thing that being married to a trans woman has taught me, it's that impermanence is real. Even basic things like gender are subject to constant dramatic and subtle shifts," writes Miriam Hall.

Yet, the men and women and genderqueer writers in this collection are doing just that by writing their stories down, sometimes to themselves in poems and essays, other times in letters to loved ones. The latter can be revealing, wrenching even, as is the case with Ann Bloomfield, who by day understands her wife is "the same beautiful soul" she fell in love with over a decade ago, but admits she wakes up at night missing the man she once knew, his muscles, his hair, the strength and security he once brought her, even if it was a perception all her own. "Now I find myself needing to be the one who is strong and protective, and it exhausts me," she writes. "Now that you are gone, what I miss the most is the ease of life that I took for granted for so many years. I never realized how intimidating it could be to be authentic until I had to introduce you as my wife for the first time. I grew up with gay uncles, and for us that was normal. However, I never appreciated how difficult it must have been for them to live in such a small town knowing that they were not viewed the same as a heterosexual couple."

While many straight women like Beth will struggle with their newfound queerness, other women, like Shanna Katz Kattari embrace that very definition of themselves and use it to claim some self-determination in their own experience. "The great thing about being queer and really feeling it as the right identity for me is that no matter the gender, sexuality, or orientation of my partner, queer covers it, and I don't need to reexamine my attractions based on my partner."

There are opposite sex couples and same-sex couples in this book; the latter—as Justin Ropella does in his essay, "How My Partner's Transition Gave Me a Schlubby Ape-Man Complex"—often presents unique takes on the transitioning couple paradigm. Ropella opines about how having a same-sex partner come out as trans* can make us rethink not just our sexual orientation but also our own maleness or femaleness; how in same-sex relationships a transition can be seen or felt as casting off what we are. Every choice his girlfriend makes, every snide comment about body hair or ugly men's clothes, makes him wonder if she feels the same about *his* body hair, *his* flannel clothing.

For others, the sameness is the attraction. Konnor T. Crewe writes about being in a trans* relationship in which both men are trans*, albeit his partner began "transition" in the 1970s, and he in 2010, when both men are middle-aged. He admits his own jealousy over his partner's ease and comfort with passing, hair growth, inhabiting his maleness. Still, as middle-aged men, their medical issues (like diabetes), compounded by poverty from having two trans* wage earners living together, go beyond transition. It's a reminder that at the root of all this, our trans* partners, are just people, two people (sometimes more as in poly relationships) in love, managing life and love and family and the expectations of ourselves and others.

That is perhaps the sweetest reminder why this book is titled "Love, Always." Isabella Abrahams giddily recalls, "I fell into Trystan, and we have never completely pulled our cells apart. He is my tether, allowing me to fling myself just a little over the edge, flirting with the fall." It reminds us of that rush of excitement, the adrenaline of falling for someone. That at the root of these stories, even the ones that end in breakups and heartache, are merely two people in love, merging, blending and growing if they last, sure, but initially falling in love without regards, in many ways, to gender.

Anne Totero's beautiful poem speaks to loving a trans* person more than they love themselves at the moment, something all partners of trans* people encounter, even if for just a day. Raised in a culture that misgenders, misunderstands, and misuses trans* peoples' lives, internalized self-loathing and recrimination are battles many trans* people face still. But their partners willingly sign up or—as in the case of Helen and I, stay around—for that battle because of the love. "I found my El Dorado in your skin," Anne writes. "Tracing your scars that you paid for just to feel a little more whole." She continues, "Thank you: For fielding the foolish inquiries of trans love. For showing me twice as much mercy as you've shown yourself. For a patience only my fingertips empathize with when I touch your wounds. For being exactly who you are right this second."

That's all we ask for.

Diane Anderson-Minshall, author of *Queerly Beloved: A Love Story Across Genders*
Helen Kramer, author of *She's Not the Man I Married*

Introduction

Jordon Johnson and Becky Garrison

Despite the increased media coverage of trans people that points to telling more holistic positive stories about lived experiences, scant coverage has been paid to partners and spouses. Rarely do we hear from partners of a person who expresses their gender differently from their assigned gender at birth or embody a trans identity.

Conventional wisdom of the medical profession would encourage couples to divorce when one partner decides to transition gender. However, research conducted by Dr. Colton Meier at the University of Houston indicates that of those participants who were in a relationship when a partner transitioned, only 50 percent of those relationships have ended.[1] They also found that for about half of the pairings who ended their relationship, transition was merely a catalyst for other issues that had been brewing already.

The takeaway? Relationships are complicated and take tremendous amount of commitment, communication, vulnerability, and strength to endure, no matter what.

---

1 Meier, S., Sharp, C., Michonski, J., Babcock, J. & Fitzgerald, K. (2013), "Romantic relationships of female-to-male trans men: A descriptive study," *International Journal of Transgenderism*, 14, 75-85.

Preliminary research indicates that couples who stay together through transition have found their match or soul mate and are able to engage in open communication throughout the process.[2] When a couple chooses and actively works on staying together, partners found that their trans loved one became calmer, easier to be around and sexier as they settled into living their gender identity authentically.

Love, Always offers a personal side to this data through a compilation of personal testimonies examining the challenges and joys of loving a trans person. In the stories, letters, and poems here, we glean insight into the emotional, interpersonal, social, medical, financial (and other) challenges that partners of trans people face. In these stories we read how couples navigate shifting identity labels and relationship status, public disclosure, child-rearing, sexual intimacy, and relationships with extended family, friends, and work. On a more personal level, these stories delve into intimate details of the ways transition impacts partnerships emotionally, mentally, spiritually, and sexually.

We encouraged contributors to self-identify their race, sexual orientation, gender identity, and other descriptors. Hence, readers will find some slight differences in word choice and capitalization of terms, yet we decided to allow their voices and words to be heard. At times, readers will witness a contributor's struggles with pronoun usage in the appearance of both masculine and feminine references within a story. This bears testimony to the complexity of embracing partners through the transitioning process. When we received diplomatic permission to reprint a previously published piece, these pieces were republished in their entirety.

We chose to use the term "trans" rather than "transgender," as it moves beyond the transsexual/transgender dichotomy and includes all who do not feel they fit into the gender binary. Some

2 Keo, B. (2011). "Relationship satisfaction of partners of female-to-male trans men". Thesis manuscript.

contributors use, "trans*," to denote the spectrum-like quality of trans identities.

Love, Always is the first book of its kind in the arena of gender and family studies. We hope readers see themselves reflected in this book, are enlightened by its raw honesty, and feel curious to learn more about trans couples. Moreover, we hope this book will spur a dialogue for more discussions of how gender transitions affect our partners, families and relationships.

At this historical juncture, much of the public writing about partnering with trans people is by the cisgender female partners of trans masculine men and nonbinary people—a phenomena no doubt influenced by cultural messages about both femininity and masculinity. There is a preponderance of female-identified writers here, with fewer voices of men who either partner with trans women, trans men, or nonbinary people. A partner's transition still isn't something that spouses, girlfriends, and boyfriends choose to address publicly.

As editors, we can only share stories of people who are ready to share their experiences—and the stories told here point to larger societal issues of why so many trans people (and their partners) feel they must remain quiet. This is especially true for those who are undocumented citizens.

We also recognize that more white authors than authors of color are collected here. Although we were diligent in trying to represent the vast spectrum of partners' lived experiences, these imbalances reflect dynamics present in many fledging conversations, and are undoubtedly influenced by racism, classism, whiteness, and sexism. We readily acknowledge the opportunity for future possibilities of conversations about partners of trans people beyond what is present in this anthology.

Just as gays and lesbians moved out of the margins into the mainstream, our hope is that awareness for trans people and their partners continues to grow.

Intimacy

To Sweet Potatoes and Mangoes

Briyana Davis

I'd been picking up floating rubber duckies, checking each bottom and looking for a match. The whole time I was holding number thirteen in my hand, but these ducks are only one through ten. I try on labels, stretching and tugging at their edges, but none fit. There's always something slightly off. I'm trying to win rigged carnival games. This term is a ring that won't pass the tip of my finger, while that term is a shirt with no place for my head. Words that fit like a hat with no space for my curls. Labels that suit me like tights with no shade for my skin. I cannot squeeze into a system not made for me to fit.

Queerness is curious. White gay men carry (straight) brown girls. You know, those "hags" carrying bags full of insecurities. I too sat with long nights and tears, with no space for the glances that weren't returned. There was no mirror to glimpse that real reflection of myself.

We are conditioned to think we should, can, and will only want one thing—the "opposite" thing. I spent years thinking and assuming I wanted boys, men. It was as if Eve woke up and suddenly realized she wanted oranges all along. Except maybe I wanted kiwis, mangoes, or blueberries. Maybe I want carrots, or a sweet potato.

I found myself in the midst of a garden.

At first, my uneasiness with labels seemed to be a fear of being gay, lesbian, or bisexual. Pansexual made no sense to me. How could gender not be a consideration when men had made no sense? How can you not see gender when it is written on our bodies, slapped on sidewalks, and scribbled across stories—when it is everywhere?

But your face, though pained from heartbreak and distant from rest, sang to me. It was a song silent to my ears but harmonious in my heart and through every inch of my brown body that for years had ached to feel the way it was supposed to—loved and desired and wanted.

I had never heard your name and knew nothing of your past. I didn't know your major, your age, your food, your story, your playlists, your pronouns, the boxes you check, which bathroom you use, or anything else that makes up the universe that is you.

But somehow I knew.

Maybe your pain found my pain—the pain of staying quiet, unheard and heartbroken, brownish and bendy. I think we both felt not at home but what is home? And where do we park our anger?

In our home, there is space for that fire. Shame can hide in the closet until it's ready for dinner. Once fed, it can start to unwind. An embrace when understanding comes home and says its time for healing, off with a kiss and warm cup of sweet compassion.

Your resilience met my scattered. My confusion met your proud. Doubt melted into that warm darkness you dip your spoon in—comforting, soothing, sweetness.

Through soaking in your stories, your silences, and your smiles, I grew more comfortable in myself. I felt at ease in embracing my bendy-ness, in talking about my uncertainty, in not knowing what my sexuality is beyond just "queer," in not knowing how to truly define my gender, in acknowledging how my background affects the ways I do and do not dress and carry myself.

We are so many things. We are different colors in different seasons, amps and octopuses, bookshelves and green onions, breath and tears, and poetry in every moment. We become more than just characters. Nothing in us stands alone. We cannot separate our color from our pain, our queer from our voices, nor our minds from our homes.

The labels do not make us. The queer and brown runs through our blood and breaking that down, at times, seems fruitless. It is a challenge to convey our fruitful truths while navigating the boxes, assumptions, and expectations carved into the world we currently inhabit by the white, the cis, and the hetero. How do I black girl come out to a family that does not discuss sex or dating? Was I ever black girl in a closet? How do I black girl explain our genders and that there are endless genders when the black people who love me know the word "queer" to be a slur? Perhaps they use it and do not know it is a slur. If I am femme today, will they see us as heteronormative tomorrow? If I wear a tie today, will they think you have changed me tomorrow?

Making my way through this maze is easier with you by my side. We create space for each other to run, turn back, crawl, nap, and take breaks for smoothies. You have given me the strength to burst into flames and let my radiance overpower any weed trying to take root on this body that is mine.

Just Add an "A"

Melissa Contreras

When I first met her, she was a very attractive but painfully shy young man. She looked younger than her actual age of twenty five. She was crazy smart. She was fascinating. She had *stories*. She laughed at everything I said. She was cute and sarcastic as hell. But what really made the butterflies go wild inside me was her smile. That knee weakening, knock out smile. I was smitten on our very first date.

During that first date, she rather casually mentioned that she had struggled with gender dysphoria, but it seemed to be a secondary piece of information in our conversation as we discovered we both went to the same queer bar that featured a prolific drag show we both enjoyed.

I was so excited to find a guy who wanted to "dress up" and role-play—my first boyfriend in high school *loved* wearing make-up and skirts and fucking with gender every day. I had a soft spot for feminine men anyway. I had visions of girl nights when we would do our nails, dress up, and go out together. Our sex life was amazing right away, so the faint thought that she might have been a closeted gay male quickly faded.

We were inseparable. We watched every movie we could find with a transgender or cross-dressing theme, no matter how bad they were. She owned every Eddie Izzard DVD there was and I watched them all. I was totally excited about the idea of having a cross-dresser boyfriend.

She hadn't been out in public "dressed" as a woman and was terrified of it, assuming she would never "pass." But we found a regular meeting of self-identified "t-girls" (this was the name of the group and how they identified themselves) who met at the same bar we went to, and they had an exclusive part of the club where they could be themselves—dressed and made up to any degree they wanted—and be accepted completely. She wanted to go, but the first hurdle hadn't been cleared.

She hadn't dressed for me yet. I encouraged her to dress for me. I told her I was really looking forward to it. We were at her apartment and she knew this was "the night." She had shown me her blond wig, a long piece with bangs. There was a vintage dress, a beautiful red gown, that was slightly too big for me and I thought it would look good on her.

I sat on the couch in the living room while she was getting ready in the bedroom. We drank Midori cocktails. She was nervous. I was nervous for *both* of us because I was hoping she would look...okay? I worried that she would look ridiculous and that I would have to work really hard at lying and pretending I thought she looked great. I am very grateful that didn't happen. I worried that she wouldn't go through with it—that her fear would overwhelm her—and I couldn't bear that either.

When she came out she was wearing her wig, but back in a ponytail. She had on makeup: eyeliner, shadow, and lipstick. The dress fit her perfectly. She was beautiful. But make no mistake, it sure wasn't the wig or the makeup. My heart just melted because I was so struck by her fragility, her vulnerability. She was showing me how she saw herself. *Her identity.* She was like a trembling baby bird that I wanted to scoop up in my arms. Yet, she was so very brave. I instantly fell in love with her about ten more times during those first moments.

Her terror was only partly diluted from the Midori, but we were soon on the couch, giggling nervously and I was playing with her hair, the wig, like it was her real hair, and I told her how pretty she was—and didn't have to lie—but I desperately wanted her to *know* I thought she was pretty. We talked about what girl names she liked and identified with. Her final choice entailed just adding a single letter to her boy name. Something so simple contributed to a completely new identity.

That night, my desire to make her *feel* like the woman she wanted to be overcame my feelings of doubt or fear; I just wanted so badly to be with her and make her feel loved. As I held her and kissed her, I knew I would do anything to protect her and defend her against anyone who would try to harm her in any way. She was my favorite person. She was worth fighting for and worth any sacrifice I had to make to stand up for her.

I am Looking for You

Andrea Briechle

I am looking for you

I am looking for you
looking for your true self
hidden behind the expectations of a gendered world

I am looking for you
seeing my own face in the mirror
being changed by your presence

I am looking for you
when I walk the streets, watching people
living roles they never question

I am looking for you
and I am not afraid
for I can sense you deep within the body that irritates you

I am looking for you
although sometimes I am lost in the labyrinth of gender roles
and do not know how to call you

I am looking for you
beyond the appearances of a body
I have learned to love and caress

I am looking for you
I watch you closing
till my own self takes up your dance

I live in Germany, where I grew up in a middle class, liberal Catholic, academic family. Then I flew out to study medieval history and to find a place to build my own nest.

Recently, at the age of 33, I fell in love with a non-binary trans* person shortly before their process of "transition" started to became a serious matter. It did not bother me much when the love of my life turned out to be trans*, although it was a bit strange to be confronted with my seemingly "deviant" sexual interests for the first time and realize that the label "homosexual" did not work either with my new partner.

Yet, since I had not been sure about my sexual orientation for a long time, I was prepared to fall in love with a *person*, not a sex or a gender. This worked out nicely when my trans* love found me. Since then, I have been trying to free myself from any gender-labeling. For me, living with a non-binary human being has been a truly liberating experience. It stirs up powers by showing new options and unexpected choices for a fresh look at everything just by constantly questioning gender—one of the most fundamental classifications unfortunately adhered to in the western world.

I've always liked playing with gender roles and my partner saves me from too much conformity to standard norms and behavior. However, it makes me sad and angry that it is so difficult for my partner to live as their true self just because people are not used to or do not like the notion of a non-binary model of gender. While people may easily identify me as a cis-female and it is fine for me to be addressed with the gender pronoun "she," I like the utopian idea of a world where gender does not matter and where it is not constantly invoked by our use of language and our behavior.

Admittedly, while it may be a bit presumptuous to look and search for my partner's "true self" as expressed in the poem, my quest has been more than rewarding as our relationship is the best thing I have ever found.

Tin Porn Star

JAIME M. GRANT

Before

In the waiting room the whole undertaking felt suddenly, surprisingly huge. Too big. *Double mastectomy with aureole/nipple grafts.* I felt on the verge of some kind of shattering cry—like somehow M. might be overstepping some cosmic biological line in the sand. I mean I fell in love with her in this body, and now she's altering it permanently, purposefully. What if she hates the result? What if after all this, the body still doesn't reflect her internal, gendered self?

The truly surreal moments start when she's signing in and we see that her intake forms designate her as male. There's a big M in all of the "sex" boxes. Her "diagnosis," down the page is female-to-male transgenderism. She signs everything. None of these terms quite reflect how she thinks about herself. All day, the carefully trained and perfectly respectful staff refer to her as "him," while I say "she this" and "she that" here and there. They take my gaffes in stride, assuming perhaps that I'm one of those partners who is resistant to her lover's gender transition or that I've experienced transphobia so often in medical settings that I can't make the shift in a trans-friendly environment. On my end, every time I slip, I panic a second, thinking that we're nine tenths of the way there and I'm going to get us thrown out at the door to the surgical suite. *Aha! She's no transsexual! You must go home!*

We can't go home yet. This trip has been almost seven years in the making even if I've only been on the journey for about a year. I've sat with her as she's worked this choice over in her mind again and again, reconfiguring it, considering different surgeons, deciding and revising, and then revisiting it all again. It's taken me months to get my own head around it: M. identifies loosely as female—as a butch, a bulldagger. But if you boil down her sexuality, she's pretty much all man—a top, a dom, the guy running the show. There are no check-off boxes for this, anywhere. Even the medical professionals with the most experience with "gender variant" patients don't have much tolerance for the folks in this queer middle. Like those choice-driven bisexuals in the "born-gay" movement, genderqueers throw a wrench into the idea that by surgically revising key gender signifiers, they're heading toward a gender destiny that was somehow screwed up by an accident at birth. My lover isn't abandoning her birth gender by reconstructing her chest, she's reinventing it.

On the night before the surgery, we sat in a neighborhood Thai place and passed our fears quietly back and forth across the table. We reassured each other, fell for each other all over again. As she prepared to take one of the biggest risks of her life, I understood that I really couldn't do without her. That even more so than all of the passion and crazy sex of this unanticipated, perfectly romantic year together, this terrifyingly bold move toward a more fully embodied self has cemented my commitment to her.

During

We get to the SurgiCenter at around 5 a.m. The whole thing will take about six hours—zip-zip, drive-through chest reconstruction. The uber efficient staff checks us in and I realize we're in some kind of twilight zone-ish surgery lane—not a real hospital, no overnight stay, out of view of people getting "regular" mastectomies. I'm pondering this as a brisk, dykey nurse hooks M. up to all of the various lines that will monitor her well-being over the next several hours. When she stretches one of those blue puffy surgery caps over her forehead, I feel slightly faint.

Dr. Brownstein parts the curtain and steps in. After months of phone calls and charts flying from coast to coast, this marks the first time we've actually seen him. He's a man of few words, which we both knew before choosing him for his superior craft at recreating the chests of girls who have long dreamed of racing through their summers shirtless. He opens M.'s robe and traces dotted ellipses on her breasts. They don't seem particularly precise to me: fat, wobbled Sharpie lines. M. is already woozy from whatever's in her IV, and I feel a little panicky that she doesn't seem to notice. I realize that *I* am in charge of noticing after all of this lead-up and I am suddenly, completely unprepared. He closes the robe, pats her hand and leaves us. These are my last few moments with her.

M. wheels away from me down the hallway awash in fluorescents. The butch nurse hands me a prescription for painkillers and directs me across the street to the pharmacy. I practically run to the elevator, relieved to feel the cold San Francisco morning hit me when I step into the street.

The pharmacy is full of sick people. M. hates painkillers, she'll be a bear about taking them. I start to think about ways I might convince her when a very sickly, ancient man navigates his way into a chair. He falls and a woman several years his senior hoists him up into the chair with great disapproval. I grab my pills and make haste back to the shiny waiting room.

Finally, after a long five hours in the SurgiCenter, we roll her out onto the sidewalk in a wheelchair. I've called a cab to get us home and when I make a clumsy attempt to shoehorn her into the backseat, she bats my hand away.

We get home at last and I settle her into bed. She's groggy, not very mobile. She naps for a time, then stands, sways a bit, makes her stubborn, don't-baby-me way to the bathroom on her own. Despite all the medical camouflage, the swollen padding at her chest that travels all the way to the waist, I can see her. I watch her move away from me and I think—there's her body. I recognize it—even as it's not quite fully realized—I can see where she's headed. The shape of her, the heft of her, the clean, sturdy line of her. She's moving toward herself, the self she's been forming, one insistent step at a time, all along.

After

Dr. Brownstein's office—nestled against an unassuming off-ramp of the main highway into San Francisco—appears to be the anti-doctor's office. Coming up on the industrial looking building, we're initially puzzled—there's a plumbing supply shop on one corner and a storefront church across the street. I'm almost surprised when we find Brownstein on the intercom/directory and are finally greeted by Mary, his thoroughgoing warm administrator.

Mary leads us into the suite and I'm disoriented for the second time in ten minutes. A huge upholstered yellow chair that's Alice-In-Wonderland sized takes up the lion's share of the entryway. If I weren't so nervous, I'd enjoy the joke. Beyond the chair, in an open room dominated by large windows to the right sits Dr. Brownstein, his hands clasped together thoughtfully under his chin. Only two yards away, he doesn't acknowledge us. A computer screen winks behind him.

Mary leads us past the Wonderland chair but away from Dr. Brownstein into a room defined by a half-wall. In this room there's a long leather examining table and cabinets neatly stocked with medical supplies. Now, it seems, we're not in Wonderland at all but Oz. The Wizard sits in full view just a few feet away as my partner removes her shirt, revealing a chest binder stretched over sutures and gauzy padding.

In a minute or two, Brownstein gets up from his chair and strides over to us in the examining room. He unzips the Velcro fastener, surveys his work carefully, makes an approving grunt or two, and refastens the binder. He decides to remove the "drains" a day early. The removal of these two plastic leads that suction blood away from the major incision site delights my lover who hasn't had a decent night's sleep since the surgery two days ago. When he finishes, she practically leaps off the table she's so excited, while Brownstein moves with some kind of mysterious determination back to his desk.

We'll come back two more times over the next eight days following the yellow brick road back to the room with the giant chair and the rather small man who holds the secret to finding our way. Unlike Dorothy, whose lessons seemed so clear after the tornado that ripped her from the safety of her life in Kansas, my lover's path is uncharted. There really is no "home" to return to after making this journey—only a new place in the road that we can't fully anticipate or describe.

Mary confirms the time for our next appointment and leads us back toward the yellow chair. In the entryway, a boyish girl in a multicolored striped cap awaits her time with the man behind the curtain. We step out into the brisk sun of a San Francisco afternoon, giddy.

Two days later, we get the stitches out. This time, Dr. Brownstein was actually sitting in the big yellow chair. He appeared to be answering his mail. We were greeted at the door to the suite by his barky, white-muzzled old dachshund, Frank. Mary led us inside and I don't know how I missed it the first two visits, but there's actually a life-size tin-mannish statue in the entryway. Only it's a tin-woman, with huge torpedo-shaped tits shooting out of her chest.

I was shocked by her—shocked that I could have ever walked past without noticing her—and shocked by Dr. Brownstein's increasingly unsettling sensibility. Here's a man who is performing countless mastectomies on men who by some biological misfire were born women, or on women and other gender outlaws who find their breasts incongruent with their sense of self. And he's got what amounts to a tin porn star greeting you at the door, her steely nipples jutting into your path.

The sutures came out fairly easily. Twinges here and there as he tugged on some of the more stubborn lines. M. gave a protesting groan or two, but it all came off fairly quickly. We had several hours before a friend arrived for a couple of days and I thought, good, she'll have plenty of time to get a good look at the new chest, take a shower, have some time to adjust. But no, she just wanted to go downtown, get breakfast, and hang out.

So we got home in the late afternoon and she finally got her first shower since surgery only minutes before K. called us from the train station around the corner. And just as I'd anticipated, M. had a big moment or two with the new reality. A flash of Frankenstein. A what-have-I-done? moment. I held onto her, then tried to give her some privacy, and then dried her off, and held her again. She cried on me some and then I had to race off to the metro. I thought, God, this is so wrong, she needs more time; but I think—internally—she deeply knows what she needs and giving herself just a minute or two for the terror, the possible disappointment, the fear, that's all she wanted. We spent the rest of the day eating and playing low-key tourists with K. It was great.

But God, for me—those few minutes. I left her in the shower and I thought: here it is. You've found the person you know you're supposed to be with and here's the impossible challenge. The surgery isn't going to deliver. She's going to find herself in a body that's even less congruent than the one she just abandoned. She's going to lose this giant swaggering self-love that drew me to her so powerfully.

I felt like I would split in half and then I just pulled myself up: I can meet it. Whatever, however. This is what love is. I don't care what's next, how hard it's going to be. This is the love of my life and even if her (or my) worst fear is realized, I am on this path for good, and I'm grateful to be here. And however she comes to see herself, however she comes to experience this change, I know I'm lucky. I am living the luck.

Ever After

After the surgery, I think I had no expectations—or more like an expectation of nothing. But that very first day, just two hours after getting her home from the hospital, I'd gotten her some soup and cheese and then she lay stiff and stretched across the bed. I took the tray off her and she said: *climb up here for a minute.* How could I be surprised? I climbed up and hovered over her like a cat and she pulled my breast into her mouth and sucked and sucked on me. I shivered and came almost immediately. My breasts feel different now that they're the only breasts in the room—iconic, girly, *necessary*. I felt slightly embarrassed—like, here she is nursing on me for comfort and I come like a rocket.

And then, those first tender post-surgery days when we were shuttling back and forth to Dr. Brownstein: I wanted to suck her off every day—to assert some kind of familiarity into this foreign territory, to reassure her somehow. But I worried that if she came really hard, she'd bust her stitches and ruin Brownstein's lovely, expensive work; so, I'd take her cock into my mouth ever so gently and suck until she was hard, no major explosions. And then later, as we lay in bed, my back spooned against her, she'd push her hand inside me, work me up and down and all over. I thought: this is how we'll have sex when we're in our eighties. Simple sex. Not-very-physically-demanding sex. Languid, lovely, comforting sex.

Finally, last night, just two weeks after the surgery date, we got down to it. The sutures had been out a week, the surgery tape that had been in place for another week removed. I rubbed her scar line with lavender oil and aloe. Lay my head on her chest. For the first time, I could feel the enormity of the change. She climbed on top of me as I dragged my nails across her back and her whole body felt different, recalibrated. She came at me with the grappling fervor of a first time fuck.

We went at it for almost three hours. Occasionally the words *double mastectomy with aureole/nipple grafts* would float across my mind. But the whole idea seemed so misplaced as I held myself against her hard, level chest. A mastectomy would be completely devastating for me. I've always had a direct connection between my nipples and my clit. But for M.—whose breasts have been nothing but a burden, a gendered albatross—finding a way to let go, to re-create them, has already, in this briefest of recovery windows, brought a sense of possibility that veers toward the miraculous

Apparently

K. Ann MacNeil

Remind me,
when I have had a predictable gin and tonic,
to tell you about
how good you look to me,
with your chest wrapped under a small, white t-shirt,
before fireflies
but after dinner
with your three, tiny nieces running barefoot around your yard,
with ice melting
and
how guilty I am of letting myself think about categories
like husband
and father
until I have to shake my head to clear it.

An Accident at the DMV

K. Ann MacNeil

I like the idea of you as a boy.
With M instead of F on your license
(accidentally scammed from a DMV,
when the woman there read your wrapped chest and new hairline
and lowered voice
and checked the box for you).

I like the irrational legality of it.
Married by Elvis,
in a silver convertible,
at a chapel,
in the drive-through,
with your dog named for the king in the back seat,
with virtual well-wishes streamed in by phone.

I would finally wear my new-to-me white go-go boots.
My hair, "turned up against laws of nature and physics, maybe," you
have said.

You in white, suede bucks.
Champagne at a stand and eat buffet, at a nightclub, really.
Our die-hard fans, sprinkled in among the ranks of strangers.

A ring,
rescued,
by you,
for me,
from a pawn shop.

A Wedding I Meant to Have

K. Ann MacNeil

After Vegas, maybe we would have another wedding, in Chicago,
my twenty-years-in the-borrowed city,
graciously and generously,
at Doc's mum's school,
on the grounds,
near the Lake.

Our family members,
chosen and of origin,
in thin dresses and not-so-serious suits,
assembled and waiting for old school cues
to stand up,
to solemnize,
to witness,
to cry, a little, maybe,
to queer the day.

With our nieces (all eight of them, from seven down to just born),
and the boys (two nephews between us, one each),
in cotton dresses and shorts, as their parents would,
in late, late August (or early September)
with petals threatening to stain fingers and hems.

And my daughter,
who would look suddenly grown,
and radiant,
and happy for us,
with a wide bloom in her hair.

"Seems to me,
that if a body carries a torch for us for twenty years,
we ought to acknowledge it."
This, unbidden, from my father, when he explained why he liked that you had visited
(not called) him, north of Boston, to ask for his blessing, before.

Imagine that.

At dusk,
with my Gemma's girlhood-now-eighty-years-old-at-least mason jars,
some blinking with candles,
some potted with grass to attract whatever fireflies endured,
some spilling over with (more) roses,
and a jazz trio (I doubt the block association would allow more),
and a minister,

a woman,
as butch as humanly possible.

And then picnic food
and carrot cake, vegan except for the frosting,
thick and quite possibly too sweet,
made with friends and merriment and thrift the week before,
in the school kitchen,
served cold,
on mismatched, chipped plates,
on fraying, bleached linens on the grass,
with a few rickety tables,
all borrowed from my two oldest straight girlfriends,
whose own glittering Chicago weddings made me ache for one,
finally.

And your favorite drink,
that and no other for anyone that night,
a bourbon Manhattan,
a boy drink, definitely,
a farewell to summer drink,
served in (more) mason jars.

A litter of hand-initialed matchbooks,
for cigars, good enough ones, domestic, short and thick,
banded and inscribed
with resourcefulness, cheek and hope.

Music until late,
with “Harlem Nocturne” at least,

with speeches and poems and dancing
with a five dollar bet paid by you to Frank somebody,
now that you were hitched, inexplicably and legally, no less.

You in linen pants, and me in yet another dress,
this one a halter,
with whatever was left of summer roses,
messy ones,
open
and almost falling apart.

Fractured Identity

Jeffrey Zweig, II

Dear Hajime,

You've asked me maybe more than once how I could be so accepting of someone "like you." I recall you told me a few months into our relationship that at first you were afraid I was using you, that I was a "chaser," a temporary passenger on the journey of your life. Obviously over time, I've shown I actually liked you and wanted more than an easy fling. But to get to the present I had to return to the past, which meant combing through some unsavory bits and memories I'd like to share with you. I would not call this letter a confessional or a roadmap. Perhaps it is somewhere in between?

Before we started seriously dating, I had to answer some questions for myself. Was I to be designated as *gay*, or at least *bisexual*, according to society's ideals of gender because of who you were? How would our relationship affect my life and its many facets? Of course, questions like these breed and forced me to confront and break barriers instilled in me at an early age.

Barriers based on fear and doubt controlled me, so well that I avoided anything to do with issues or situations relating to me that were not considered "normal," straight, or cis-male oriented. Experimentation that questioned my sexual orientation and gender identity haunted me for years. I'd even go as far to say I was paralyzed because I felt threatened by those experiences, because of the increased harassment and bullying, I already suffered in the Indiana town I grew up in.

But then an epiphany came to me, which was my first gateway to the freedom I secretly desired.

I'd like to tell you about a friend, who was the first truly androgynous, gender neutral individual I had met, though he sided with male pronouns. He was my first real-life introduction to what I would consider a transgender individual. They introduced me to the term genderfuck, which was something he called himself and was proud of. He'd bend his image to fit his wants and live as he wanted without caring what others thought. He didn't care that he lived in a shitty apartment, had little money, or struggled. He was free, and that was better than anything anyone else could offer him. When he was free, he was complete.

Through his example I got a taste of freedom without the fear, which held me for so long. I've been chasing this kind of freedom ever since I moved away from that Indiana town. He was so tired of the system that he had to forge his own path—just like you had to. I just didn't realize it until years later after you and I had met that I had to do the same.

I bring up my old friend because between the echoes of this person ringing in my head and your current struggles in a world of red tape, you both serve as reminders that a person, no matter what they wear, how they present themselves, their sexual orientation, or their family structure, is someone deserving of love and respect. I've never seen the point of restricting the rights of one law-abiding, decent person over another. You never tried to overthrow the government or declare war on gender, but you fought to become who you're supposed to be and how you actually wanted to live.

When I heard about your past, I have to admit you seemed fearless to me as you chose to move your life in vast new directions. You would say you were just "being you," and were actually quite terrified when you first started transitioning. What I eventually grasped from those later conversations was that despite that fear, you did not let it rule you. You accepted the hand you were dealt and owned it, made your choices, and moved on with your life even in the bleakest of times. You wanted your freedom just as they did, and that's inspiring.

Speaking of moving on, here in March of 2014, we're now less than a year from your sexual reassignment surgery—the biggest part of your transition to date! We're excited, nervous, and hopeful for the changes that will come not just physically but the possible emotional completion and peace of mind you will get from synchronizing your brain and body together and hopefully defeat dysphoria and the like. One more recent realization I had was that surgery would not change anything for me in our relationship.

In fact, I always recall when we first met, which was before you even had any of your feminization surgeries. I had ended a mono-relationship a few months prior and was going to these polyamorous meet-up group activities regularly. On that February day last year, you sat across from me eating a salad. We chatted a bit and exchanged nothing substantial in our conversation. However, the interactions you had with the others, helped me like you instantly.

It didn't matter that it hadn't been long since you had been going "full time" as a woman. You may still be getting the hang of some things, but you seemed confident, and you left a mark in my memory. You were indelible not just because you were cute, but because I know so few people geeky enough to break out their *Magic the Gathering* deck and play with others at an event not meant for such awesome geek-dom. Also, you were not afraid to show your affection to your primaries in public. These actions represented a glimpse of the person I wanted to know better—one who accepted themselves and didn't apologize for it because what was the point of hiding anymore?

So I contacted you about five months later, and now here we are about eight months in. This glimpse of the "me" before there was an "us"—does it provide all the answers? Of course not. Some of the fine details are lost in time forever. Perhaps this will satisfy some curiosity about a past scarred from pain that belonged to a man with a fractured identity.

I didn't answer the questions I posed to myself in the past in this letter because I've come to find that those answers don't matter. They are bred from outdated ideals. Like you, I have come to accept who I am and plan to make the most of it no matter what happens because it's my life. My happiness is what matters in the end and I answer to no one but myself at the end of the day.

You have taken the time to make me feel a part of your ever evolving life. For that, I am grateful. I will follow your example and refocus on forging my own path wherever that will take me.

With the love I have to give from one of your loves,
Jeffrey

Finding My Truth

VANESSA ESPINO

How do you describe what it feels like to fall in love? I am not sure how it happened. I know that my life changed the moment I met M. I never planned my life like this but then again, no one plans to fall in love.

The best way to describe this ephemeral feeling is that it's like watching a dancer express their way through a piece of music you have never heard before. As they move through the empty space, each contraction and flex of a muscle becomes so much more than a choreographed dance; it becomes a communion with the music…and all of a sudden you feel emotionally moved. You understand what they are feeling, what they are saying without a word uttered. You come to know the person through the way they're expressing their passion through their body, through their artistry, through their soul, and sending it out into the universe—to you in the audience to catch.

That is what love is to me. An unspoken indescribable connection between two souls that sparks the moment they meet. Some call it kismet, others destiny or fate, I call it—truth.

I met M. online, not as rare today as it was ten years ago. But even now with the wide array of social media sites available to anyone with an Internet connection, it's still hard to find truth in connection. In fact, the night I met him on a dating website I was taking my profile down. I was tired of being bombarded by illicit webcam invites or the occasional sexting innuendo. I had decided that spending my time communing with the screen of my laptop could be better spent writing or doing something with actual people.

Our chat started with a simple "Hello" and then followed by a question that would change my life: "Are you into FTMs?"

That's it. That was the first thing he said to me. That was the spark. We have been speaking to each every day since.

I had no idea what the hell he meant. The Internet dating world is filled with an alphabet soup of acronyms, some of which are "kinky fuckery" conversation starters. *FTM* was one I hadn't run across before.

M. kindly asked me to read his profile and I still didn't get it, but the word *transgender* did ring some bells for me. We began a fast friendship which felt a little like talking to a friend from my childhood.

I had no intention of being in a relationship with anyone and neither did he; we were both just looking for someone to talk to. But chatting quickly turned into texting and emails, which then evolved into phone calls and Skype sessions. I remember being hesitant to answer his first call. As the phone rang, I wondered if the person in my head and on the screen would match the voice I heard on the other end of the receiver.

What if he didn't? What if the person in my head sounded different than the person on the phone? What if he sounded the same? I remember taking a deep breath before answering and then I heard his voice, "Hello."

M.'s tone was bright with a slightly anxious energy that let me know that he was just as nervous as I was. Hearing his voice felt more intimate and sensual than texting and emailing.

Shortly after that first call, we naturally started calling each other pet names and our phone calls stretched late into the night. Looking back it was quite adolescent, constantly checking my phone for a message from him, but now it all makes sense. M. was my first real prospect of a relationship. I didn't date in high school or college because I was too wrapped up in my love of theater. My social life revolved around rehearsal schedules, production meetings, and tech weeks. Bars were for late night cast parties or the occasional taco Tuesday with friends between classes. I never really had that first love experience of youth until meeting M. and I was already in my mid-twenties inching closer and closer to thirty.

To my surprise he was feeling the same way.

M. had begun transitioning four years earlier and was in a relationship when he made the decision to take his first steps to becoming a man. As he became more male, his relationship with his girlfriend got messier and finally dissolved in a lot of emotional misunderstanding and mistrust. So for him, I was also his first girlfriend as a man and first straight girlfriend, at that.

M. was passing as a man by all accounts; he had his driver's license changed so at least the state recognized him as such. Testosterone replacement therapy had done its magic by lowering his voice, masculinizing his features, and giving him the facial hair he had always desired as a child. One of our first late night conversations centered on his desire to shave and how much he wanted to be like his father. I could hear in his voice how much his desire was rooted in insecurity and a constant need for self-assurance. This was something I had never encountered talking to the opposite sex because, as a cisgender woman, I don't need to be assured. My femininity is never constantly questioned like it is for M. whenever he meets someone new, it's a luxury of self-assurance that M. is still searching for. For him, the reassurance was not about vanity but rather a need to know that what he saw in the mirror was what I and the rest of the world saw as well. I did see him as the man he is, regardless of his insecurities and dysphoric anxiety, that's just one part of his whole life.

I am the oldest of three children to my forward thinking yet semi-traditional Mexican parents. I'm the first daughter and the first grandchild on both sides of my family. Both sets of grandparents immigrated in the 1950s and 1960s to start a new life and live their version of the American dream in Southern California.

Growing up, there were a lot of expectations I perceived were my responsibility to fulfill. My mother expected me to finish college, find a good job, travel the world, and be a good daughter. She also included that my free time should be spent with family and that I should remain a virgin until marriage. Her credo became a road map for my life. Culturally, it wasn't so far off. Mexican women have always been expected to be strong, family oriented homemakers, and exist in a primarily patriarchal social structure. I was fortunate to have that traditional Mexican cultural experience turned on its head. All of the women in my family were strong and it was a matriarchal household where the men deferred to them for the most part.

So when I told my mother I was interested in a guy I had met on the Internet, let's just say we weren't having heart-to-heart conversations about feelings. We had more of a, "Well, if you end up in a ditch somewhere make sure you are wearing clean chonies," conversations.

My mother is a daughter of second wave of feminism and self-reliance and strength are paramount for her as a woman in the list of things she wants for my younger sister and me. For the first time I found myself in a burgeoning relationship; a relationship with a man who was born a woman, a man who needs to have his masculinity reaffirmed daily. Hence, my perception of what a strong Mexican woman is, was challenged because to be submissive is not something that comes easy to me and certainly isn't how my mother raised me. So I kept his identity as a trans man to myself and my family only knew him as I saw him—a guy I met on the Internet.

The first month of conversation flew by faster than we realized and our long phone calls turned into a daily occurrence. Whenever we had a spare moment we texted, sent selfies, and played phone tag until the day was over and I heard his voice again. But it wasn't enough: we had to meet. At this point, I was living in northern California and he was living 400 miles away in Southern California.

Fortunately, a theater project popped up and I had a work-related reason that my mother deemed suitable for me to travel. I took the train down to the Central Valley, and with every stop down along the way I felt a nervous energy starting to swell in the pit of my stomach. By the time I was getting ready for our date, a little voice in the back of my head kept telling me to put a spare pair of "chonies" in my purse.

Before I knew it, M. was there. I don't remember if he spoke or I spoke but I do remember grinning like a fool and then he kissed me and on some level I knew. He kissed me even before I could tell him how handsome he looked and before I could acclimate to being in his car without knowing what he had planned. In that instant, something clicked and I felt safe. It was as if I was going to dinner with a best friend, not a first date with a man I had never met in person.

We walked through a historic part of town and had dinner at a jazz club. As we sat listening to the music, there was a moment during the band's rendition of "La Vie en Rose" with him right behind me when I couldn't think of a better place to be. I didn't see sparks or feel thunder clap above my head. Rather, it was sitting next to him, listening to the trumpet player riff on the familiar melody when it crept up on me. From that point on, I realized that the time M. and I spent together was something special, something to be cherished. When he left me at my doorstep that night, something inside me had changed. While I didn't know it then, I came to realize later that from the first moment we kissed, my truth and purpose in life would include M.

The next hurdle came a month later over the holidays when I invited my new Jewish long-distance boyfriend to Christmas. Let's just say my mother was less than pleased. Even though I was well past 25 years old and educated, she felt the need to reiterate the birds and the bees to me in every conversation.

At this point, I had decided to leave all personal disclosure of his personal information to him. It was nobody's business who he is. There are many (within and outside) the trans community who have opinions on what it means to be out or stealth. For me, it's a personal (and political) decision every person should make for themselves. It wasn't my place to say anything to anyone. In the days leading up to his visit, I rehashed all those ideals my mother instilled in me and pitted them against what M. needed in a partner and what it meant to be a strong Mexican woman. Nothing added up nicely.

As I thought over every permutation of the conversation having to do with M.'s identity, either M., my parents, or I would end up hurt, embarrassed, disappointed, or worse, shamed. At this point, M. and I decided that meeting my parents for the first time was not the right venue for an identity conversation. The holidays were pleasant and my family was welcoming, though skeptical. But overall, our visit was good and I got to spend more time with him, which is all I wanted. It was the best holiday I had in years. I was happier than I'd been in a long time.

Now I was keeping a secret that I wasn't sure I wanted to keep. After a few overnight visits, my mother started peppering me with questions about pregnancy, which increased this mounting tension I felt every day in the pit of my stomach. I was constantly pulled between wanting to tell her everything about my new relationship and not wanting to disappoint her with something she might not be able to understand. Then, as time wore on the tension mounted with the problem of keeping M.'s identity secret to the woman who was the cornerstone of my life and identity. How could I find the right words to explain his identity *and* my choice to keep it from her?

I felt like a straight woman hiding in the closet with no way out. M. was getting closer to the next step of his transition, top surgery, which became a constant topic of our conversations. I found myself watching pronouns—which was never a problem before—and talking in code to keep my family from catching on and finding out his truth. While M. was transitioning, I was going through an identity crisis of my own trying to figure out who I was in this relationship.

I have always identified as a straight woman. I am a girlie girl of sorts who hates sports and loves feeling feminine. I love wearing high heels, the sexual power and elegant sweep of the shoe to my leg, even though I can't walk in them to save my life. Being in a relationship brought out and made me more conscious of that side of my personality.

My relationship with M. brought up many questions I'd never fathomed before. *Am I a lesbian because he was a woman? Am I pansexual? What is my number on the Kinsey scale? Am I straight because he is a man? Am I bisexual because our intimate relationship is so good? What the hell am I? As his girlfriend, do I belong in his community? Am I an ally? Am I gay? If I tell my parents who he is, will they think I am a lesbian and will they reject me? If I wear makeup and dresses, will they think I am straight? Who was I?*

When M. met with his surgeon Dr. Crane for the first time, I sat in his San Francisco office holding M.'s hand. As he listened to the details of the procedure, I wondered, *"Do" I look like his girlfriend?* Through all the incessant questioning, I would always ask myself: *Does it matter?* Some days the questions bothered me, while on other days I would ignore them. But they were always there lurking in the corners of my mind.

After a year, it was time to take that next step in our relationship. Being in a long-distance relationship was wearing on our patience and we both desperately needed more physical intimacy on a daily basis. M. asked me to live with him. I knew if I was going to take that step I would have to have the conversation I feared with my parents. I respected my parents too much to take that chance without being completely honest about how I felt about him and who I was.

So one night after a nervous call with M., I sat down next to my mother who was watching television and kind of blurted it out. She got quiet and asked all the politically incorrect questions: "How long did he know? What was his name? What kind of genitalia does he have? Is he having surgery?" With each one, I felt disappointment wash over me.

Then she asked the predictable question: "What does that make you? How long have you known?"

I told her that he confided his gender identity to me in our first conversation. Then, she got quiet and went upstairs. I remember it like a vivid dream I was watching from the outside. I sat on the stairwell that led to my parents' bedroom door. Like a maudlin child I waited for my punishment to come down from above. I was afraid they would never talk to me again. Many people don't talk to their families. They move away and only connect on birthdays and holidays.

In that moment, I had to find the strength to say that I am choosing to follow my heart even if it means leaving my foundation, my family, behind. I fully realized what it meant to be in love. Every time I told M. that I loved him, I was also giving myself the permission to be myself, and that little voice stopped asking questions. Fifteen minutes passed and my dad opened the door and sat on the landing with me. He said something that I will never forget: "I don't care what he is or what you are. All your mother and I want is for you to be happy, and if he makes you happy then that's all that matters."

How do you describe what it feels like to fall in love? For me, falling in love is finding the best part of yourself and giving it to the person you love. It's like a dance and the music is the journey, a communion of two souls that create a whole heart.

M. is still on his journey of transitioning and continues to evolve and find himself every day. I've found my truth and my true self through loving him and can only hope he finds his with me.

Third Time's a Charm

Jennifer Miracle

My love…

Never could I ever have imagined the life I have with you, which makes me so very excited for the life we will have together in our future. When our paths first crossed almost 17 years ago, I was searching, uncertain of my own identity in terms of my sexual orientation. I had dated mostly cisgender men at that point, with the exception of one woman, and was in a relationship with a man at the time. I remember there was always something about you; something that drew me to you, but at the same time, somehow intimidated me. You were so intense. You seemed to have a confidence about you that was so grounded and stable and you didn't give a shit what anyone else thought of you. Some things never change.

I definitely wasn't there yet, as I was still dealing with my own, "I like boys, but I also really like girls" dilemma. So, when you propositioned me that night for a kiss, I gave you a safe response that I couldn't do that, as I was your resident assistant and besides, I had a boyfriend. Then, of course, I turned around and dated your roommate for four years. I'm still not sure why you're even still speaking to me, much less want to marry me. However, you did not hold it against me. Instead, we all remained friends, spending time together beyond the residence halls. You actually came with your roommate to visit me during my internship and will not let me forget that we made you sleep on the floor.

Why are you still speaking to me?

As time passed, we all went our separate ways as people do and as fate would have it, I found you on Yahoo personals in the summer of 2004, seven years after we'd first met. I remember seeing your photo and saying out loud, "Holy shit! It's Amber Boom!" and thinking "Wow. Those eyes! God, she's hot."

I messaged you, excited to reconnect and hoping to visit and catch up. You were very receptive; we met and, although it was never intended to be a date, it turned out to be the epitome of one: dinner, putt-putt golf, and ice cream.

I remember meeting you at the restaurant and being a little taken aback by your striking masculinity. Although it was evident from your online photo, there was something much more powerful about your energy in person. Everything about you came across as masculine and I can remember being a little uncomfortable with that—although not necessarily in a bad way, but rather in a way that challenged me. I think it was more about my insecurity with my own identity than anything to do with you or yours. There was a part of me that still felt like being gay meant being a woman who liked women. Feminine women. "I mean, if I was going to date a woman who looks like a man, why don't I just date a man?" It's astounding how small minded we can be sometimes. Yet, I'm thankful for having been in that place at some point, because it equips me now to answer that question from others about women who date masculine women.

Maybe that was the barrier that kept me from opening up to you at that point in our story. Maybe it was just that it wasn't our time yet. In any case, I cannot blame you for being disappointed when you came to visit me a week later and I blew you off. It was never my intention to hurt or mislead you, however; you were not crazy. What you felt from me that led you to believe things could go in a different direction was real. Although you remembered it much more vividly than I did, the fact that I invited you over for "beers and a movie" tells me that, at the very least, I had every intention of making out with you.

While I will always hate that you were hurt by that situation, I do think it was meant for my attention to be drawn in a different direction at that point in my life in order for me to arrive on my path, right where it perfectly met yours for the third time, another seven years later in the absolute best condition for loving you with every fiber of my being and more importantly, allowing you to finally love me.

The first weekend in Athens was the first time I'd met you in person as Ethan. I was so excited and at the same time so nervous to see you that I, Ms. Director of the LGBT Resource Center, managed to fuck up the pronouns literally within the first minute and a half. It had been so long and yet I was still fully aware of the chemistry that we always had. Before you even arrived I was clearly drawing the boundaries, letting you know that while I did not have a guest bed, I had a very comfy couch that I didn't mind you sleeping on or I had a nice queen size bed that I didn't mind sharing if you could behave. You said you'd sleep on the couch. Having just started testosterone replacement therapy less than three months before, you said you didn't want to put yourself in any kind of tempting situation.

I will never forget how great you looked as you walked up to the hotel where you were meeting me to hang out with some of my friends. I had that same experience I'd had seven years before when I found you on Yahoo, "Damn, he's fucking hot." With that thought, I consciously put up my guard. Little did I know that by the end of the weekend, my heart would totally outdo my head.

Having been burned twice by me before, you had put up a bit of a guard of your own in terms of not having any expectations about the visit. You also let me know your feelings about the previous encounters by "teasing" me about having blown you off. I had never known how much those two rejections had stayed with you until that weekend. In fact, I had forgotten about the second one altogether until you reminded me.

As the weekend went on, I quickly found myself feeling that same "thing" that I had felt with you in the past growing stronger as the days went on. Only this time, there was something much more comfortable about it. I didn't find myself feeling intimidated or uncomfortable with you. Rather, I found myself feeling quite at home with you, which in itself perplexed me. At that point, I had not dated a male-identified person in well over 10 years. I mean, I was a well-established lesbian. Most people in my life at that point had only known me as a lesbian.

The more time we spent together, the more I felt drawn to you and eventually, realizing how much in the past my actions had affected you, I brought up my past behavior and apologized. I think that was my first step, although I didn't know it at the time, to allowing myself to love you. It definitely dissolved the boundary I'd been holding between us and led to the most amazing kiss I've ever experienced. The rest, as they say, is history—or I prefer to say "our story."

The point of your visit had been for a consultation with your top surgeon who I'd recommended. I attended your appointment with you and we've reminisced about how we both felt as if we were already a married couple despite the fact that we had established that basically, *what happened in Athens, stays in Athens*. It was simply casual sex between friends. Or was it?

The following weekend, I flew home to Michigan to walk in my graduation ceremony for my master's degree. In the meantime, based on my reaction to your kiss on the curb at the airport, you had determined that the weekend in Athens was all it was and all it would be. That once you'd gone home, you'd never hear from me again, despite the fact I'd said I would see you in Michigan. However, this time I did not disappoint you. I called and invited you to the graduation. Despite having to work midnights that night, you made the three hour trek to Mount Pleasant to see me walk the stage. You stayed for dinner and I invited you to meet me at church in Ferndale the next day.

It was at church that everything seemed to change. I don't know if I can put into words what took place there, but it was as if our souls were united, and the energy flowing between us was like nothing I'd ever felt before or since. Pure. Calm. Rush. That's how we described it to each other. I became aware of the fact that I was still resisting what was so clearly the calling of my heart and I remember making a conscious decision to stop doing that and let you love me. Not only that, but I also remember promising myself that I was going to embrace every single thing about you. All of the things that had ever challenged me or made me feel intimidated or self-conscious—I was going to love every bit of you. And I do.

It was at that point that I began to work through what this meant for my identity. Again, it had been over a decade since I'd dated a man. I remember saying to you, "My family's going to be so confused," in both amusement and a little bit of apprehension.

For whatever reason, I felt some kind of need to explain myself. I remember initially responding to people's puzzled looks when they would hear your name or I would talk about my boyfriend with the explanation that you were transitioning, but then I felt very uncomfortable with that. On one hand, I think I was struggling with the fear of being perceived as even more straight than I already was and feeling compelled to explain myself. Yet, on the other hand I felt that outing you—aside from being totally not my business to do—undermined your identity as a man. It took me a minute to figure it out, but I eventually began responding to, "But I thought you were a lesbian?" with "I was," and leaving it at that or explaining that now I'm in love with a man.

It did really fuck with my identity for a minute, though. Suddenly, *lesbian*—a label that had felt good to me for at least a third of my life—no longer worked for me, because I clearly was attracted to more than just women. *Straight* hadn't worked in eons and decidedly would never work for me again. *Bisexual* still felt too binary to me. *Pansexual* and/or *omnisexual* technically worked by definition, but just didn't resonate with me personally. That left me with *queer*. The irony of this is that just four years earlier when I first landed my dream job as the Director of the LGBT Resource Center, I could not say *queer*. It was not a nice word.

The take-away from all of this was that labels are for other people. I love you and that's all that matters to me. Call me whatever you want. I love Ethan. And you feel the same way. I remember you saying, "You can be a lesbian and be with me. I don't care what you call yourself as long as you love me."

Of course, we've had lots of conversations about how our story unfolded and of why things happened the way they did. I've shared with you how I have wondered if the reason things felt so right the third time around was because you felt so right with yourself. I remember saying to you, maybe even during your very first visit to Athens, "Man, you have always been Ethan." By that, I meant that you were exactly the same person I'd met 14 years earlier. Your soul, your spirit, your personality, truly you were always you. I see you so much clearer now. However, I think you had to see yourself first.

One of the things that I love the most about you is that as much as the world tries to box us in, you continue to seek and explore yourself, not as a particular gender, but as a person. You are the embodiment of authenticity and that is what connects my soul to yours.

As we continue this journey in life, pretty consistently perceived as a cisgender, heterosexual couple, I am forever grateful for being blessed with the courage to live authentically with you and the opportunity to continue to open people's hearts and minds to how we as humans can experience one another.

You are my love and my inspiration. I love you.

An Unexpected Wedding

Audrey Silver

Planning a wedding is a hectic time for anyone; there is so much that goes into making the day exactly what you want. The Perfect Day. The amount of work and planning that is required cannot be imagined until you are faced with having to do it for yourself. This was something I learned as I was planning my own wedding, a wedding which I never really thought I would have.

I know many women feel this way. They get discouraged and begin to believe they will never find "the one," let alone get married. I knew for most of my life that, even if I found that one special person, we still couldn't get married legally. It was the reality for same-sex couples that I had come to terms with. But this changed a couple of years ago and opened a path for me that I could have never imagined.

Two years ago, I was single, fresh out of a few not so great relationships and interactions with potential partners, and I decided it was time for me to take a different path in my search for that perfect partner. It was once again time to try the dreaded online dating scene. I was not especially excited about this option, but one day I got up the courage and decided to go for it. Looking back, it was the best decision I ever made. In just a few days, I got my first message from her, and she changed the course of my life forever.

She was very upfront and open with who she was and that is part of what attracted me to her. Knowing that she was a transgender woman didn't particularly bother me. Nor did it excite me either. Her gender was simply another piece of information about her like her hair color or height. Perhaps that makes me unusual; I am probably not the best person to ask about that, but I was more interested in her as a person. I am not one to judge who she is. Was I nervous when we met? Of course, but that seems incredibly normal. Who wouldn't be nervous to meet someone for the first time?

There was no hiding my nervousness from her; I talked and talked about nothing at all and she listened and did some talking of her own. It was all remarkably natural somehow. It certainly was not forced. I knew from that very first date at a restaurant which I have since learned she hated, that we could have something good together. Our relationship developed very naturally and quickly from that first date. There was just something about her that made me feel at home. She made me feel like I could finally be myself, that it was oaky. And later I came to find out that she felt exactly the same way.

We had been together less than six months when we knew we would be together forever. It was that year when the Minnesota bill to legalize same sex marriage passed, and it was a few months later that the Supreme Court made the DOMA decision. The combination of these two things set me on a path that I never anticipated: planning a wedding. A wedding that some might consider very untraditional—not only a lesbian wedding, but one where one of the brides is a transgender woman.

As I mentioned, wedding planning is quite a task, but I was faced with some additional challenges. Being that same-sex marriage was new in our state, I knew that there might be some vendors that would not be as accepting or inclusive as I would have liked and could have possibly refused to be a part of our day. I also knew that, while I didn't see it as an issue, I needed to have a conversation with all the vendors about my bride-to-be being transgender. I knew that she was nervous about being accepted for who she is and I didn't want any surprises for anyone. This was an important day and we had the same right as any other couple to have it be the perfect day of our dreams. Honestly, I was surprised by just how accepting and happy people were for us. From the photographer to the make-up artists to the decorators to the venue, everyone was not only accepting, they were excited for us and wanted to help make the day special. It was truly amazing.

Everything was beautiful. Just thinking about it and how perfect it was still makes me a little teary. Yes, there were a few bumps, a few hiccups—what wedding goes off without a small bump or two?—but at the end of the day it didn't matter. Everything was beautiful and it was ours. She was mine and I was hers and it was all more than I ever dreamed possible.

Was planning hectic, especially towards the end? You bet. The details all start to take over and for small moments it is easy to forget that the small details matter less than the big picture that I was getting to marry the woman I was meant to be with forever.

The day felt like it was over in an instant and, while I may not remember every detail (or got any food at the reception), I will never forget the feeling of that day, how pretty she looked in her dress and how happy I was. How happy we both were.

Whale's Belly

Sofia Rose Smith

This week, I took their words at face value. When she told me on Tuesday, "I think I wanna get top surgery," I breathed in an imaginary future with top surgery in it—with my partner no longer having breasts; with saying goodbye to four years of touching and licking, eight years of looking and seeing; of saying hello to something new and flat, to the world not round but flat.

It's been days and months of them in mirrors. "They" is not an exclusive pronoun, but on Tuesday, I thought they said it was. Mirrors and big hands covering boobs, squishing them, pulling up and to the side; playing; pretending they, the *tetas*, are gone.

I have watched my partner in the mirror in this way; not in my way, not in the careful placement of eyeliner and shadow, the oil I run through my waves of hair; not in my mirror face, the one my best friend knows the way I know the coarse feel of the long, black hairs on my belly, the hairs I used to bleach and Nair and shave, so that they would be invisible; so that I would be hairless as I should be. I let them be, now, I don't want to change them; my lovers love them, I accept them.

I accept them more than I accept the dark spots and scars on my high cheekbones; wishing in the mirror that I could wash away the many years of acne; wishing I hadn't let the blemishes go untreated, wishing mama had been there to slap some sense into me. I smear the chemical cream on nightly; my skin is addicted now, even as I turn thirty next year. Nutritional healing, homeopathy, yoga, and acupuncture didn't work. So in the mirror I spread the medium brown tinted sunscreen. I hope my face is camera ready. Clip my hair up just so, wild mocha-colored mane flowing down my back. Some days, lipstick, most days not. Every day, a dance with my reflection, my image, the shape of me, the perfume on my neck.

For her, the mirror has been merely a coincidental meeting, brushing teeth. Face washing not a ritual, but a splash. Out the door in five minutes, not fifty.

Their cream skin and freckles.

Their flat tummy and long limbs.

Their breasts like afterthoughts.

The last few months, they became more acquainted with that mirror. I watched them watching. I was the mirror too, sometimes. As was she for me so many days before, "how do I look," I must've asked a thousand times.

So how come it feels different from here, when the tables are turned? When they ask me, "How do I look," hands covering nipples, and I tell her, "You look beautiful, both ways."

Crossing the street and riding up the escalator yesterday, I tell her that this is a mystery for both of us, a process of discovery for them and for me. I don't know what might come up, if I'll feel sad or happy, joy or grief, all of the above. I imagine I'll feel all of it.

They tell me "they" isn't exclusive, today; I can use "she" and "he" and "they."

I tell them this feels different when it's my partner: my intimate love, my family; different from the allyship I can much more easily embody with friends or strangers, clients or colleagues.

It is different, she says.

Embodiment.

Today she went to get the eggs, she forgot the paper bills. She asked if I could make the coffee, she toasted the sourdough muffins, flipped sunset orange yolks in the cast iron.

The daily minutiae; the crackling of oil. The sunlight through the windows; the scrolling of our smart phones; the anger, the arguments, the frustration; the fear around centering white trans* masculinity in this, our house, our bodies, our lives.

The fear of it.

The ways we've avoided those spaces on the outside; the single-issue, gender-dominant, white washed spaces.

Like the one in the book I'm reading, the book she read yesterday.

Where is our book?

The one that shows us our reflection?

I guess we are writing it now, with each other.

Our messy house, my clothes piling up on the desk. Her radio mics on the coffee table. New sheets, a red cotton blanket, woven white sand colored pillows from Target.

Otis, our cat child, our mothering of her.

Mothers, now parents, now papa, now hubby.

"I wanna be your hubby," she told me yesterday.

I knew she would never be my wife.

I was inside of partner.

I hadn't held hubby yet.

It's different from this angle.

From inside of the whale's stomach; her words like pebbles thrown to water make waves and ripples in me that I can't quite name.

I'm inside of it.

Can't quite see it.

But I feel it.

We are here.

Creating

Loree Cook-Daniels

Dearest michael:

I love the life we have created together.

I love how our shared passion for creating a truly inclusive community for ourselves and our loved ones—the "ourselves" that is so much greater than the people we know and the "loved ones" that embrace people we have never met—brought us together in such a powerful, life-changing way.

I love revisiting the night when we spoke so deeply, our souls recognized each other and ignited. We both knew then that our worlds had shifted, that there was no way we could go forward without remaining deeply involved with each other.

I love reliving the image I had of myself driving back from a counseling session not long after we had made that profound connection. I felt like the goddess who holds her palms high to the sky while from them spring endless fountains of positive, transformative energy. You made me feel like I could make anything happen.

I love how we managed to transmute that glorious transcendence into very, very practical moment-by-moment support and coping as our world crumbled beneath us and nearly all our support structures fell away, and we were daunted into silence and invisibility by the devastation. It was a time neither of us would want to re-live but it helped ground us thoroughly in what it's like to live in a world that can seem incredibly painful, hostile, difficult, and lonely.

We took those feelings like we have taken so much of what we have experienced, and mined them deeply and repetitively for insights into how to make the world a better place for everyone. We were not always sure we would survive what we were experiencing but we never hid or ducked from what was coming at us, at least not for long. I love how we continued to turn to face the challenges so that we could learn from them.

I love how unwavering we were for the 13 years it took us to reach our number one goal: keeping the environment around our child as stable as we possibly could while he grew to maturity. This was not a role you bargained for but it was one you stepped into with all of your tremendous determination and creativity.

I love revisiting my multi-sensory memories of the many, many times we cuddled together on the floor or the sofa, sharing the pain and keeping each other going. Sometimes we moved some deep psychic pain out and away, and sometimes we just felt each other being there. I love how there were even times when all we were doing was sharing what happened that day with no catastrophes or upheavals to report or "process." I love how this is happening more and more often.

I love how we are reclaiming our home. We originally pulled it together in crisis with an eye toward raising an overactive, grieving child who needed literal and metaphorical space. Now we are in the midst of making this "empty nest" ours. We have torn down the desk that never failed to remind us we had assembled it in tears, mourning the losses of our butches, who had always been the ones to wield these strange tools that Ikea took for granted. We have packed up the kid's toys and books and tucked them out of sight.

We are clearing space, literally as well as metaphorically, and creating room not just for doing but also for being—chairs built for resting, a television we even occasionally allow ourselves to watch, a whole room for spiritual connecting, sight lines that lead to views and images that bring us delight and peace.

A haven.

A nest.

A place for nurturing *us*.

I love how we are tentatively, but bravely inching beyond the twosome we have been for so many years and beginning to bring others into our work.

It is hard to ask people to help and ask them to share the vision when we have so often experienced those who not only refused to help but worked to pull down what we were building. While it is hard to be vulnerable yet again, it is also necessary to our spiritual and organizational growth. I love that we are daring this huge-for-us step.

I love our many conversations trying to adapt our community's changing terms and understandings to our own. We have struggled together with the word "ally." Who does it silence? Demote? Acknowledge? We've watched with interest and then concern as "cis-gender" emerged and became for many an epithet and yet one more way to divide the world into "us" and "them" with ranking an implicit and unavoidable consequence.

When we felt pressure to begin referring to half of our constituents as "transmen," we struggled with how that usage seemed to erase your own genderqueer identity. You have dabbled with "they" as a "preferred personal pronoun" and I with the label "genderqueer," both as ways to upset others' assumptions. Neither of those terms fully reflects us, but accuracy seems unattainable. How do we explain our own complexity, let alone the diversity of our community when everyone wants simple, understandable "definitions"? I love how we continue to engage with these dilemmas.

I love how despite our efforts to always be on the politically correct side and our unwavering opposition to stereotyping and bias, we sometimes permit ourselves some "bad ally" time. How many times have we come back to the table to complain in a whisper about an extrovert in the bathroom: Who *taught* these people their bathroom manners, anyway?! How often have we privately commented on one of our friends whose head seems perpetually somewhere among the sky's wispy clouds? *Might they*, we often wonder, *be able to edge a little closer to the earth the rest of us live on if they would occasionally take a grounding bite of meat?*

I love our joking about your hormones and mine. Is it your "man juice" that is making more of my chin hairs sprout, or my menopause? Which of us is hotter—you on testosterone or me in a hot flash? Why is it that despite your trans-ness and my apparent "cisness," I show more stereotypically male behaviors than you do? Me ask for directions? Are you kidding? According to a local expert, your penchant for writing thank-you notes comes from your female upbringing. Why didn't mine lead to the same outcome? I love the fact that we can tease each other about the many, many ways we do and don't fit what both the mainstream and trans communities say we are and should be.

I love how we are able to laugh at and joke about your penis. I am deeply thankful that this part of your body is a joy to both of us, a flesh and a concept simultaneously that we can and frequently do make the heart of a loving, connecting tease.

I love how we are slowly, slowly considering moving out and away from the pain we and our community have carried for so long. We've begun to ask ourselves and each other, "What does 'thriving' look like? What is this thing called 'joy'? With all the pain there is in the world, do we have a right and the ability to begin to move into a lighter, happier place? If we do so, can we help bring our community with us?"

I love how despite our lack of answers, we remain committed to asking the questions. I love how we are beginning to believe that we and our beloved community are worthy of all the effort it may take to forge those answers.

I love you, michael. I love the life we have created and the lives we are creating. I love being your partner in life.

Your loving partner,
Loree

How Sex Changed—Or Not

Elspeth H. Brown

Dear Sis,

Thank you for all your support ever since Max has gone through his transitioning. As you know, his decision to transition after our 13 years together as a queer, female-bodied couple took me a bit by surprise. While I've always been turned on by his masculinity, I wasn't prepared for all the emotional and sexual changes that medically and surgically transitioning from female-to-male would bring.

For understandable reasons, Max wasn't comfortable putting into words what he was going through at the time: He needed his space. But I felt isolated, alone, lonely and, at times, rather freaked out. My main source of support in life is Max. He couldn't be there for me during the most intense part of the transition and I get that. You, my sister, were my main confidant during this period and I can't thank you enough.

As you know, however, my scholarly self kicked in as a response to his transition. As I found hardly any information that spoke to the experiences of partners, I decided to interview partners of trans men who'd been with their partner before and during some aspect of transition. I ended up chatting with 35 people in the U.S. and Canada from every walk of life who were in poly, monogamous, or open relationships with a trans man. I needed to do these interviews and found that the partners I spoke with needed to talk.

My deal with them—and to myself—was to share what I've learned. So this letter is a start. (All the names here are pseudonyms.)

I want to write this letter about sex and desire. It's a topic that came up in all of the conversations I had but one that people don't usually talk about without some prompting. The main question I was curious about was: "How has sex changed, or not, in relation to transition?" I asked people about changes in desire and attraction, touching, sex roles, shifts in sexual orientation identity, to strap on or not, changes in sexual relationship structure (open, poly, monogamous, etc.), new names for body parts, kink and BDSM, as well as the mechanics of sex like foreplay, orgasms, oral sex, and penetration.

None of the material below is drawn from my own sexual history. Normally, I would adhere to feminist practice by situating myself in this narrative. However, since this piece is written in my own name, I'd be violating others' confidentiality by telling my story. I have a lot more I could tell you but here's just a snapshot. I know you're busy and don't have two days to read this! I don't make any claims that these stories are "representative" of larger trends. Rather, this is just what some folks shared with me.

Since so many trans men have top surgery, it's not surprising that many of the partners spoke about their relationship to chests, boobs, and nipples. Here, as in so many of these stories, there was no common narrative, though it's fair to say that for many couples, the trans person's pre-surgery chest was an erogenous no-go zone.

Take for instance, Amanda, a young white woman who attends a women's college in the U.S. with her trans male companion among other poly partners. She described the first time when she encountered Jason's pre-surgery chest. "I was very nervous at the beginning of our relationship before he had top surgery," she told me. "The first time we ever made out with like touching and stuff, I accidentally touched his breasts and didn't realize that they were a no-no zone. When I touched them he was like, 'Don't do that.' I didn't really think that he was saying 'no' because he didn't want me to do it. Instead, I thought I just had done it wrong, because I'd never been with a female-bodied person. So I tried to do it a different way, and he was like: 'I just need you to go away now.' His chest became sort of a territory that I didn't get to cross."

Yet, on the eve of his top surgery, maybe as a goodbye ritual, things changed. Amanda recounted, "The night before he had top surgery was the only time I was actually allowed to touch his breasts, which was very, very uncomfortable because I'd been avoiding them for months. He told me to motorboat him. It took me an hour to build up the courage!" This erotic touching was a "goodbye, boobs" moment for both of them.

Other partners described the delightful transformations that took place after top surgery, when partners could explore their loved one's body more freely without being concerned about harming their partner's sense of self. Kara is a white working class femme who had been a dyke for nearly 30 years before her partner transitioned; she now identifies as queer. I spoke with her soon after her partner had chest surgery.

"It's wonderful, because he's so happy," she said. "I can't get him to put his shirt on! I never saw his chest. Yeah, the first thing I did was I listened to his heartbeat. Like, I want to actually put my face to his chest and I want to hear his heartbeat. In the past, I couldn't hear his heartbeat because of the binding and these fucking T-shirts. I don't want to see a T-shirt in my bed again! So yeah, that was huge, where now I can't get him to get dressed. It's like he's always got the shirt off, but he loves it. He loves his chest. He's thrilled with his body, he's finally happy."

It's possible to be thrilled for one's partner about top surgery, of course, and still miss the boobs. Helen, who was in her late forties when I interviewed her, came out as a lesbian at age 17 in the working class bars of a de-industrializing steel city. She is the only partner I've interviewed who still identifies as a lesbian even though her trans male partner transitioned five years earlier. When Helen expressed her deep love for her partner, she also confessed to me: "This is the thing, how much do I miss breasts! Oh, my God. I have to feel my own sometimes. It's horrible (laughs)."

At the same time, Helen described their mutual joy at his top surgery: "I was elated and so happy for him. Just so happy to be, you know, even a part of somebody coming into themselves so visibly. That it [top surgery] was really just an amazing experience for me, and I was really glad to be a part of it. I was glad to be able to have the money to fund it and I was glad to be able to just see it. I was glad to be able to be there when he took his shirt off for the first time in the sunshine and felt the sun on his chest. He was just was so excited."

At the same time, however, Helen's attraction to female-bodied people hasn't evaporated. As she explained, "Part of what's happened to me is that I'm not as sexual as I used to be. That's because I'm not as attracted to him as I was when he was a woman. I love him so much, and I still look at him and think he's gorgeous. However, that kind of heat is something that we have to really consciously work on. I know it's me. I mean, I'm gay, right."

I'm telling you Helen's story mainly because it is so unusual. You'd think most of these partners would report some degree of missing sex with women given that the vast majority of people I interviewed self-identified as lesbians or dykes at some point. But you know I haven't found that to be true at all. I almost feel like we need a new language to describe the sexuality of so many of the partners I've interviewed, who invent new genders and sexualities as we all go along. The closest term I've found that can account for the fluidity of our sexuality is "queer," which not incidentally is the term that most partners have settled on, even if their male partners identify themselves as something else.

For example, Andrea described herself as a "tomboy femme" and her partner Everett as a "bear." As she explained, "Everett is a bear whose favorite color is pink. We both got beach towels and I got the orange one and he got the pink one. It's that sort of stuff that makes him queer enough for me or that makes our queernesses match so well. Part of the normative story about trans guys is that they have to leave lesbian community and do that process. But Everett also was a really bad lesbian for a lot of the same reasons that I was. Because, he really is a gay man. The girlhood he had was the girlhood of a very nerdy boy who's trained to sing opera."

Their robust sexual life hasn't changed much in relationship to transition, except right after surgery. It happened soon after top surgery. Andrea was worried about the fragility of Everett's new nipples. "It took a while for me to feel comfortable kissing them or being intimate with that part of his body in part because I think that it had shifted into a medical field. So it took a while for me to feel comfortable sort of reclaiming it as a sexual field. I sort of separated it into this part of him that I'm taking care of in ways that aren't sexy at all. So it took a while to come back to it being a part of my sense of his sexual self. And now I feel a lot of tenderness towards his scars and towards his chest, because it reminds me that we did that together. His chest is a place where we felt really connected to each other—in the doing of that part of transition."

Then again, I found some of the stories around transition and sex quite sad. Neema, a queer woman of color, spoke about many of the changes she underwent with her partner Richard over their seven years together. Neema observed that she was a queer stone top with Richard: "A lot of our sex was about me engaging and exploring topness, which I hadn't done before to the extent that I was doing it in this relationship." According to Neema, this development allowed Richard to release his formerly stone butch top position and become "embodied in a way that he just never had up until that time."

Although this was a wonderful development for both of them, over time Richard stopped paying attention to Neema's body, preferring to simply enjoy the sexual services she provided him. By the end of the relationship, "He was having sex [with me] but I wasn't having sex. Like, I was his rub and tug girl at the massage parlor. Like it really felt that way, but I wasn't getting any money out of the deal."

She tried to shift the dynamic, but she found herself blocked. As she recounted, "It was like he didn't know my body or he no longer knew or had interest in my body. I had felt so silenced and so voiceless in the relationship. Even for me to say, 'to the left,' or 'harder,' or 'softer'—it felt too dangerous to do for fear that it would end in yet another argument or yet another freezing out."

And then to make matters more complicated, Neema added, "There was some BDSM stuff there. So, you know, me being harsh, or angry or whatever toward Richard would become part of the scene." She tried to get him to cuddle more, but at the time—a view that Richard may have since shifted—he explained to Neema, "I can't do that, I can't do that, because men and boys don't do that." In Neema's experience, intimacy could only happen after he achieved an orgasm. "So after I serviced him and he got off and then I could be held, there could be cuddling, after that there could be that kind of intimacy." The pain in Neema's narrative is still palpable even though they broke up several years ago.

A few partners I interviewed were female-bodied when their partners transitioned from female-to-male, though they have now transitioned themselves. Kevin is a disabled trans man who began his transition at age of 48; his trans male partner Robert came out as trans and gay at age 17, hooking up with gay men in New York City as a teenager. While Kevin hasn't had a chance to do any of that exploration, Robert wants to stay home and play house. Kevin tries to get Robert to go out by saying, "Let's go party. Come on, let's go to that place that you used to go to." At the same time, Kevin observes, "I'm in an old guy's body and I can't do anything about it."

As a female-bodied person, Kevin gained weight as a means of protecting himself emotionally and physically. Now that he's transitioning, he lost much of the weight, and expresses apprehension about undergoing surgery. "I have degenerative disc disorder because of my weight. I need all these skin surgeries and top surgery and, God, when am I going to have the time or money to do all these surgeries? If I had a lot of money, I could get the works. Then maybe I could have some kind of second childhood, like one of these Hollywood people that is able to hike their skin up as though they have it tied up with a bow or something."

In the meantime, Kevin feels sexually trapped and reluctant to do the exploring that he identifies with coming out as a gay man. Both Robert and Kevin "have a poly outlook on life," but they haven't explored much independently or with a third person. As Kevin explained, "It'd be nice, I suppose, if we found somebody we were compatible with, but it just seems way too complicated. I don't want to add somebody else to our dysfunction."

These are some of the harder stories I heard. Overall, while most people reported some changes in how they had sex, many reported no significant changes at all. Of course, couples that have been together for a long time independent of their histories of transition have different types of sex across the length of their connection. Hence, assuming causality is always tricky. But it was really important for me to hear the tremendous range of responses to my questions about sex, since these stories helped me make sense of my own changing erotic landscape.

Much love,
Big Sis

The Best of Both Worlds

Kaylin De

On a clear and breezy Friday evening in April 2013, I met the man I am going to be happily married to for as long as the fates will have us (a seasoned expression for the wise—dwink!). We unexpectedly met just three months before I turned 30. The occasion is one to be treasured because we had contemplated skipping Philadelphia Black Gay Pride where our paths first crossed. He was there for work and support purposes, while I was there to socialize in my new community.

Immediately, I was drawn to his presence. He was talking about a musical artist whom we both adore when I interjected into his conversation with another vendor. He is a tall, smart man with a glowing face and smile and was wearing a bright yellow sweater that displayed his confidence. His voice was low and smooth; a joyful sound to grace my ears. He made me laugh and feel warm, although the glass of Moscato wine I was drinking probably complimented the feeling in that moment.

Within in the first few seconds of our conversation, he introduced himself as a transgender man. His honesty was attractive. I did not expect that level of full disclosure so soon in our conversation; it was reassuring. Due to the nature of his business as an insurance vendor that night, he suggested we meet for dinner and discuss future plans. It is important to note that he was networking, while I was flirting; both totally missing the hints in our dialogue. The conversation lasted perhaps twenty-seven minutes. I went home and waited for him to contact me. Being the thoughtful man that he is, he did not contact me for a dinner due to my busy schedule nearing the end of my degree program. However, I could not wait to speak with and see him again. I emailed him within three or four days requesting our next encounter.

At my insistence, we went on our first date less than two weeks later. Before the third course could arrive, I felt like the entire course of our lives had changed. We shared many things about ourselves which people often find out much later, or not at all. He shared his dating, professional, personal, and spiritual history.

For the first time in my life I put all my cards on the table the first night and revealed my truth. He learned that my last relationship with my first girlfriend ended after nearly three years. Even though I was preparing to leave the country to teach English abroad for a year, I was interested in dating him. I admitted that despite not knowing him there was something about his presence that captivated me. This was/is a new feeling for me. I have been attracted to men and women alike, but never like this before. I am aware of how cliché this sounds. He accepted my proposal and we have been inseparable ever since.

Although we are in our second year of partnership and still getting to know one another, it feels as though we understand and accept one another, especially in fits of anger and unforeseen disappointment, like people who have been familiar with one another over the span of several decades.

This is where the notion of being two-spirited has multiple meanings for me. Our relationship dynamic has transcended our gender; the dynamics are about reciprocity, meeting a mutual understanding and achieving balance in every dimension of our lives. The way we relate to one another is gendered to some extent; yet, on another level, I have never experienced anything close to the balance we have in any previous relationships.

As my partner and I respect the merge of masculine and feminine aspects that exist in both of us, it is clear that a balance occurs when the energy is shifted. An example of this naturally emerges when we are in heterosexual social spaces; I am expected to behave in a feminine manner. Therefore, it is not unusual for me to cater to my partner by fixing his meals or refilling his beverages. Even though the action might seem minor, he does not take it or me for granted. Only when we are alone do I feel comfortable releasing my two-spirited self. In my dating past, I often felt strange because my natural responses and self-expression were perceived as "masculine"; for instance, embracing him from behind. Being myself in this two-spirited relationship means I can freely express my emotional, physical, and psychological self without worrying whether I am being too "mannish."

I consciously choose not to define myself with labels, as I observe how people are placed into identity categories that leave little room for flexibility, expansion, or evolution. I want no part in the stifling oppression of titles that make other people feel comfortable. Even a queer identity, which is supposed to be conceptually expansive, has its limits. I am a queer individual whose life exceeds the mold labeled as "queer." I am a woman who adores women, after spending much of my life loving and lusting after men. I am in love with a man who once presented himself as a woman. For me to love him, I need to fully embrace his past, his present, and our future.

Our two-spirited relationship guided me with the tools to explore the many facets of who I am as a person. One of the many things I love about my partner is the intellectual, emotional, and spiritual depths of our conversations. Our exchanges have taught me more about myself and the world. I am not sure if my partner's gender has anything or everything to do with our ability to cultivate a friendly space of intimacy in our relationship. Our safe space allows us to discuss and share sensitive topics, perspectives, memories, and desires. What I do know is that I have never experienced such firm tenderness with a partner. He is the best of both worlds. I am so happy and proud to be in this loving relationship with my future transgender husband. I welcome the new perspectives that his approach to life reveals, as well as the growth I have experienced on a spiritual level.

I thank The Divine for bringing us together at exactly the right time. We believe we were made for one another; we are equals in this world.

Until the day I met my man, I thought I would be single (but dating) until I was in my 40s. I thought that my chances of cultivating a meaningful relationship with someone were diminished by my dreams of traveling and living in various countries. Not wanting children also seemed to lower my opportunities of discovering my soul mate in the prime years of my life. Now, as I live and love my man in this incredible partnership, I am amazed and ecstatic at meeting the one who was designed for me. He is a person who has transformed into a giver of sustenance.

The nutrients that he provides are not just for me, but I am thankful that they exist when I am in need. Since the age of 26, I have come out to several trusting people in my life. When we share our news with my immediate family, I am hoping they will continue to support me as they did when I told them that I like and date women. It is my prayer that my parents will embrace us as a couple even more, once they realize how challenging life can be when ignorant people in society deem you as a threat or a negative presence.

As a queer person, I have remained silent at work when discussions about transgender issues arise due to fear. Often people wrongly assume I am a "straight" woman and say hurtful things about the LGBTQI community in my presence. Being present in this relationship has opened my eyes to a growing culture that deserves respect, visibility, and support from all who have ever felt like an outlier. As I continue through my transformation, I aim to be emotionally stronger to speak against the opposition. It is hard to decipher when and where I should disclose my identity, especially to co-workers because people may react with prejudice. However, my identity is complex and doesn't begin or end with my queer status. My experience as a cis-gender woman has taught me that everyone belongs to a variety of cultures. I happen to be a woman of color, who loves wo/men and is in love with a transgender man. Yet, that is not the totality of who I am; I am also a writer, educator, and scholar. I am also a daughter, sister, surrogate mother and will become a wife in the near future. I am thankful to be in a relationship with such a great and loving man.

Reader, if you take nothing else from my declaration, meditate on this: if you want love in your life—real love—be open to whom you are naturally attracted to; do not allow the notion of how others will perceive or mislabel you to stop you from being with the person that you enjoy life with when you are alone and together. Love yourself enough to love yourself unconditionally. Write a list of what you *need* and *want* in a partner, consider if you are a good balance for that mate. I know from experience: you must be a mirror of the things you desire in this life because we attract who we are.

The Mirror

Amanda W.

Soft, supple movements.
A brush of hair, you slide your bangs behind your ear carelessly.
Pat, pat, pitter, pat.
You're beautiful, and you don't even see what the world sees.
Applying your make-up, afraid of the looks and stares,
Don't hide.
Don't cry because you can't change certain things as fast as you wish.
Patience love, pitter pat.
You glow, you're alive—oh how my heart leaps and jumps for your joy!
I look away so you don't catch me watching you, staring into the mirror
wishing you had "real" women features.
You are more feminine than I will ever be. Could hope for.
Pitter, pat, pat...almost done.
Perfection, pitter.
You are what you want to be, believe and love yourself
the world will follow.
Pat, pitter, pat, pat.

A Femme's Chrysalis

Isabella Abrahams

The Beginning Spark

We live in a binary plane and there is a certain acceptance of either/or, good/evil, yin/yang. We need better options and we are just beginning to have glimpses of the many possibilities of how gender morphs and manifests itself. We all come to this life with an agreement to experience this adventure, this three-dimensional school, starting in our own personal ocean, programmed to grow into this human body. The mother bathes us all in estrogen and progesterone in the womb causing some to go back and forth in gender assignment several times. It can be an archetypal battle, the first initiation into the hero's journey. Some lose this first battle, only to have to recreate themselves again later by taking hold of the gender reins. They ride into a new country, crossing the borders, taking a new identity, like a spy in possible enemy territory. It is not a choice, and it is brave and sometimes dangerous. To challenge convention is a revolutionary stance and can result in the firing squad. I hold myself as a witness and an ally and sometimes as a fellow spy. I carry the story of my beloved, like coins sewn into my clothes. And sometimes some of that story passes through my femme lips, secrets kissing the air. This is one of those moments for ears that are ready.

The Dangerous Dance

I always felt the most comfortable when walking on the edges of cliffs, on the tops of high fences in the murky between-world, neither here nor there, but somewhere in the middle. So I looked for a partner who knows that dance and enjoys throwing me up to the clouds, secure that I may or may not come down into their arms, and that either way, it was okay. I did not really believe that I could be matched in this way until I set my eyes on my beloved, Trystan. On meeting him, I felt the call of the moment. I tried to circle slowly, but centripetal forces pulled me in, a storm that I could not fight. Nor did I want to. Within minutes of meeting, we were in each other's arms, electricity lighting up the air between us. There was a forever quality about our embrace and I had a hard time staying on the ground, which began to fall away beneath me, leaving me to walk on the edge of myself. I fell into Trystan and we have never completely pulled our cells apart. He is my tether, allowing me to fling myself just a little over the edge, flirting with the fall.

There were ripple effects from this energetic crash into each other. Some would try to rip us apart, seeing that we are a formidable force and, we had to do spiritual battle, but the inevitability of us, built a shelter, fending off the daggers of curse. There seemed to be these rites of initiation that we had to pass to earn the right to be together. Going through this experience gave us a warp and weave of strength that has seen us through many challenges. We arrived into each other whole individual beings with proud scars of lessons learned and earned painted on our skin like tribal tattoos.

As a femme, I have the choice to cover my scars with painted colors, a proud peacock. However, I had to watch my gender outlaw Papi layer those scars with invisible ones, those that do not show. Judgmental eyes bore invisible holes into his black butch body, as he dared to go through those prohibited gendered doors and dared to walk down a street dressed for himself and in defiance of the gender police.

Being the well trained femme, I had learned how to transform my lover's body, avoid the prohibited spaces, and carve a breast metaphorically into a chest. It was second nature to me and I was comfortable with recreating his male identity in our butch-femme reality. This enabled me to see his surgical changes as just another episode of our imagined gender dimorphism.

Gemini that he is, moreover, I had become quite comfortable with relating to several diverse personas all wrapped in one body. It was/is like being in a relationship with several different people, which made it easier to process his transition as adding another persona to the already existing constellation. It had always existed as a metaphor and option in my mind, so when Trystan's physical pain began pointing us toward top surgery it was really not about transing his body.

After his chest surgery, we were soon to discover a remarkable truth as the scroll rolled itself out like a red carpet welcoming us to a new premier. The truth did not have to be spoken. It floated around the room, around our home, and on the plane to Europe with us. The words came out of my mouth with a mind of their own, the color of dark molasses, taking years of moments to pass through my lips, rich and sweet. There was something between us. At first, no definition presented itself and the words just lingered, naked and raw, filling the air between us. But words can be like lovers and I found myself in a *ménage à trois*. So "something" travelled with us from country to country, as my lover left layers of skin, pain, and definition behind. He came back to America, naked, new fresh skin and in transition.

I wear metaphoric glasses that allow me to sanctify the mundane. Everything we do in the same place at different moments of time, over and over again become ritual. So many aspects of transition are ritual and I proclaim myself as witness of this process, anchoring transmutation into the blood and bones.

Dreaming and Speaking in the Shift

Change does not happen until it is imagined, called in, made manifest. So many words and dreams were shared between our lips, laid down in a bed of contemplation. The dance of negotiation is a sexy sharp edged tango, and stiletto heels wound. I believed that I could not move into acceptance beyond top surgery. But I learned what I can stretch into, as challenge knocks on my door, and over time I shifted into a new agreement with myself and Trystan. I have always prided myself on the ability to transfigure reality and I took this as another magical challenge. To do this, I had to ask my soul some important questions. My soul reminded me that we are energetic beings trapped inside our physical bodies to experience lessons, to experience life. So, I moved out of these worldly definitions, up and out of my femme dyke persona and I saw this being that I loved so dearly through new eyes. Gender was simply the wrapping of this beautiful package of soul seed. From this perspective I could see that I chose this journey to learn about this level of love and a new gratitude sat gently on my fear of this change. Without this calling I may not have had the opportunity to shed my own layers and boxes. I cannot always hold this, and like everything in life it is a work in progress. I have times when I long for the comforts of my past perceptions. But in a world where we are learning how to surf the tsunamis, change must become a dear friend in order to avoid becoming a fearsome foe. It is a fractal of a shift and reflection of something so much larger and timeless.

Quetzalcoatl

The operating table is a sacrificial altar: the anesthesia, an inauthentic swap for shamanic journey, the surgical tools, a bloodletting that culminates in the sacrifice of one life for another. This is the initiation that I have seen my Papi go through so many times now.

For thousands of years, bodies have been laid upon altars ready for dying into a new resurrected self and sacrificed to the necessity of change. I count my beloved among these souls, laid on foreign tables in far-away lands. It is difficult to put into words the terror of watching him go into the long twilight of phalloplasty, passing him into the great architect of no time, where anesthesia takes one.

I call my Papi the rain god, as he is so enamored of the sexy wetness of storm and the spark of lightning. So it is apropos that a storm raged on through the many hours of his surgical journey, so loud that it drowned out everything except for my tears. Rain and I wailed like mothers over graves. So many hours passed—six, seven, eight—that it seemed impossible that he could emerge unscathed.

Nothing could have prepared me for my first sight of him coming out of the operating room. It seemed like there was no life present in him, color having left his mocha skin and leaving him looking like a corpse. I laid my hands on him giving every spark of life I could pull from Source, and I watched him return to me slowly. His first words were "gratitude," which he repeated over and over for several minutes, reaching out to the surgeon and myself.

On that day, the great serpent was manifested, harkening great changes to come. I have been a snake charmer before and will be again. I am not going to pretend that there have not been adjustments to this new life and it is not always easy to hold a snake. But remember that the snake holds the sacred secrets and hisses them in its own time.

Transmogrifrication

Animal joined us now though, with the new strength and rawness of testosterone coursing through his body. His need to chew and gnaw and growl brought an ineffable pre-verbal level to our erotic communication. It also brought me to my own levels of transition which was unexpected. Something grew within the lacy leather of my femme self, not about gender, but about lioness self-definition. There was never a question that I would remain a femme dyke. The outlands that I live in allow for this, as many in my tribe reside in these unexplainable complexities. Testing this beyond these safe radical limits of the Bay Area is uncharted territory, excepting travels where I use glamour hypnosis to banish the mendacity of blending in like a camouflaged lizard, spitting just a little too much glitter in others' eyes.

Well, this is the story I tell myself, creating the only fabulous world I can live in. So I search for that spark of visual recognition from my sisters doing the transition tango with their lovers. We are a secret society with our own rituals and initiation is not for the faint-hearted. Conformity attempts penetration, returned to its sender like a laser meant to redefine the molecules of matter.

A New Street Dance

The Sephardim Jewish skin that I live in is a form fitting sexy dress of privilege. When I choose, I can invoke the cloak of invisibility that allows me to dance around judgments and assumptions. I am allowed to look others in the eye with my magic looking glass without invoking fear, and I have the magical keys to the forbidden gates of knowledge cities that take pride in exclusivity. I am fortunate and humble with these offered gifts. I try not to take them for granted but use them for benefit of all. I have come to see that a responsibility comes with this in my relationship. My lover has turned himself inside out to reveal the black man that tried to form in the womb. We are here to re-write the world, the possibility of transmutation glowing in the reflection of new windows to new worlds. This brave decision has thrown him into a world of being feared and judged, way before he walks close enough to be known for his true self. Part of my spiritual contract with my love is finding ways to protect him, without emasculating him. At my best, I can try to hold up my superpower gauntlets and wave off the sharp knives of racist innuendo, the bitter tongues of hate. I can act as ambassador for the country of our relationship when soldiers advance. I can distract with crystal houses built with femme glitter that transport us to safer lands.

And so I commit myself to this contract in body and soul. The bridges that we build today take us into our evolutionary future. The brave and amazing metamorphosis that surrounds me is only the beginning of what we are all destined to become. All parts moving into wholeness.

Challenges

Love Always, All Ways

Jessica Lynn Johnson

I am sitting here with God, legs crossed in my best yogic pose with my scoliosis spine as straight as it will stretch, staring out of my living room window that sits just above the altar that my Love and I built together.

Breathe in. Breathe out.

Our altar is where our two very different worlds merged every morning over the past year and some change. The scent of his incense would fill the room as the smoke tickled the face of Ganesha, caressed the framed photo of his Guru Ma Jaya Sati Bhagavati, floated lovingly around my Jesus and Mary candles, and finally settled sweetly upon my Holy Bible.

My mind flashes back to his handsome hands tracing these ancient Biblical pages. This was a book that had been wielded as a weapon against him, rather than a lamp unto his feet and a light unto his path.

"Let me read that verse again," he would say, grappling to understand Christianity in a new way because I, the straight virginal woman he wanted to marry, was a self-proclaimed "Jesus freak." His eyes earnestly darted across the well-worn pages while his mind churned toward resolution, and I felt my heart fill with elation as I shared this part of my identity with the least likely subject: a mostly-straight-transgender-yogi from the queerest of communities.

I cannot say I am surprised by any of what transpired between us. Isn't it exactly how God always, all ways, seems to work? Mysteriously. Never as we planned. For we are not the doers and God's ways are not our ways.

Back to reality. The present moment.

Breathe in. Breathe out.

It is an unusually chilly Los Angeles morning. I watch the palm trees outside my window ferociously swaying in the Santa Ana winds, and I find myself very still. I am still in shock. I am still missing him. Still devoting...but now devoting alone. Not entirely alone, of course, as God is always, all ways here, but alone in the sense that I believed this man was the love of my life. Yet, only days ago, he packed up all of his things and went back to Atlanta, taking our dreams of a big life and an even bigger love with him.

Breathe in. Breathe out.

Haunting silhouettes of his gorgeous transgender body creating yogic poses on my living room carpet flash through my mind. He drops into his downward facing a dog and I see vividly the tattoo across his wrist that reads, "Don't Worry." Through my hot tears, I try to take these words into my soul, deeply, giving my grief to God, surrendering my anxieties, my questions, my anger, my longing, my expectations, myself. Hoping, trusting, and being.

Breathe in. Breathe out.

I must muster up the faith of a mustard seed. God's Word tells me that's all it takes to move mountains. I want to believe in God's love for me the way I did as a child. I want to believe that God will move this mountain and pour out loads of love and mighty miracles because...

God is good...right?

Breathe in. Breathe out.

I pray for the peace that surpasses all understanding. I ask God for the assurance that what my Love and I shared was divine, that all of the signs and synchronicities we undeniably witnessed all along the way were real, that they were proof of the spirit moving in and through and all around us, and that we were not wrong to love each other. In my opinion…

We were perfectly correct...right?

Breathe in. Breathe out.

"It's just a thought," I remind myself as the questions, accusations, and taunting voices circulate in my head. His Ma, the Guru, gave him this teaching, and he passed it on to me. A simple, yet immensely valuable practice for a spastic, spirit-filled woman whose mind is rarely present and is always, all ways, thinking two steps ahead. "It's just a thought. It's just a thought."

It. Is. Just. A. Thought.

Breathe in. Breathe out.

I sit before our altar, now bare of his spiritual trinkets that traveled south with him, yet the intertwining of our souls echo eternally in this space. It is one of those forever truths that cannot be packed up or flown away on first class. It is, it was, it always, all ways, will be.

Breathe in. Breathe out.

Lord Jesus, heal me! For all of the heaven this man brought into my life...

This. Hurts. Like. Hell. Heal me, Lord Jesus.

It wasn't a lack of love. We both worked harder, loved better, leapt further out of our comfort zones than we ever had for anyone in our pasts. We fought, we forgave, we tried on, we sought to understand, we came toward, we moved away, we gave it to God. Over. And over. And over. Again.

So how did it get away from us? How did it slip away from our grasp? Why couldn't we keep it? God please let me keep it...let me keep him…

It's just a thought.

Breathe in. Breathe out.

I try to find solace in the only thing I am certain of—God. I inhale God's truths; I exhale the world's lies. All of the lies that plagued us over the last year, the lies that eventually became insurmountable, all these lies start to leave my body one breath at a time...

Breathe in. Breathe out.

Inhale love.

Exhale the email from my aunt expressing her "concern" over my "participation in a same sex relationship" that, by her estimation, would undoubtedly lead me into a future that fell far short of God's glory.

Inhale love.

Exhale the traditional Christian rhetoric of my old megachurch claiming that God was the angry jealous God of the Old Testament, who was both enraged and betrayed by my interfaith and quite queer romance.

Inhale...love.

Exhale the roadblocks that this megachurch placed at every turn as I tried to begin LGBTQ ministries, prayer groups, discussions, outreach, support...

Inhale...

I can't find my breath...where is my breath?

Exhale this megachurch finally asking me to step down from years of faithful leadership, because they could no longer "entrust it to a gay person" in my care because of my stance on LGBTQ equality.

Where is my breath?

Exhale losing my entire social and spiritual community, not to mention my sense of worth, my spinning moral compass...

Where is my breath? I can't breathe...

His Christian sibling who assured us that our "sin" was no worse than her "sin," who handled him hastily and harshly just before disowning us both entirely.

I can't breathe...

Exhale his militant friend's assumptions that I must be "one of those Christians" with an agenda to change and control him, that all of my needs and requests and values and ideas and dreams for our love must be flawed and from a privileged place and therefore, dismissible.

I'm suffocating...

Exhale the self-imposed pressure I endured to make sure that this relationship lasted. That this relationship must work. That we had to make it work! In fact, we had to make it work all the way down the aisle!!! Because...

What did it mean if we failed?

That wouldn't make them right...right?

...

God give me breath, give me Your breath, Your breath of life...

...

Breeeeeeaaaaathe iiiiiin...

Breeeeeeaaaaathe oooooouuuut...

Breeeeeaaaathe iiiiin...

Inhale all of the unique ways I have experienced God when this man walked into my life. Christ was there when he stood trembling, yearning to heal this very old wound, alongside me in an old wooden pew at my new church—my vibrant, progressive, inclusive, life-saving, live-giving Metropolitan Community Church.

A congregation made up of everyone who had been thrown out, tossed aside or chased away from God because of the hate and ignorance displayed by those who claimed to represent Him. Here we all stood together in the most radiant rainbow I had ever seen.

The Holy Spirit was present as I stood back stage with my baby right before his keynote speech, holding his hands in mine and praying to our God, who is the same God, that Ze'd bless my Love with words and confidence while he relayed his message to an auditorium full of fans. God was in the awe that I felt for my partner as I watched pure light fill the room with every educational word he spoke about the trans experience.

I swear that Shiva and Shakti were both there when he and I finally met in real life for the very first time after falling in love online for months. God was in that Vegas hotel room where I'd requested two queens and kept my clothes on...but I did touch him. My hands dipped beneath his pajama pants. I had never been more aroused in my life. He told me...

"You know exactly what to do with my body."

And I did. I did know exactly what to do, because this was bigger than us. We were both just in the flow. We were vessels. We were not the doers. It had all been divinely mapped out long before either of us were even a thought in the other's mind.

It was no random act that I had grown up knowing and loving a transgender best friend, it was no accident that a relative of mine transitioned from male-to-female behind the scenes of my childhood, nor was it a coincidence that my Love needed a new face for Christianity after years of pain brought on by that religion. And that face was mine. I was his angel, he was my prince, and God was the mastermind behind all of it.

It was part of the master plan when my Love would read to me night after night from Ma's book *The Eleven Karmic Spaces*, or chant next to me in his Ashram as his Swami blessed us. All of this took me to a more intimate understanding of how big God really is.

My Savior was there, when my Love told me of his adventures in queer culture and his years of sexual liberation. I followed suit, divulging my thoughts on the sacredness of sex and my choice to remain a virgin all of these years.

The Universe surged through us every time we took a bow after one of our double-bill theatre performances, interlacing our fingers, arching our backs, and together, laying our talents and our stories at the world's feet. It seemed our paths would be interlaced forever. Forever in mission, forever in love, forever in God's limitless possibilities.

Breathe in. Breathe out.

The ego, the devil, whatever you call it, begins to steal my peace. Run away with my joy.

"It didn't last. It's over. You failed. You were wrong. You sinned. You are sin."

Breathe in. Breathe out.

It's just a thought.

I recognize in this moment that a loss of this magnitude is bigger than me. I invite the Holy Spirit in. I acknowledge the divine intervention it will take to mend my heart, to replace all of the lies with love. Love, the truest truth.

Breathe in. Breathe out.

Kinder thoughts make their way into my consciousness. I recall my friend Sofia's words as she treated me to breakup blues sushi just days before...

"So what if it didn't work out. You two still changed the world with your love. It will always be true that a queer transgender yogi fell in love with a straight Christian virgin. That happened. That will be true forever."

Breathe in.

Inhale the truth that God is a God of love, that God is love, that Jesus was actually a man who stood on the side of the oppressed, who surrounded himself with those deemed by society to be outcasts and misfits, that Christ himself fervently argued against pompous religious zealots! That the real Jesus, the Jesus that I believe in, the Jesus that I am in love with and want to emulate, that Jesus would be on the side of marriage equality, that Jesus would be marching proudly in a gay pride parade, and that Jesus celebrated with us when we found our love, and he cried with us when we lost it.

Breeeeeaaaaathe iiiiiiiiiin.

Breeeeeaaaaathe oooooouuuuut.

Out. Out of the muck. Out of the closet. Out of his arms. Out of the water.

A fish out of water.

Leaping into something new.

Brand new territory surrounds me as I sit here ending my meditation. While I have been a Christian my whole life, for the very first time in my life I am defining for myself what it really means to be Christ-like, to actually do what Jesus did. To be an ally. To be a little queer and embrace others in their queerness. To know love, and be loved, and be love, and to surrender expectations of what that love will look like, who will possess that love, and to remain wide open for whatever package that love may come in.

So let it all go.

Breathe in.

Breathe out.

It's just a thought. It's just a thought.

It. Is. Just. A. Thought.

Surrender.

I quiet my mind as best I can, as a brand new yogi.

And I wait expectantly upon the Lord...I wait for God's gentle whisper.

Breathe in. Breathe out.

It's just a thought.

Breathe in. Breathe out.

It's just a thought.

Breathe in. Breathe out.

It's just a thought.

...and then...

A. Bright. White. Light.

...fills my mind...an endless blank canvas...holding all of the possibilities, all of the love, all of it, always, all ways.

God is in all of it, in all of us, in every inch of every perfect body, in all the world, in all the love, and all of that love is mine, to have, to hold, and to freely give as it has been given to me...

IF

I will surrender to it, if I will just...

Trust.

How My Partner's Transition Gave Me Schlubby Ape-Man Complex

Justin Ropella

When your partner transitions genders, you become acutely aware of things you might never have considered before. Not long after I found out my partner is a transgender woman I began to take a hard look at my own sense of self and identity with some of the same focus she used on herself. What I found surprised me.

The overwhelming majority of partners of transgender women I've encountered are cisgender women. As helpful as their perspective is, many of the unique challenges they face are things that don't translate to my relationship. I've heard stories about helping their partners with things like makeup, hair, and clothing, or of catching their partners using their supplies to try things on their own. I can't relate there. While I can help shop for things she needs and give my opinions on what I like, I'm ultimately a man who has been with men for most of his adult life. My knowledge of and assistance with makeup and hair is limited at best. I've had the same $14 haircut since approximately 2001 and shop for clothes almost exclusively at chain discount department stores. I'm not exactly a pinnacle of style here.

It's been interesting how this process can make a partner like me strangely self-conscious, though. I've always been rather comfortable in my skin—comfortable enough, anyway. Sure, I'm overweight and certainly didn't hop out of the pages of a magazine (wait, is *Midwestern Schlub* a magazine?), but I've always adopted an attitude of liking what I like in terms of style. I never really thought too hard about it or cared too much, and I was fine with that. While I've gained and lost weight several times over the years, I never really had any huge physical hang-ups about myself, either.

I had been mindfully working at living a healthier lifestyle during the time in which she came out, so perhaps that put me at a heightened awareness of the physical aspects of what was occurring. Whatever the cause, I found myself internalizing things I would have never cared about before. As my partner talked about her dysphoria and pointed out all the ways she's uncomfortable presenting as male, I found myself assessing the same traits in me and starting to feel a bit uncomfortable too, albeit in a different way.

As her focus on body hair removal progressed, there was more than one occasion where she talked about hair in particular places like her hands and feet being repulsively ugly. I realize, of course, that she's holding herself to a feminine ideal and embracing her true gender expression, but in those moments I couldn't look at the hair creeping down my arms onto the back of my hands without thinking, "Huh. Is this really off-putting? Am I some sort of disgusting, hairy-handed ape-beast? How have I not noticed this before?"

I stood in front of the mirror and thought she might be onto something I just hadn't noticed, and that I should do something about it. I impulsively grabbed the clippers to trim my chest hair in order to test out what a difference in body hair would feel like on me. As it turns out, it just felt itchy and not much of anything else.

I don't have the patience or desire one needs in order to deal with body hair removal—aside from the quick manscape here and there, of course; I'm not an animal.

The same thing happened with clothing. As she talked about how difficult it had always been to shop for herself, she said things like, "Men's clothes are just so boring and ugly. I hate the clothes I've always worn. I hate plaid. I hate giant, clunky guy shoes." Her list of hated, ugly clothing items was not short. While I know she's innocently relating how repressed she's felt in not getting to wear the clothes that she would truly feel comfortable in and that would represent her actual gender, her list of horrible, ugly, disgusting, boring items covers, oh, about 90 percent of my wardrobe. I found myself standing in our closet, looking at my clothes, thinking, "She thinks everything I own is ugly."

Especially since I know that's not what she means, these really are rather stupid thoughts. She doesn't like those things for herself because they represent the repression and disappointment she's felt her whole life. That has nothing to do with me. I should be as comfortable and confident in my own sense of self and style as I ever have been, right? While I logically know I should do that, I still now find myself second-guessing my own tastes and nitpicking myself in the mirror—a very new, very strange phenomenon for me that is still taking some getting used to.

This has happened in other areas too, as she disparages her "boy-mode" identity and her more telling masculine features. I see the things that cause her so much pain and discomfort reflected in and projected by me. Perhaps I'm compelled to adopt her views on them in some kind of subconscious caretaker effort to make her more comfortable, or perhaps I'm just feeling a little unsure of myself as I adjust to fluctuations in my own body. Either way, it's been strange for someone who has historically given very little thought to these things to be suddenly so very aware of them. Maybe someday I'll again be able to walk into a store and feel comfortable with my only serious criteria for a purchase being (1) whether it covers what I intend it to cover, (2) whether it complies with my office's dress code, and (3) whether it is on sale.

On second thought, she might be doing me a favor here.

Lost in Transition

MIGNONNE POLLARD

I said, "Yes." I said, *yes I would be there* with Nick through the operation and afterward. Of course, I would be there!

I had not planned on falling in love with Nick. I was happy in my Black lesbian world, limited but safe. I knew the rules of the game, people's histories, where I fit in that world. I was married to a Black woman stationed overseas in the military when I met Nick, though I had divorced by the time of his surgery. While I did not want to fall in love, all of a sudden there was this person who reminded me of myself before I came out.

Nick made me feel like when I was in my twenties living in New York City and traveling to and from Europe. He had similar features to my long lost love, a Frenchman. My buried and forgotten history came alive, and that history opened the door for Nick to walk into my heart.

When an earthquake hits, sometimes there is a small tremor as the earth shakes beneath your feet. It is the warning before the books fall off the shelf, before you look for the nearest doorframe, before your whole world comes crashing in towards you. Nick was my earthquake, and my life will never be the same again. I can no longer hide in small confines of sexuality, gender, and race. My world came crashing down and it has taken me three years to rebuild it. It has taken me three years to come to a place of acceptance to write this love letter to the man who changed my life forever.

At first it was innocent. I was "off limits." He was "safe" living with Karen. I had known Nick when he was Nicole. The irony is that my ex-wife and I wanted to invite her over and become her friend. We wanted to expand out of our little world and thought Nicole was cool. Before any of that could take place though, my ex-wife and I moved overseas.

Nine months or so later, I came home before my ex-wife's tour of duty was over. I searched for meaning and purpose, and I went deep into contemplation about what I wanted to do with my life. In the midst of following my passions I met Nick. He told me a sentence or two about changing genders. I had compassion, it all seemed so natural. The change in gender seemed just *right*. I really liked being with this guy. I did not know Nicole that well, but I got to know Nick intimately.

It was innocent. We started as friends meeting over our mutual interests of making the world a better place. We shared our hopes, dreams; we worked together on creating a future. I felt alive, totally alive. He was a gentleman and always paid for the excursions although I signed the bill. You see, his credit cards read, "Nicole Gottlieb." I would giggle and say, "I don't think I look like a 'Gottlieb.'" I would get angry if a waiter or waitress called Nick, "her." *Why couldn't they see what I saw?* Nick as a charismatic, fun-loving, adventuresome, handsome man with mesmerizing light brown eyes.

After each time we got together, I could not wait until we would meet again. Our weekly meetings turned into twice weekly. Twice weekly turned into weekends—weekends turned into road trips. If we weren't together, we were Skyping or texting.

I loved being at the highest of high femmes with him. I was inspired! I went into overdrive of femininity—played every role—cooked, cleaned, and cared. I was really unaware of what was happening. I was like a magnet being pulled by an unstoppable force. I loved every moment of being with him.

Then, one day after a couple of months, it happened. We looked into each other's eyes and talked about sex—when, how, where. We talked. We *planned.*

We did not cross the line for months. I was trying to be a friend, not admitting my feelings. I accepted Nick as male long before his surgery. It is difficult to record months of conversations or the mental dance I did when Nick unbound his breasts and we slept next to one another. I loved him regardless of his body. I loved his soul.

As the months rolled by I helped Nick get over his broken heart and his failed relationship with Karen. I shared my own sadness over the end of my marriage. And on the day of my final filing for divorce, church bells were ringing in the background as Nick and I talked on the phone. I took the bells as a sign of better things to come for both of us. Let freedom ring!

We were still one month away from Nick's surgery. I believed my life was about to change into everything I had always dreamed. There really *was* a Prince Charming and we really *would* ride off into the sunset. *And nobody would know our little secret: That Nick was transgender.*

I was willing to keep that secret, too, despite my history as an outspoken woman of color LGBTQ activist. When I was living in Boston in the early to mid-1990s, I helped a group called

"Girlfriends" become a non-profit coming-out support group for lesbian and bisexual women of color. Black, Latina, and mixed-race women needed a place "just for us." I was even written up in *Bay Windows*, the local gay/lesbian newspaper. However, our group had no idea about intersex and transgender people—identities we generally viewed as a "White thing."

Then one of my best friends in Boston, an old-time White dyke from the Midwest, introduced me to Leslie Feinberg, a trans person who wrote *Stone Butch Blues* and *Transgender Warriors*. I actually met and talked to Leslie when he came to Boston in 1993 for the Outwrite Conference for LGBTQI writers. I admired Leslie primarily because he was the first White person that I encountered who understood the complexities of race and gender and wrote about Black dykes in the sea of White lesbian literature that I was drowning in at the time.

Perhaps meeting Leslie and reading *Transgender Warriors* some seventeen years before I would meet Nick was the tremor to prepare me for what was to shake my world. Of course, I flirted with Leslie and, being a gentle person, he flirted back, within appropriate limits of course. These interactions made me smile throughout the entire conference, and even now as I recall our interactions. Some of my most treasured possessions include signed copies of *Transgender Warriors* and *Stone Butch Blues*.

So, there it is—the tremor. I was open to having my whole world turned upside down.

Four years ago, I gave my first gift to Nick on his birthday: my signed copy of *Transgender Warriors*. However, after I had given him my copy, I later demanded it back and had Amazon deliver a copy to his house—I felt it was very important for him to have his own, even if he couldn't have mine. He had no idea about transgender rights and no interest back then. He was happy in his transitioning and wanted to be "incognito."

For a while I really enjoyed the heterosexual privilege that I had with Nick, it made me forget about all those years in the lesbian ghetto. When I was with him, I was free to be the most feminine me balanced by his masculine energy. It did not even bother me that people read him as a gay man. My friends would look at him and say, "Honey, he seems a little gay." I would say, "Yeah, but he is not."

Now, is that a lie? Perhaps. But it did not feel like a lie at the time. Should I be ashamed that after seventeen years of calling myself a "lesbian" that I liked being read as straight? I became unsure of my orientation. I had my second identity crisis, in my mid-forties, and I swung between defining myself as "bisexual" and "lesbian." *What does it mean to be "lesbian" with a man?*

Bisexuality won. Bisexual is the only truth I know to be true. I fell in love with a man: a trans man.

During this time, I attended an annual "Significant Others, Family, Friends, and Allies" (SOFFA) dance. I got to know a few people in the local transgender community. I felt protective of trans folks, perhaps like people did in the early days when gays and lesbians came out. Still, I never claimed the title of "Significant Other." I was more like a "Friend with Benefits."

The benefits included meeting Nick's only brother and an amazingly special trip to Nick's hometown. For me, the trip was about new beginnings. The trip for Nick seemed to be more about closure and reconciliation with his past as he was saying goodbye to his mother, childhood memories, and friends. He was releasing the last of *Nicole* while I was imagining life with *Nick*. It was the summer of 2011 and the visit took place about two weeks before his surgery.

During a two-and-a-half hour drive back from his coastal hometown to his apartment I was daydreaming about cooking his favorite meals, what to do with the dogs, and going to meet the surgeon before the procedure. He fell asleep as I drove home; I looked at him and smiled. I was ready for whatever was ahead for us in life.

July rolled into August and as the date of the operation approached, I put my life on hold. Then one week before the surgery he called and said simply, "I don't want you at the surgery. I choose Karen. You understand, don't you?"

No, I really did not understand. He had not spoken to Karen for weeks—or so I thought. We had just firmed up the calendar for when *we* (*he and I*) would talk to the surgeon. When he called, I was out grocery shopping for the meals I would prepare after the surgery.

Even though I did not understand I said, "I love you. I will take really good care of you." He replied, "I know. I choose Karen."

I could do nothing but love him from afar. After the surgery, I knew intuitively that something went wrong. I felt something so sharp in my own chest. It was a pain I've never felt before, an intuitive hit that was about Nick.

Later that same day, I got a call from a mutual friend saying Nick had been rushed back to the hospital due to post-surgical complications. I did not go to the hospital; I did not visit him at home. I could not. The first few months after his surgery, early 2012, I tried to be "friends" and even tried to be a "dating coach" for him. These were the most painful roles for me. I had to go into silence and withdraw as I let go of our past connection, like the dreams we shared on the Pacific Coast Liner in the first-class passenger car.

Back then, I had not realized that the champagne-infused life we described to each other was "his dream" and "my dream," not "our dream together." But slowly I realized I had to get off this train called "transition"; my life was a wreck. I did not know what to do next, now that I was divorced and my dream with Nick was shattered.

In every sense of the word, I had become the *transition girl.* Nick wanted me in his future on the sidelines of his life as part of a happy foursome, yet this was a life I could never imagine living.

Aftershock. Those are the tremors that happen long after the earthquake has hit.

Today, it has been three years since the operation, the time of transition, and I get to see Nick living the life he dreamed about. Now Nick is an advocate for transgender rights. He gives workshops and lectures and inspires youth to live authentically. I see him happy and in love with his French-inspired girlfriend who is everything that he wanted in a partner, a woman who knows the fullness of womanhood: a mother, a performer, a person who loves dogs and football, *a person with milky White skin.*

There is a cheesy saying, "When you love someone you set them free." I did that the moment Nick said just the opposite of what every girl wants to hear. I set him free when he did not choose me. Nick is not coming back. Our journey was never about going backwards. It was always about moving into the future and living the life we were meant to live.

I am living life thankful for the magic and dreams Nick brought into my own world. I am grateful to him for helping me feel alive again and to experience life in Technicolor after so many shades of gray.

As a result of my relationship with Nick, I now have transgender friends with whom I have clear boundaries, people who are on the road to transition right now. I am open and understanding of transgender youth. I followed the fight to "Free CeCe McDonald"—and now she is free! When I interviewed to be the Director of a Women's Center at a nearby university campus, I did not bat an eye when the campus tour was led by a Black MTF transgender youth. I was not surprised when I learned that the biggest fight on campus was for unisex bathrooms, and found out that most of the transgender youth on that campus (MTF and FTM) felt more at home in the Women's Center than at the LGBTQ Center. It all felt right; I understood. I owe some of this to the expansion of my awareness around gender, race, and sexuality to the fact that I fell in love with a trans man.

Still, I've never understood why I was rejected by Nick. I want to blame it on race. I want to blame it on the past. I want to blame it on someone or something. But the truth is: There is no one and nothing to blame. It was a time of transition. No one can take away the love I gave him. Now, that love is channeled into my larger life purpose. I work with foster care parents around issues facing gay, lesbian, and transgender youth, and have become an advocate for trans youth.

My heart has been opened wider than it has been in years. I am exposed to possibilities I never consciously imagined before. I know my relationship with Nick forever changed my life. My world was shaken, but now I stand on solid ground. I send my love and best wishes to Nick and his chosen family.

My transition is complete.

The Last Thing You Are to Me Is Invisible

Michelle Bressette

Standing in the kitchen, with warm tears brimming my eyes and a hitch in my throat, I blurted, "I know this isn't helpful, but I feel icky for you."

How could I have possibly thought that such a lame attempt at empathy would be okay? I only had an inkling that my partner had just experienced one of the most jarring episodes of gender dysphoria to date. Yet, in my desire to be supportive, all I had in me was a weak attempt to make it about me and my insecurity, as well as about how I could actually be supportive this time.

Would I *ever* get this right?

For hours afterward I felt emotionally overtaken and unable to focus on my work. I left the house that evening to escape. The last thing I needed to do was to entrench my family in the throes of my own intense processing. I felt selfish, guilty, and wounded.

I sped down Interstate 70 wailing and lost, ending up at a sympathetic friend's house. There I continued to rock and sway and vomit up my grief for a number of hours until the emotion was spent or at least softened. She offered hot Earl Gray tea laced with raw granular honey as a warm comfort. I wrapped up in a woven blanket on the couch with her unfailing strong arms wrapped around me. Her warm hands stroked my hair.

Gradually she soothed away the grief and tamed it from a ferocious growl to a low hum. At one point I remember saying, "I just don't feel like I'm allowed to be *me* sometimes!" followed by the cold hard realization of cisgender privilege slapping me across the face. The tears started again. Could I really continue to do this? Was it too big, even for myself? I really didn't know.

Three years ago I enrolled in massage school to continue developing my personal client base into a more medically oriented massage therapy practice. Recently, I'd decided to leave retail management and pursue my passions and spiritual practices: yoga, meditation, and Thai massage. My son was old enough to begin staying home alone and I was happily single and not dating. During this time I focused on myself and my career. I really wanted to see my life evolve.

My partner and I met the first day of massage school in anatomy class. We discovered we both had rowed on crew teams in college and were from the northeastern United States. We were also fiercely competitive and intellectually driven. We found common ground in an academic atmosphere, where we would have ignored each other otherwise, and began building a strong friendship.

We shared some classes together, which pleased me greatly. I knew I would have someone to commiserate with regarding the class material, instructors, or other frustrating aspects of being a well-grounded adult student. Our initial simple conversations began to grow in depth and embrace those things that intimately drew us to one another. More and more, side-by-side, we eventually discovered that we shared a passion for spiritually informed social justice and a fierce dedication to providing our massage and counseling services to those who don't typically have access to them. I greatly appreciated the evolution of our friendship, whereas with others, I had been hard-pressed to find depth or freedom to express my inner feelings. Not only was I free to express my authentic self, but our relationship required that I was *charged* with doing so.

The friendship we built three years ago is now what we constantly draw from. It serves as an intense wellspring of patience, understanding, and mutual respect we both crave and require in order to be in a truly intimate relationship. We live with the intention of being true to ourselves; we strive to be autonomous and whole as individuals. It wasn't until I was given this autonomous freedom of expression that I could begin to understand when life requires one to live invisibly.

In many respects, our meeting, growing, and loving were easy. Ze was unabashedly out when I met hir. As I wanted to thoroughly understand the concept of third gender, I spent countless hours doing my own research to fully grasp the nuances of trans life from a cisgender feminist perspective. I was present to watch hir tell a classroom full of students how to use third gender pronouns. I was "in the know" and supported hir fully, taking on the progressive gender education of our fellow students with enthusiastic zeal. I was going to be the model ally.

With the perfect timing, I was dealt with the harsh reality check. When I learned that ze was in a verbal altercation in a grocery store that could have ended in injury, I was glad I had not been there. I knew that I would have been posturing in a loud, aggressive way, possibly getting us both hurt. I was enraged that someone dared to threaten my partner in front of his young children. My suburban home no longer felt safe for my family.

Having navigated this kind of transphobia before, my partner handled the situation with the strength and conviction of someone who knows themselves inside and out, who isn't afraid to look fear in the face and skillfully convince the enemy it would be wise to back down. The level of mature stillness required not to engage physically with hate and fear, takes years to perfect, and it was just the beginning of my understanding.

When the possibility of a car breaking down, missing a bus, choosing a bathroom stall, or when any other "normal" daily inconvenience becomes a dangerous reality, being visible is a liability. I felt that I was a trusted partner, but also a tenuous liability.

I am not used to being invisible in any way. In addition to being from a loud, gregarious family, I was taught from a very young age to *own* a room when I walk into it or else someone else will own me. As a cis-gender white woman, I've spent my life being unapologetic about my aggressiveness and could afford to do so as the "protected class." This brash demeanor served me well in a male-dominated world and I was continually rewarded for it, frequently at the cost of others' feelings. I relished being able to take risks that made other people cringe. I have always been a proud risk-taker—a classic marker of unchecked privilege.

Part of this demeanor also evolved from my family's propensity to defend my loved ones the way an enraged bear would, regardless of the consequences. This was especially true since I was a single mother of a child with special needs. However, my willingness to risk my own safety and the safety of my family is no longer warranted or desired. I've struggled with taking off the coat of protective aggressiveness that I've been trained to wear throughout my life. My risky driving, mouthing off, and brusque facade are no longer humorous or helpful. Learning to let go of the combative persona I have perfected involved a lot of grief, embarrassment, and anger, as well as a willingness to take a good look at the example my partner presents daily. When your partner's safety is at stake and not your ego, you let your ego die over and over again.

Our relationship is a constant reminder of what it means to be seen authentically and what taking personal responsibility and ownership of that authenticity looks like. No longer do I need to be the biggest, loudest person in the room in order to understand my impact. I do not need to protect myself by wielding my personality like a katana, slashing through anyone who gets in my way and walking away without regard to the carnage that may result from my actions.

So, I'm learning that I don't need to become a bear or brandish weapons to defend or protect what I love. Rather, it takes commitment to become aware and humble. It takes a willingness to work on my own history because it benefits *me* to grow as a compassionate human being. I need to inhabit my body even though I was raised to believe that this was not only an undesirable place to *be*, but that my body was a tool that could be used against me. I was trained to use my body against others in order to get anything I needed.

Being in a relationship with a trans person has opened the door to a world of self-validity that I could have never touched otherwise. I have been afforded the space to take off my own oppressive clothes that once kept the real me hidden, secret, and lost. Now that I am no longer coveting and hoarding, I am open and vulnerable and thus able to bloom into my own authenticity.

Now I am free to inhabit my own body by honoring someone else's choice to truly inhabit their body. As a result, I feel more trusted, cherished, and loved than ever before *because I love myself more*. There is much more depth to my integrity and a lot less noise. The vision I now see in the mirror is mine to own—be it a yogi, femme, or cleric. The key is that I can gaze at *myself* unapologetically.

I no longer choose to claim "ally" as my identity. Only a trans person or anyone from a marginalized oppressed community can truly determine who is their ally. That attribute can only be given to me in moments of grace and solidarity, when the image in the mirror matches what I hold in my heart.

When I came home from my cathartic meltdown, my partner had no idea of the depth of my visit with my beautiful, kind friend across town. I explained to hir that I left because I caught myself trying to hijack the family with my own emotional baggage and chose to leave. Hir response was "well that was mature" and ze meant it. Ah, the progress.

The following day was bathed in glorious normalcy. Curled up on the living room couch, I was studying practical theology in the warm sun. My partner approached me to share how the previous day's events at a training for shoulder injury recovery had unfolded. Ze lightly grasped my arm, palpated my spine through my sports bra, manipulating my scapula in its natural range of motion. Ze demonstrated with firm, sure hands how other participants in the training had to move their partner's bodies when working together.

Even though all the students worked with each other in an appropriate, respectful manner, ze described how the process of working in such close physical proximity brought hir to a place of intense emotional sensation. My partner recalled an experience similar in intensity to a political demonstration in previous years. Unlike the clinical training, the demonstration included the military, helicopters, and public protests. The demonstrators from years ago had supportive, debriefing sessions and resources for processing trauma. "Normal" professional trainings don't require debriefings—or gender-neutral restrooms.

This I Believe

Ann Bloomfield

Ten years ago I was preparing for my wedding to the man of my dreams. Ross and I were young, optimistic, and in love. Our beautiful, intimate wedding was held in the mountains. The year that followed was challenging; it was filled with a taxing promotion for me, a new baby, job changes for both of us, and moving in with my mom so that we could all make ends meet.

Eventually Ross found a job, I became pregnant with our second child, and then he found a better job. His new position allowed me to finish my bachelor's degree, earn a master's degree, and start a career of my own in recruiting. At about this point, Ross became frustrated with work and was longing for a change. We started job hunting and ended up in Phoenix, Arizona.

Moving was tough. We spent six weeks living apart with Ross in Arizona and the kids and I waiting for the end of the school year in Ohio. When the big day arrived, we packed our truck, hugged our family goodbye, and set off on our journey to our better life.

When we arrived in Arizona, we were a little older, but still in love and optimistic about things to come. Once the homesickness passed and we started to make friends, I felt like we were finally where we were supposed to be.

In early November of that year Ross came to me nervous and confused. He said that he felt that he was a cross-dresser, meant to be a woman, or something else that he was not able to explain. I cried and cried and said that I could not do it. If a transition had to happen, we would need to divorce. I am straight after all. How could he expect me to live with him as a woman?

I was terrified for myself, my children, and our marriage. Both of my parents had two marriages that ended in divorce, I knew what being the child of divorce could be like, and I did not want that for my children. As a child who watched my mother sacrifice her needs for my siblings and me, I knew that I did not want that for myself. So I decided to stay and try to live in this new relationship. Upon reflection, I felt I owed it to myself, my children, and Ross, now Rhea, to try.

Day after day our life was redefined. What started as occasional cross-dressing shifted to Rhea identifying as a transgender woman without wanting to transition. When the emotional strain of being dual-gendered became too much, it was time to embrace transition. While Rhea has been able to bloom and develop and become more at peace, I have not.

I struggle living with the ghost of my husband who is now a woman. I miss the hardness of a masculine hug, the feeling of protection and looking forward to seeing Ross dressed in a suit and tie, wearing great cologne. I am disappointed that my children won't have a dad in their life. My dad was not around much when I was a kid, and I promised myself that I would never put my kids through a childhood without a dad. Now, I am dealing with the reality that two good parents are more than enough, regardless of gender.

Goodbye, Love

ANN BLOOMFIELD

Ross,

It has taken me a while but the time has finally come that I give you a proper goodbye. I know that neither of us is strong enough to do this face to face, and some things are best to be shared between me and the paper.

I want you to know that I love you and that will never change. The life that we had, even with the challenges that we faced, was perfect. I was absolutely in love with every part of you and, while I still get to have some of that and the wonderful new parts of you, I wonder when the sting of losing my husband will fade.

Many times at night when I reach over to put my arm across you I am startled by the softness that has replaced the muscular chest that I slept on so many nights. During the day I am aware of the changes, but in the night I still wake up expecting my husband to be lying there next to me. Logically, I know that you are the same beautiful soul that I fell in love with all those years ago, but emotionally I miss the man who has gone away. I loved your muscles, your hair, and the feeling of strength and security that you gave me. Now I find myself needing to be the one who is strong and protective, and it exhausts me.

I am so happy that you haven't totally gone away, and that our boys will have two parents raising them, but I miss being "Mom and Dad." Watching the kids struggle to redefine their relationship with you and figure out how to present you to their friends has been incredibly painful for me. I don't ever want them to be ashamed or embarrassed of who you are or who we are, but I sense an awkwardness—one that they don't want to bring up because they want to protect your feelings. I know that we are doing our best to raise wonderful people. I just hope that we are able to surround them with enough loving, accepting people that they don't feel like they are missing out on something because of our family structure.

The thing I miss the most, now that you are gone, is the ease of life that I took for granted for so many years. I never realized how intimidating it could be to be authentic until I had to introduce you as my wife for the first time. I grew up with gay uncles and for us that was normal, but I never appreciated how difficult it must have been for them to live in such a small town knowing that they were not viewed the same as a heterosexual couple. It is difficult for me to be viewed as someone I am not by anyone who doesn't know us well, but it would be harder to live my life without some version of you in it every single day.

I have realized that I love you more than I ever thought I could and that I am capable of far more than I ever knew. I am honored that I get to be a part of this journey with you and that I get to know the true you. I am so thankful that I am not saying goodbye to you entirely, but the parts of you that I have lost I will miss for the rest of my life.

Hello, Ladies

SHAWNEE PARENS

I don't think I ever noticed how much the word "ladies" is used until I fell in love with Ray.

Curiously, we seemed to get "ladied" more after Ray had top surgery than before he started "T" or changed his name. Were we simply noticing it more or were people trying harder to categorize us? It grated on Ray's nerves, but I tried to make sense of it and give the benefit of the doubt. "It's their service standards, I'm sure. They're required to say 'ladies' when two women are together, even if we're not both girly." At the time, he hadn't decided to transition yet. Hence, it was not inaccurate to identify us as a gay couple.

Two years later, after Ray's gender transitioning however, I've stopped offering the benefit of the doubt so generously. Now my role is, The Friendly Corrector. Not to brag, but I've become exceptionally good at saying, "Excuse me, we're not both ladies," with a smile on my face, trying to come across as both firm and kind. I don't want to embarrass anyone and I don't want tension. I really just want two things in those moments: for the pronouns to be correct and for my love to enjoy our time out.

It doesn't always go well.

One night at one of our favorite neighborhood restaurants, a new server greeted us; we didn't recognize him. Something about his manner set off red flags for both of us. Ray leaned over to me and said, "He's going to be one of those faux-sensitive-earthy-guys who calls us ladies. Just wait."

Ray was right, of course. As soon as Mr. Sensitive took our orders, it happened.

"Thank you, ladies."

There are some times when this can sound like a slur. This was one of those times, when "ladies" doesn't sound polite, but drawls out with a bit of an edge. Or, maybe that's just how I heard it. Regardless of his intent, I turned to him feeling tired and not up to mustering my usual appeasing friendliness.

"Excuse me. We are not ladies. My partner is a transgender man. But, honestly, many lesbian couples I know also do not really enjoy being called 'ladies.'"

Mr. Sensitive responded immediately: "Well, I'll just let them tell me themselves what they want to be called." His tone got smarmy, sarcastic. "But thank you for *communicating* with me. I like communication. Communication is *good*."

Then he walked away.

We seethed.

I don't know why we stayed. I wanted to stomp out or call to the manager, but I just shook in my seat. Another server delivered our meal. I ate very little, tasting none of it. I didn't drink my margarita. I just sat and stewed, furious with his attitude. Early in our relationship and well before Ray had begun transitioning, I remembered him telling me that sometimes people would call him "sir"—which he didn't mind at all—and when they realized their mistake, would get angry and rude with him. "It's like they feel it's my fault that they are uncomfortable."

Our server finally reappeared later to bring us the check. He also brought us an apology.

"I'm sorry about what I said. I went to the back and I thought, 'What else am I going to say if I can't say 'ladies?' But then I thought, well I could say 'Hi folks!' or 'You guys.'"

We were shocked.

"Or you don't have to say anything at the end," I replied, digging deep for some compassion and patience to teach. "You can just say 'Hi' and 'How are you?' and 'Thank you.' You'll never go wrong with gender neutral. It works for everyone."

His apology seemed sincere, but even so, Ray and I ruminated on this interaction for days.

Ray has been on testosterone for nine months. He craves for facial hair or sideburns, something visible that undeniably indicates manhood. His voice has dropped though, and his body has shifted—broad shoulders, squarer jaw, and harder lines on his face. My straight female friends pull me aside to tell me how handsome he has become. He's more comfortable in his skin, walks taller, and makes eye contact more. In our small Midwestern city, we are almost never called "ladies" anymore.

We got married in June and flew out a few days later for a honeymoon in San Francisco, coinciding delightfully with Pride weekend. On our departing trip, every flight attendant, TSA agent, and taxi driver called Ray "Sir." On the plane we had a hushed conversation about how to refer to each other in public. To help Ray pass, we agreed that "husband" and "wife" would be safer. But the terms stuck in my throat; I wrestled with being called someone's wife.

We stayed at "all are welcome" gay B&B where everyone was friendly, but a few people gave us curious looks.

"Trying to figure us out," Ray said.

I wondered to myself what they ended up deciding. At the wine social one night, a man from Texas asked me, "Is your friend…uh… partner…she…he…sitting here?" I laughed at how he covered all of his bases and we spent the next half hour sharing vacation stories and a plate of snacks with his partner and Ray joining us.

The big surprise came when we went out to dinner on the first night and at the end of the evening we were called "ladies." It had been so long since this had happened to us that we were stunned and silent. Ray second-guessed his appearance; I encouraged him not to let it ruin what had been an otherwise perfect evening. I wondered with hope, "Had we misheard it?"

No, we hadn't. This was a regular occurrence during our trip to the Bay area. I dusted off my line again, ready to respond quickly. "Excuse me, we aren't both ladies."

Perhaps you are wondering why Ray doesn't say something. Why is this my job? I can't speak for him, but I can tell you what I see. I see, with my heart, that when he is mistaken for a woman he folds into himself. I feel a combination of anger and sadness and many other complex and nameless emotions fly off of him. With a feeling of protectiveness I leap into action: I address the label as quickly as possible so that he can rejoin me, so that it doesn't ruin our evening, so he and the server can collect themselves and we can move on.

I frequently worry that the reason we're read as a gay female couple is because of me. Ray doesn't get it. One night over dinner I tried to explain.

"It's Pride weekend. We're staying in the Castro. Everyone in this city is primed to be looking for gay couples. They see me and they peg us as a butch-femme couple. If I look straighter, I bet they'd see you as a guy."

"What do you mean, it's how you look? You look straight."

I honestly didn't know how to feel about this.

"Look around the restaurant." We were sitting in an upscale place in the Embarcadero that seemed primarily straight. "Find me a straight woman with short hair."

"Straight women have short hair."

"Right. Halle Berry, for example. Find me one in this restaurant."

"But…but…you just look like any mom from our neighborhood."

"Um, thanks. So in the 'lesbian or Midwesterner' competition, you'd vote for me to be identified as a 'Midwestern middle-aged mom?'"

Fantastic. I was feeling sexier by the minute.

Up until recently, I hadn't considered how my appearance might affect Ray's passing. In our funky little neighborhood, which is full of families and queers, I do blend in—both with lesbians and with other moms, gay and straight. However, I know from working with a lot of straight women that there are many small signifiers that call me out as not-straight, even when I'm girlie-ed up in a dress and heels.

I identify as bisexual and am happier when I'm read as queer rather than straight. But this comes with a conundrum. If I look queer, perhaps that influences people to read Ray as female when we're out together. As Ray becomes more undeniably masculine, will we cease being recognized as a butch-femme couple? It is more likely that folks will simply conclude I'm a straight Midwestern mom. Not that there's anything wrong with that.

In the end, being called "ladies" repeatedly did not ruin our honeymoon. I gave the correction each time and it usually went well. One server craned her neck around almost comically to get a good look at Ray's face; another vanished for most of our meal. As we left the grandstand at the Pride parade, a fellow reveler yelled, "Happy Pride, Ladies!!" But those were just small moments.

We had barely been back for two weeks when we began daydreaming about another vacation.

"Let's just go lay on a beach for a week. Do one of those all-inclusive things where they bring you cocktails and snacks all day."

For fun, I did a quick online search for "LGBT all-inclusive resorts" and discovered, very quickly, that a large number refer to themselves as "gay and lesbian," which does not include us.

"Baby, what will we do?"

Ray shrugged. "We'll have to go to a straight resort. And people will just think we're straight."

Nobody would call us "ladies." But I wonder how at home we'll feel?

Cocoon

S.J. Sindu

I am the stepping stone
the rope that saves the drowning transman
        Don't worry, baby, I got this
Testosterone throbs in your blood
rides on your cells
as they soar and dip
through your body
through your brain
anger and sex
like any other man

I can give you hormone shots
a horse needle through the leg
        Don't worry, baby, I got this
I'll stand by your bed
before surgery
and tell you I love you
with or without breasts

I can use phrases like
double bi-lateral mastectomy
metoidioplasty
urethral lengthening
phrases that morph in the mouth
and taste like metallic saline
taste buds dissecting themselves

I can make you feel like a man
until you no longer need this trophy
          I am the fucking Camaro
I can suck you off
know enough to ask before touching anything
know to call it a penis
call them balls
cringe when you refer to your uterus
pretend you don't have one

I can let you fall fast
fall hard
head over heels
because I'm there
at the point when you are neither
that cusp of change
before the world turns inside out
and shows its seams
the string unraveling
tying in on itself
like a surgeon's stitches

I can be the guide that holds your hand
the voice that whispers sugar cane

even when I am trapped in the saccharine
          drowning
          invisible
caught between the carbon bonds
poisoned by phenylalanine
during tea time
spiraling, draining
like blood in a bathtub

I can tell you I see stubble on your chin
when all I see are shadows
satisfy a sky-rocketing sex drive
          Don't worry, baby
Of course your hairline's not receding
And yes, your penis is bigger than it was two hours ago

I can tell you I love your scars
          Do you want to see mine?
remnants of internal bleeding
cut by your manhood
          This is your story
but I am the pages you mark
with the ink of transition
branded
the discarded cocoon

I wrote this poem five years ago on the heels of an emotional break-up with my first long-term partner, a trans man who medically and socially transitioned while we were together. At the time, I was exploring my own gender and struggling to come out as gender variant in a heteronormatively gendered relationship.

Since then, I've dated other trans men and come out as genderqueer. I've supported many others through transition and done grassroots organizing around trans issues. Still, I find this poem relevant not only to my own experiences as a female-bodied queer person who sometimes dates trans men, but also to the experiences of many other partners of trans men whom I've supported and befriended.

The poem speaks specifically to partners of trans men who are medically transitioning. Some of these trans men feel an intense need to fit into normative social roles and see their partners as extensions of, or foils to, their own gender. The poem speaks to the experience of partners who have the supporting role in an unbalanced relationship.

It speaks to the lies we tell as partners of trans men because we love them and want to mitigate their suffering. It speaks to the overall cultural anxiety caused by body and gender dysphoria. It speaks to overcompensation, hypermasculinity, misogyny, male privilege, and other issues present in the transmasculine discourse. It speaks to the social power shift that occurs when one partner transitions and the ways that change can reverberate throughout a relationship.

Mandy and Me

Kathe Burkhart

"In sum, true homosexuality… could occur in the case of a man and a woman who would both be gay, or a man and a woman who would both be lesbians.…So that even homosexuality is repressed homosexuality since its imaginary is heterosexual"

Guy Hocquenghem *The Screwball Asses (1973)*

I met her in the bowels of the Internet on a fetish website. It was winter and I was lonely, having just filed for divorce from my partner of fifteen years.

A month and a million emails later, we finally met in an East Village cafe. It was the first time I had ever met anyone in person whom I had met online. Mandy had cancelled our first date, which was on Valentine's Day, showing the sensitivity of a wrecking ball. Mandy is a beautiful, completely passable pre-op transwoman and musician who worked as a real estate agent. She had transitioned in the mid-90s.

There was chemistry between us right away. At one point, she had to go to the bathroom to loosen her corset so that she could breathe. I was enchanted.

We were together on and off for about three years. I called her my mermaid. I used to joke that on a good day I got two for one, on a bad day, I got a bitch and an asshole.

She dresses like Mary Tyler Moore, a "career woman," in a fitted suit with support hose, body shapers, and stilettos. She assembles her designer label wardrobe mostly from thrift shops. Her breasts are well developed and her body is further feminized by the foundation garments and the redistribution of body fat. Like Candy Darling, she is not a modern woman, but an outmoded throwback to another time.

"You dress like the enemy," I used to say, teasing. "Would you actually hang out with anybody who dresses like that?" I asked her.

She explained that it was just about passing in public and the public humiliation and/or danger that she might experience if she didn't pass. When we're out together, she winks at me with a twinkle in her eye when she "passes" with straight men; she *loves* it. I don't ever raise an eyebrow, because I'm so proud to be with someone that strong.

She was quick to explain to me that she's not interested in men; she's a *lesbian*, and that's her excuse for why she won't suck my latex cock. What kind of a lesbian will I make? I find cunnilingus irritating after a few minutes.

Her greatest fantasy is to be a beautiful woman, a living doll so desirable that no one, man or woman, can resist her. A femme fatale, a covert secret agent who slides off a pink, estrogen-fueled cloud.

To a certain extent, I worry that she confuses feminism and femininity, not quite grasping how gender roles can be reinscribed through an embrace of stereotypes, what might be called *feminin*ism.

Whether we are more heterosexual or homosexual is constantly in flux. We are both phallic women, connected by our mutual dysphoria; masculine hands, broad shoulders, class position and work ethic, through our soft breasts and lips; we are weird fraternal twins. I think one thing that freaks her out about me is when it gets to be too gay male for her sometimes. I was born this way, intersex, and she was not; still, sissies and tomboys have a lifelong bond.

I had to learn to recognize her verbal cues: when she calls with a fake European accent and pitches her voice up, addressing me in French as *Madame* or in German as *Meine Freundin*, it is always a booty call.

I love the waves of femininity that wash down her face an hour or so after she takes her hormones, watching it pulse, like plasma or a lava lamp. She is my inverse proportion. I'm her inside out and she's my outside in. The gender play is irresistible, priceless, electrical; I feel her his-and-hers energy coalesce with mine. This ecstatic full spectrum sex is like having both a boyfriend and a girlfriend at once to the tenth power.

I take her to the doctor for testing and hormones and pay for it. I can't even afford to go to the doctor myself. I spend the day waiting for her in the depressing HRA office during the holidays while she applies for SNAP and general relief. I take her to Callen Lorde for medical care.

Mandy is unprepared and has to go uptown for her documents. We're supposed to meet at 2:45 p.m. in front of the Whitney Museum. The Whitney is closed. She has no phone.

Mandy calls saying she's being sexually harassed at work. They taunt her, playing "Walk on the Wild Side" and snickering. I would kick the ass of anybody who would get in her way or try to insult or harm her.

I drop everything, including my sister's birthday present, and take the train uptown to 68th and Lexington Avenue, put her in a cab, bring her home, buy her wine and sorbet. She calls Lambda Legal and we watch a movie. I tell her I love her and caress her. To my astonishment, she gets up abruptly and runs out on me.

Queer heterosexuality with kink is way out on the front lines. No matter how ready we might be for it, the world isn't quite ready for us yet. Our new queer world is still too science fiction for most people. This is still a really hard thing to do.

We talk about going to Amsterdam together, where I've lived part of the year since the mid-90s. She'd be able to get better, cheaper health care there and get out of the rat race. Three summers come and go but she never comes. She wants me to pay her way but I can't; I can barely afford to support myself.

We dream of doing a performance in the Red Light District to make phallic women visible, because there are no hard cocks to be seen in those windows. T-girls and men do not work there openly. She'd be the prostitute and I'd be her pimp photographer. She would pass all day in the window but for a certain number of hours per day, she would untuck. Her services would only be for women. I would make beautiful photos of her trident unfurled, bathed in the warm red light.

Mandy knows that I'm leaving for the summer soon, so she texts me. She comes and we have a bottle of wine and we feel so good in each other's arms. I believe her when she says that she has loved me all this time.

Mandy tells me she stopped taking her blockers and is taking it easy on estrogen. She is one hot mess. She spills red wine all over the place, spraying it onto the pristine white closet door, madly flailing her arms about in bed with a leopard skin print chiffon scarf around her neck, soiling the carpet.

She spends the night with me and sleeps with her phone in the bed. Two texts—or alarms—go off in the middle of the night, waking me—but she sleeps right through them.

I wake up when she leaves at 8 a.m. without saying goodbye.

"Good evening, Madame, on this balmy arctic eve. Call me," she texts, "from an unblocked number."

I make her a salad of quinoa, haricots verts, sundried tomatoes, bell pepper, parsley, and mint. She goes gaga for my cooking. We cuddle and kiss and play with the cat. She spends the night and I barely sleep.

Mandy awakes to the alarm on her phone at 8:30 a.m. on a Sunday morning saying she has to go to Queens for a change of clothes. She takes a long shower and refuses to either make or have coffee with me, so I see no reason to get out of bed. She comes to the bedroom door shoeless with her coat buttoned up to kiss me goodbye.

She comes to a benefit with me and someone recognizes her from the past, all eyes are on us and she acts like my boyfriend. Outside on the street she's my girlfriend again, but inside I almost feel like I'm with my ex-husband because she starts asking me, "When can we leave?" as soon as we arrive.

It's the second Christmas that I'm home alone and she calls. I haven't heard from her in months. We talk for an hour. She has her own place and says shyly that she is sorry and wants me back.

"You broke my heart," I tell her. "You broke *my* heart," she says. "But I loved you," I say. "I loved you too," she says. "Still do." And I feel bad when she tells me that she really wants me to be her partner because I don't know if I'm up for it anymore. I remember how she mistreated me. A leopard doesn't change its spots.

Allowing myself to indulge in a romantic fantasy of her as my dream partner for a second, I conjured the image of us living a revolutionary life together. But it was a life that she couldn't afford to live. The loss of earning potential and income combined with the high costs of electrolysis and other procedures like waxing, manicures, pedicures, hairstylist, hormones, tests, and doctors would took their financial toll.

I worried too much about what I didn't know about her, especially whenever she disappeared.

I don't think that our issues as a couple had much to do with her being trans except for the hole that it burned in her wallet. I think I would have had the behavioral issues with her in whatever form she took. Being trans was healing and empowering for her—except for the price.

Dear Mister

M.E.

Dear Mister,

You took my name and when you did, I thought you were the one with whom I would grow old.

But when you tried to take my voice, that—*that*—is why our relationship ended; not because you transitioned.

When you opened up my computer and read my journal entries and confronted me with, "This is *my* story," I knew our relationship had already dissolved. It was no longer "us," but "me" and "you."

There was always you.

In that moment I felt the suffocation of what I had been holding for so long to protect you from exposure: silence. That was more painful than any of the times you told me you thought I was really a lesbian—your words, not mine—when all I wanted was to be your partner. Or that you liked me five pounds lighter, which I now realize was a projection of your own discord with your female body, not mine.

We fought about many things. We stopped having sex even though you'd tell me you had trouble looking me in the eye because the "T" made your eyes wander uncontrollably down women's shirts. We were transitioning together, you see, but all you could see was you—and cleavage apparently.

I could see the end coming but I never really had a chance to say goodbye to you—the old you, the one with whom I fell in love.

It was like walking in to find a new roommate when I entered our home and came upon you with a needle in your hand, building up the courage to inject yourself with your first dose of testosterone. I stood by you then, even though my feelings of betrayal caused my voice to crack when I urged, "You can do it."

You told me that we would talk about that day. You never gave me fair warning. Even if I didn't know what our future would mean, I wanted to be at your side to wait and see.

But you did it without me. I had only moments to take you in as I would remember the old, familiar you. I gazed over your smooth, strong jaw and your curves, and I listened so intently to the timbre of your voice to commit these things to memory, as they would surely be going away. And I was okay with that. All I wanted was for you to see me, hear me, believe me, when I said I wanted to be by your side.

It took me a long time to forgive you.

You told me that you wanted to be pioneers together. This isn't the story I hoped to tell, but it is mine.

Goodbye.
M.E.

Body Parts

Loree Cook-Daniels

Marcelle keeps showing me pictures. "What do you think of this one?" she[1] asks. "Or this one?"

"I don't care," I answer. "Whatever you want." She is disappointed; she wants me to get excited and say, "*This* is the penis I want you to have!" It is important to her that I be as enthusiastic about her new body as she is. She wants me to be turned on, flushed with anticipation of what her new body will do for me.

I can't fake it. It irks me, frankly, that some of this change is, for her, sexual. *Men*, I think, *obsess about penises, not women*. I've always liked the fact that Marcelle didn't have a penis, because penises tend to distract men. They start getting excited at what they're feeling, and quit paying attention to what I'm feeling. I much prefer dildos or the flexible fingers of an attentive butch. I'm not thrilled about the competition that a sensate penis will bring. I don't trust Marcelle to not get carried away.

1 This essay was written at a time when Marcelle had made and was announcing his decision to transition from female to male, but had not yet done so and was therefore still using "female" pronouns.

And so it begins: the transformation of Marcelle from caring butch to uncaring male. When we would have this conversation, she would be incensed. *Why do you think I'd ignore you*, she'd demand. Even my mousiest voice probably couldn't bring itself to whisper, "Because that's what all men do."

The power of our internal images, of the prejudices we hold in our mind's eye, is incredible. Marcelle is angry that some of the women in our couples' support group, to whom she was a fine member for over a year, now see her as alien, not to be trusted or even admitted into their presence. *What has changed about me*, she demands, *except that they now know my gender identity?*

She's right, of course, but I am also beginning to understand the terrible potency of our internal categories. I'm learning to overrule everything we actually know. It matters not that I've lived with this person for twelve years, or that we've shared more than 4,000 days together. If I let my guard down even for a second, the Marcelle I know is replaced by a man who carries her name and nothing else. Instead of displaying all of Marcelle's characteristics with just a slightly altered appearance and new pronoun, this man bears no resemblance to Marcelle.

Instead, he is a mosaic of 37 years of prejudice. My prejudice.

It is painful living with a mirror. The two hardest things about this transition is facing the fact of my stubborn, decade-long refusal to accept my lover and facing the fact that I have way more prejudice than I can possibly own up to. I thought I wasn't prejudiced about men. I thought, having taught an early and controversial university class in bisexuality, having been the men's advocate in my Women's Studies program, having dated a man and taken the flack when I was "Lesbian Co-Chair" of a highly visible group, that I had bested all such bias. I thought I was "over" gender, that I had grown past the need to categorize people by their genitals and attribute psychological traits on that basis.

I was wrong.

I am amazed at the beliefs this transition is bringing to light, laying out before me to own or disown. I am amazed about a behavior I breezed over one day is magically transformed into something sinister the next, based simply on whether I am seeing Marcelle as Marcelle, or as the composite of my fears.

The intensity and number of assumptions and biases this transition keeps flushing out of my deep, dark interior frightens and weakens me. If I have all these prejudices, I think—someone who has worked so hard at being unbiased, who understands that no one can be summed up by a single attribute, who preaches regularly that we must see people as individuals and not as representatives of some artificial category we've constructed—if I can think these fantastical images apply to the person I've loved for twelve years, then what am I asking of others? How can I possibly ask them to see Marcelle as Marcelle, and not as some mythical Man?

And so I know that, although Marcelle is right—nothing has changed about her, so why are people so upset?—I also know that the issue is nowhere near that simple. We are not talking about penises here, or pronouns, or the rejection of femaleness, or a desire for male or heterosexual privilege. We are talking about people facing themselves. We are not, it turns out, asking them to see Marcelle a certain way; we are asking them to look at themselves in a certain way. We are asking them to take a good, long look in the mirror of Marcelle to recognize and own their invisible assumptions about women and men.

That any of us rise to this challenge at all is a miracle.

And as for those penises, dear, try me later. It seems I'm a little too caught up in my head right now to deal with flesh and blood.

Transition Envy

Konnor T. Crewe

I tell my story for those who are in trans*/trans* relationships. I think finding support when you are in such a partnership is very difficult. Support groups exist in limited quantities in metropolitan areas for spouses of male-to-female people, and while I was initially transitioning, there were none for trans* spouses of transgender people. I felt like an outsider in both trans* and spousal support groups and the lesbian community had already pushed me away. I was quite alone.

K.C., my partner, started living as a man in 1975 and started transitioning hormonally in 2006. My own social transition started in 2006 and my hormonal transition started in 2010. So when we met in 2007, he had a 30-year head start in dealing with the issues of living as a man. I still felt like a baby when I met him and so many things were new to me, whereas for him, some of my discoveries were old hat. His attitude was, "Been there, done that, got the t-shirt to prove it," and he did not really want to go there again.

I will say that there are advantages to having a trans* partner. It's nice to have someone show you how to give yourself your first testosterone shot. K.C. told me what to expect in my transition, guided me in finding appropriate doctors, and eased me through the scariest parts of the process. However, in some ways I felt like I was being cheated of experiences that he didn't want to indulge in, like my adolescent exploration of clothes, presentation, and interaction with other people. He simply didn't need the same kind of validation as me.

My early social transitioning phase was very different from my partner's experience. He started so much earlier than me and came out from a different background. He faced more hardships and developed a tough exterior. To me, he always seemed like the cool kid and I was the nerd. We were opposites in many ways.

I came out as genderqueer before I jumped to hormonal transition. I changed my clothing, hair, and body language and dealt with the psychological aspects of coming out.

Coming out in the Midwest and with a religious right upbringing meant that I had a lot of baggage of internalized transphobia. I carried a burden of shame and conflict. My anxiety was already ramped up because I worried about his safety.

My partner and I were committed to being out about our trans* identities; we weren't stealth in any way whatsoever. However, I didn't understand that being out *with* your partner, doesn't mean that you get to *out* your partner.

Early on, I made the mistake of outing K.C. without asking him. I was so happy at the initial stages of our relationship that I wanted to tell everyone. I guess I never thought I'd actually find someone like me and K.C. was such a hottie that I thought I had won a prize in catching him and had to brag.

When I finally realized my error of outing him, the recoil of dealing with people's transphobic reactions depressed me and I feared for my own safety. In one fell swoop I endangered him and messed up my own head.

I was dealing with many new experiences I didn't understand and my own issues about being trans*, a lot of guilt and self-hatred because of my conservative background. My feelings were very complex and created a great deal of trouble for me about going out in public.

Some of the complexity in working through my transphobia was because I'd just lost a previous partner to early onset dementia. I was so depressed about the loss of K.H. that the loss of K.C. seemed certain and I wanted to keep him close to me. My internalized transphobia made me obsess about trans* violence and victimization. I became so frightened of losing K.C. after losing my former partner that I had to be hospitalized for anxiety. My fears were magnified and distorted beyond reality.

Until you've been outed or read in public as trans*, you can't really understand how much it will affect you. I'd been outed as lesbian before but I think there was a personal safety element back then that has changed since I transitioned. In the U.S. gays and lesbians have gained a fair amount of social acceptance in many places, so the fear of being outed as gay doesn't carry the same emotional weight.

I underestimated the depth of my reaction to how people act towards trans* people. I was so excited about having a trans* partner who understood my issues that I didn't really think about the consequences of both of our emotional reactions. I was so enthusiastic that he thought I was going to end his survival in my naïve exuberance.

K.C. was frustrated that I did not have a basic understanding of trans* etiquette or of what he'd gone through since the 1970s to ensure his safety. I had to learn more about his personal experience of living as a male back then and about trans* etiquette and culture, before I could understood where he was coming from. I missed out on a huge part of alternative popular culture; I had to get up to speed to understand.

Now, I ask K.C. if it's okay that I tell a particular person he is trans* or let him tell them himself. I let him review and edit my story here to respect his safety and privacy.

Transition Envy

In the early days of my transition, I felt some "transition envy" towards my partner. Even though I didn't suffer severe jealousy issues, I was a little envious of his beard growth, top surgery, ability to pass, and greater masculinity. He'd also been living as male for 30 years which I wanted for myself too. The depth of his life experience and freedom to be who he was were profound and awe-inspiring.

He had lived as male since the age of 17 and I didn't start transitioning until I was 46. I felt cheated, jealous, and resentful for a long time. Rationally and intellectually, I knew that I shouldn't compare my progress to another person's. However, emotionally I just wasn't there. I needed some affirmation of my own progress to get over my jealousy of him. Hearing people tell me I looked male or referring to me with male pronouns soothed my feelings and eased my relationship with him.

K.C. had been confident of his maleness and ability to pass for years and I wondered if I'd ever get there. In retrospect I feel pretty silly about my envy. I had a lot of unjustified anger at him which wasn't fair. His life was very difficult and he paid a price for his freedom.

However, I needed to find other people who were on the same mental plane as me, but the ones I met were much younger. I felt alone in the early stage of my transition, even though my best friend and partner was another FTM. Except for him, there weren't many people who could give me the affirmation I needed. There were few social spaces where I could experiment with gender.

Although his validation was comforting, I wish that I could have gotten support from other people. Knowing more couples and having a chance to talk to them personally would have helped tremendously.

While my partner paid a heavy personal price for his transition, I, on the other hand, tried to please my parents and conform to their values. I got a college education, tried out heterosexuality, and had a child. But beneath the surface of my success, I was agonizing emotionally and became increasingly unhappy and depressed as time went by.

Around the age of 30, I experienced a 180 degree shift when I came out as bisexual and then lesbian. Dealing with my sexual orientation issues was easier than my gender issues at the time. By focusing my energy on my sexuality and opening my own mind, I paved the way to tackle my gender later. Now, I think of myself as queer.

Years went before I came out, transitioned, and stop being depressed and suicidal, but my path detoured in 2000 when I attempted suicide and finally realized that I didn't need anybody's approval but my own.

In contrast, K.C. didn't attempt to please or gain approval from anyone, which I admire tremendously. Early on in adolescence, he recognized that he could never please his family and has been liberated from them ever since. While he took care of himself, the ostracization from family took its toll, as he has physical ailments and severe Post Traumatic Stress Disorder (PTSD) resulting from the hard life he's lived.

A gender minority in the 1970s, his health care, education, and other basic needs were neglected. He is an intelligent, creative, and street-smart person who never got a chance at a decent education.

But how could he, given the attitude towards trans* people back then? We are so close emotionally that I feel his disempowerment on a cellular level. I might not have had the resolve to survive that harsh climate for trans* people. So my envy of his braveness is tamed by my understanding of the pain and struggle he went through and the scars (emotional and skin) that he still carries.

Competition

I lived a double, compartmentalized life but I finally realized I needed and deserved to be happy, and, while my relationships with family, friends, and partners might suffer, I needed to live an authentic life.

In 2010 K.C. gave me a mental kick in the pants. I had gastric bypass surgery to reduce health risks that could occur with transitioning and started taking testosterone.

Being in a trans*/trans* relationship is interesting with its own unique challenges. Like our dynamics, for example. It's like riding a roller coaster with both of us experiencing mood swings and emotional ups and downs at the same time. Riding the waves is wild and fun, but also challenging.

Testosterone can ramp up feelings of competitiveness between us. We've butted horns over issues like whose surgery and doctor appointments come first and take precedence. According to K.C., my personality has changed since I started testosterone. He says I've became more assertive and less compliant. The power-balance in our relationship before I started hormone replacement was shaken up and he's right. I do speak up and express my opinion more now, but thankfully since we're both aware of testosterone's tendency to amp us up, we've also learned to laugh at our head-butting issues.

Before meeting K.C., I was started to feel increasingly disconnected from my lesbian community but when we got together, I was immediately shunned and made to feel I didn't belong there after

16 years of "sisterhood." At the time, I was still passing as female but K.C. looked definitively male. My friends were openly hostile to him and couldn't understand our relationship. They thought I had "betrayed the cause." In the end, I lost most of my lesbian friends who were my social network and emotional rock for many years. I grieved and felt lonely for a long time. K.C. became my closest friend during that harsh period of rebuilding my life.

When two gender minorities make up a relationship, the couple is more likely to suffer from poverty and lack of healthcare than other kinds of couples. My whole life has been a constant struggle to get ahead, save money for surgery, and simply survive.

K.C.'s top surgery was paid by my previous employer's health insurance. I waited to have surgery because I wasn't ready at the time. But I was able to get a hysterectomy and oophorectomy later since they were was covered. Both of us want to complete gender reassignment surgery, but we have to prioritize and take turns with whose transition goals are more urgent because of money and health issues.

We live hand to mouth most of the time and feel like we're up against overwhelming odds, but we try to remain hopeful that things happen when they are supposed to and trust the greater universe to provide for us.

We deal with non-transition health issues too because of our age. K.C. is diabetic and has chronic pulmonary disease. I've had three hernias myself and been diagnosed with Benign Fasciculation Syndrome. As we've aged and new health issues have popped up, some of our transition goals have taken a back seat so we can deal with these other problems.

At the risk of sounding cliché-ish, things do get better. Despite all our challenges, I'm happier than I've ever been in my life. I moved from the Midwest to Massachusetts to find good trans* health care, a progressive environment, and new friends. Although I still struggle socially, I love my new life and have found ways to contribute and feel connected to the trans* community.

I resolved my jealousies of K.C.'s transition when I started seeing progress in my own hormonal transition. I don't feel envious or insecure anymore because I'm passing as male now. My internalized transphobia has evaporated. With lots of exposure to all different types of trans* people, over time I've seen that while tragic things can and do happen to us, being trans* is not so imminently dangerous as I'd initially thought. I am no longer afraid of leaving the house or fear that dangerous people are lurking in the shadows waiting to harm me.

Moving to Massachusetts has helped because it's a more socially progressive environment. I have more peace of mind than when I lived in Illinois. My depression also vanished when I started transitioning hormonally, which was miraculous since I'd lived most of my adult life with depression.

While I wasn't able to find a support group for trans* partners to attend in person, I did find help online in the *Trans Over 40* Facebook group, which has been very helpful.

I want to conclude on a hopeful note. If you are the trans* partner of a trans* partner, there is support for you, even if it's mainly online. And if you are the partner of someone who is transitioning in their forties, fifties, or sixties, know that there are other people out there who are going through the same thing. *You are not alone.*

Dearly Beloved Wife

Moe Wendt

Dearly Beloved Wife,

When I met you in 1986, I thought you were a man. Soon you told me you liked women's panties when you masturbated and I thought you were a sensitive man. I had a little nightie given me by my ex-mother-in-law that I had never worn. So I gave it to you. I still thought you were a man and I thought I was a woman. Years passed.

We had kids and we kept our secrets from them. You liked high heels; I liked to be on top. When you told me you were fantasizing that you had a vagina and I was inside you, I said that was funny because I was fantasizing about having a penis and being inside you. We thought we were having spiritual sex (and we were) but we didn't think we were transgender.

You shared yourself with me—your fantasies, your desires, your experiments. Remember shaving your legs and chest, fingernail polish and applying makeup? Thank you for that.

I wasn't always kind and I am sorry for that. Although I've told you often that I am sorry for my intolerance of your desire for breasts,

I'll say it again: I am deeply sorry that it took me so many years to really hear you. We might have avoided a lot of pain had I been braver early on. But you know we were both scared. It all seemed so unreal, so far away, so impossible. Yet here we are: you with the breasts and me with a new flat chest.

I was interviewed in 2014 for a report on trans relationships. My interviewer asked me whether I would have transitioned if I had not known you. I hope so, I answered. But I don't know. Nearly half of my life has been with you; it's hard to imagine any other. It's humbling to see I was blind to myself for years without knowing that it's quite possible. I could have gone my whole life living as a woman. I would have remained that quietly angry, hard-working person who had trouble connecting with others. You inspired me to see myself. You trusted yourself enough to bring yourself out where the world could see you. Your example helped me to think that I might be able to do that, too.

Our medical transitions have put such a spin on our sex life that we have not quite landed yet. When I recall your dysphoria before your genital surgery, I naively thought we'd find peace once your body aligned with your mind. I knew I would miss that penis, I just didn't realize how much.

Before I began transitioning, when I thought I was female and we knew you were, arousal seemed like an act. I wanted to be sexual with you, but you didn't behave like I had always known. I tried to take an active role but I didn't have any real juice for it. I got more and more depressed until finally you reminded me of my own gender dysphoria, and how I might need to revisit that question. Thanks for that too. And thank god for transition; we seem to be finding our way sexually, at least a bit.

It amazes me how we have come to open our marriage after all these years. I remember we always thought the idea of a big poly family all loving each other and sharing ourselves sexually sounded cool, but not doable for us because of our mutual jealousy and possessiveness. But when our sex life crumbled into dust, we had to do something. Knowing myself as trans* has allowed me to know my fantasies and how they have always included me watching you with other people, as scary as that has been.

So when you spend time flirting on the Internet, I am okay with it. You have my blessings. I wouldn't say we have accomplished a poly relationship yet, but I feel truly open to it in a way that never seemed possible before. Like the poem you wrote many years ago, "Love is Big."

Your loving husband,
Moe

A More Enduring Gift

LEAH GOLDBERG

I was at a wedding last weekend fielding questions from a lesbian couple about my partner's transition. Normally, I don't mind doing this. I could talk about Chaim all day without getting bored. The questions usually take the same trajectory:

"Was he out as trans* when you met?"

"No."

"How long has he been out?"

"Well, that depends how you count."

"Has he had surgery?"

"Beg your pardon, that's not really any of your business.

"So, what does that mean for your identity? Are you straight now?"

It's the last question that always trips me up. It's especially difficult when it comes from other queers because until recently, I viewed Chaim as my ticket to acceptance into queer communities. I usually respond with some variation of, "I was never really a lesbian to begin with, so it's not as hard for me as it might be for others."

But that doesn't capture the full story. My sense of my own sexuality has always depended on having someone to act as a mirror and reflect me back to myself. I didn't realize being bisexual was an option until I was 15, by which time I had already disqualified myself as a lesbian. I had recently discovered the thrill of romantic attention from boys and felt that if I wasn't bothered by it, I couldn't be gay.

But the summer I turned 15, one of the girls in my bunk at summer camp was open about her bisexuality. The poor girl had a crush on both her best friend *and* her best friend's boyfriend, and moaned dramatically about it to anyone who would listen. I hung on her words and suddenly the intense feelings I had for my own best friend made sense. Realizing my own bisexuality shifted everything.

Although my interest in women quickly overtook my interest in men, my identity was mostly set by the people I dated. A few months after I got home from camp that summer, I met the first trans* person I would date, although neither of us knew it at the time. Later, we would joke that we met when she was male and I was straight, and we were both wrong. We ended up dating for nine years.

In the second year we decided to open our relationship so I could experiment with women. I was curious to know what it was like to be with a woman sexually and felt increasingly frustrated that my bisexual identity wasn't accurate or real without sleeping with a woman. Because my primary relationship was with a man moreover, I still wasn't sure I was a lesbian.

Then, when she finally told me she was trans*, again everything clicked into place. I started to let go of the bisexual label and consider if I could identify as a lesbian.

Through all this, no one ever saw me as anything but a straight girl. My partner didn't come out publicly as trans* until after we broke up, and we were frustrated that we were read as straight when we knew we weren't. When I did come out to the occasional friend or coworker, I was almost always challenged by gay people and straight people alike. A straight colleague at a summer program once asked if I was a "confirmed bisexual." A gay classmate who saw me at anti-Proposition 8 rallies in 2008 was surprised when I mentioned an ex-girlfriend and said he thought I was "just a really good ally."

Having nothing but my own insistence to stake my place in queerdom, I felt like I didn't really belong anywhere. I wasn't gay enough for gay spaces; the minute I mentioned my boyfriend, I was treated like a fraud. I was lying in the rest of my life too, both at work and with my family, who assumed I was straight. I didn't know anyone else like me. It became stifling.

I was in the middle of this crisis of visibility when I started hooking up with Chaim. He still comfortably identified as "soft butch" back then: short floppy hair, boat shoes, bow ties, feminine name, and pronouns. I thought he was unbearably adorable. With him, I finally felt seen, which was ironic since he was the most masculine person I had ever been with. When we walked around holding hands, I got the nod from other visibly queer people on the street which made me happy. But increasingly, I was giddy just holding his hand.

I fell in love with him at the worst possible moment. My primary partner and I had been seeing each other long-distance for two years, and I was driving across country to be closer. On the way, I stopped at Chaim's family's house to say hello to his parents. He wasn't there, but I was excited to see the place that's so meaningful to him.

Somewhere between seeing his childhood room and photos of him riding horses with his mom, an ache welled up in my chest like someone had punched me in the sternum. I didn't think things like this happened in real life. I walked around the house in a daze and wondered what was going on. Later that night, I identified my feelings as an unrealistic struck-by-lightning moment of falling in love.

I struggled with what to do about my feelings for the rest of the next year. I found myself burning with jealousy every time I saw a lesbian couple walking their Boston terrier or shopping for organic produce at the co-op. I wanted to be gay and I wanted everyone to know it.

Ultimately, I left my partner and moved back east, intending to be single for a change. I hoped it would clarify my sexuality: If I'm on my own and I can date anyone I want, who will I date? What kind of person draws me most? Part of me desperately wanted to be a lesbian just for the sake of simplicity.

That didn't last long. A few months later, Chaim got a job in my new city and we started dating finally. It was glorious. Not only did I get to spend time with Chaim, but I was finally able to come out just by saying "my girlfriend." I told my entire family, and even brought Chaim for Thanksgiving. I was comfortable and felt solid.

But Chaim was in silent turmoil. I don't remember exactly when he started considering gender reassignment or when I became aware of it. But I do remember holding him on late nights to help sooth his pain and listened while he talked about using his initials as a gender neutral nickname.

At the same time, I was alarmed at the idea of him going on testosterone. I was also attached to his old name and liked his body as it was. It was difficult to hear how he wanted to change things about himself that I loved and found perfect.

And I worried about what the changes would mean for my newfound comfort in gaydom. I thought I'd finally figured out who I was and was enjoying being recognized by others. He had given me a beautiful gift. Was he going to take it away again?

A turning point came when Chaim went to an FTM support group and met another trans* guy who was still early in his transition. They guy was married with two kids and he and his wife had a strong identity and community (from the past) as a two-mom family. But that changed with his transition and his wife experienced something similar to what I was now going through, but even more intensely because of the many more years she'd spent rooted in lesbian communities. But they weathered the storms together and are making it work.

Meeting them felt like a reencounter with my old bisexual self from summer camp: an opportunity for my life to make sense again. I've learned that people do survive and remain secure in their sense of themselves while their partners change genders. I never needed to become a lesbian for my ex, nor do I have to change myself for Chaim. The only definition that matters is mine. I can have my own queer identity that's stable and secure regardless of my partner's gender. Seeing myself reflected in other people has helped solidify my conviction.

So, no, I am not straight now. But then, I was never that attached to a lesbian identity in the first place, so it's not as though I've given anything up with Chaim's transition. Even if his transition takes away some of my hard-won queer visibility, it also gives me the chance to recognize myself in a variety of changing contexts, which is a more enduring gift.

Personal is Political

Laura Harrington

Not too many months ago my husband Joe and I were talking about anonymity on the Internet. There had been a story in the paper about employers demanding that prospective job seekers turn over their Facebook logins, Twitter account information, etc. in what human resource personnel might say is an effort to minimize risk in employment. As a union rep in many workplaces who's seen the ramifications of employers obtaining what many people see as very personal information, I fall on the side of "Mind Your Own Damn Business" and so does Joe. So you'd think that the conversation wouldn't have been controversial or even moderately difficult. Unfortunately, it ended up being too painful for us both. One of those moments we might label as a "potential growth in the marriage" moment.

Joe made a comment about disassociating his name with anything that could be tracked to him online, particularly a few trans projects he'd had before. He doesn't see himself as trans. He sees himself as male and he wants only to be seen as the heterosexual male that he is. I support that but, to me, it feels as if, in supporting his needs, a huge part of who I am is being suppressed. When he grandly stated that he doesn't want the world knowing he's associated with *Significant Letters*,[2] which was originally our baby, something flipped for me and the selfish, self-centered child in me stuck out her tongue at him, stamped her foot, and the fight was on. And it wasn't the first time.

But before we go any further into domestic squabbles I suppose it would help to understand *why* I was mentally stamping my foot.

I came out as lesbian in the late '80's. A child of the educated, academic, fervent, feminist movement. Birkenstocks, Levi's, wire-rimmed glasses and spiky short hair. No make-up, no high heels or skirts, and NO MEN allowed. I sewed the banner for the first International Women's Day in Eugene, Oregon. I guess that made me a feminist Betsy Ross. Mine was a time of *Heather Has Two Mommies*, political battles over whether it was even okay to be gay—let alone get married—and the phrase "The Personal is the Political."

I embraced that phrase and took to the world. My life became a tool for helping to change the world one person at a time. I've done pretty well in this matter. It hasn't always been easy. I've had to take lots of deep breaths on many occasions. Standing on a stage as the keynote speaker and staring out at an angry crowd of Occupy Seattle protesters while inviting them to come with me to welcome Jamie Diamond, then CEO of Chase Manhattan Bank, to town isnt something that comes naturally to me. (I swear, I did *not* mean to incite that crowd to start a riot. I just wanted them to make some noise!) But something funny happened along the way to living my life by the personal/political mantra. It became a part of who I am. I turned into exactly what my college professors were hoping for. I became a loud-mouth, bad attitude, question everything, in-your-face dyke for whom challenging the patriarchy, myths about queers, and just about every other social injustice you can name was just the way it

2 *Significant Letters* was a 2012 anthology project that planted the seed for this anthology, *Love, Always: Partners of Trans People on Intimacy, Challenge & Resilience* (Transgress Press, 2015).

was. I became the mantra—only now I happily embrace makeup, heels, and skirts.

The other thing that happened to me in college was exposure to the concept that gender is fluid. I was in an English major class. I got to take courses on the Transgender Warrior and (thank you, Dianne Dugaw) Warrior Women in popular balladry. I fell in love with those supposed warrior women that I now believe were really finding ways to express their true maleness. What I didn't realize then is that I have a real, biological attraction to transgender men. It feels very different from my interactions with biological men (to whom I have *no* attraction) and even women (they really need to be *butch* for me to even look). Along my path I met many FtM guys and had the absolute pleasure of dating a few. But these guys openly embraced their transgender space. I had never met FtM guys that didn't. So I hope you'll all forgive my naiveté in assuming that Joe would as well. Boy, was I wrong!

In 2010 I was in a workshop for Significants at the Gender Odyssey Conference in Seattle, Washington. We were talking about ourselves and the struggles we have with our relationships and losing our identity. Sound familiar to some of you? I made the statement that I had spent the last 20 years being out and proud and that it was a hard-won identity. The world looks at my little family and sees a husband, a wife, and a son. They don't see the challenge that we are to that patriarchal structure our society has bet everything on. They don't see the subversion that we are. They think we're heteronormative. And my husband likes it that way, but I don't.

Ironically, I chose this path of invisible subversion. I thought I knew what I was letting myself in for. After all, I know people who have transitioned and their loved ones, it seemed to me, maintained their own identity. I reasoned that I, of all people, was prepared for whatever came. For the most part I was right. I haven't had to face the challenges that many of the partners I have met have dealt with. Joe was transitioning before I met him so I haven't had to face the reality that my wife is now my husband. My child has only ever known Joe as a man so I didn't have to explain to him that his step-mom is now his step-dad. We even have the bonus of Joe being a role model for my FtM son. Heck, for that matter, my ex-wife is even supportive of gender diversity, so I haven't had to face that particular uncomfortable battle (don't worry, we aren't *that* good—we still hate each other passionately). The reality is that on that mythical grand scale of all things, I've had it pretty easy.

I think the answer is fairly simple. I worry. I worry about the world my husband and son live in—the one that denies them insurance coverage for the necessary medical care they need, that tells us the story that "Boys Don't Cry," and that simply doesn't understand them—will destroy them. I see an opportunity to tell our story and to keep changing the world one personal interaction at a time. I want my husband and son to be safe, whole, and happy. I want the attraction. I want my husband to be recognized, to have a name that doesn't hide behind bi-sexual, heterosexual or even queer. I want our relationship to have the validity that society affords to even the most dysfunctional, hurtful, heteronormative relationships. We deserve at least that much and I want to have it without having to hide. I don't want to have to censor myself in my office. No matter how it happened or how his body looks, my husband is a *dude*. He deserves to be recognized as who he is and to have the strength of his resolve to be who he is known and acknowledged by our society. He is a brave man. He deserves acknowledgement.

I think the answer is that I'm pretty good at telling stories and that I really do believe that telling our stories is the way we can change things. And I spend a lot of time on the sidelines of the transition. I can't wave a magic wand and complete Joe's transition for him—or my son's for that matter. It's a path they each have to journey in their own ways. That leaves me feeling pretty helpless. And I intensely dislike feeling helpless. Sometimes, I feel this overwhelming urge to shout out about us. It's the one thing I can do, aside from giving them my unconditional love, to help make their journeys easier—maybe.

I think the answer is also that I like me as I am. And when anybody tells me I have to hold my life and the lives of the guys I am so damn proud of as a secret, it runs contrary to who I am. It's hard to be on the sidelines. Being silent on the sidelines is pure hell. So the little girl sticks out her tongue and stomps her well-shod foot at the man that the adult woman has vowed to love, honor, and cherish for the rest of her life and the issue goes on with something that resembles a truce. Maybe it'll be resolved eventually and maybe it won't, but, ultimately, we're talking and we're loving. In my opinion, that is enough.

Living in the Present

Lacey Losh

My partner Ali and I are community organizers in Lincoln, Nebraska and our relationship is going stronger than ever through the process of her transition. We had our fair share of challenges. Discovering the desire to transition was a long process for Ali and accepting these changes was difficult for the both of us, not to mention our families.

We met in college over 10 years ago, became fast friends, and quickly adopted one another's friend circles. I'm a family-centered person and, due to years of depression and repressed gender dysphoria, Ali was having difficulty making her relationships with family members meaningful. Once we started dating, I encouraged her to work hard to continue relationships with her immediate and extended family. I knew there was a long family history where I wasn't present, but I wasn't about to watch my partner write off her family if there was a chance of cultivating healthy relationships with them.

To this day, Ali has worked hard to keep those relationships strong and growing. The news of her transition may have opened more doors to her issues with her family than anyone expected. The most important thing is that they're continuing to improve their relationships and make time to be in one another's lives.

Ali and I married in a secular outdoor ceremony performed by a friend five years ago. We were surrounded by our families, friends and coworkers. This was well before Ali's transition or even her conscious discovery of the desire to transition.

We lived a happy life together, though all throughout our relationship I felt like there was a problem I couldn't put my finger on. This problem didn't stop us from loving one another and certainly didn't inhibit our ability to enjoy one another's company. However, this did stand in the way of comfort, open communication, and trust.

In the first years of our marriage, we drifted apart very slowly until finally we sought comfort and trust from other people and not from one another. Once we recognized this, we attempted couples therapy through a free, limited-session program offered by my work. While we both feel that the therapist didn't meet our long-term needs, she did help us recognize some of the key issues we needed to work through, such as developing better communication and trust.

We sought help in recommended readings and the relationship-building activities suggested in our books. Ali slowly revealed to me that she had feelings of gender confusion and considered herself genderqueer. This was pretty easy for me to understand, as I see the problems of our society imposing binary gender options and I have recognized and celebrated a wide spectrum of gender identities for many years in my friendships and my community.

We decided Ali should continue therapy because of its benefits, but see a different therapist for her gender issues, as well as the depression she's fought against for most of her life. After a few months of therapy, Ali revealed to me that she'd prefer feminine pronouns but wasn't ready to use them outside the comfort of our home. For me this was the most difficult part of the process. It is not my place to "out" my partner, especially when she was unsure of how she felt and wanted to proceed. Still, keeping her identity secret from the people I care about forced me to deal with her gender issues, including my own accompanying worries and anxieties, without the benefits of a support system.

We're not wealthy people, so we have trouble affording Ali's therapy sessions. I joined her for these sessions in the beginning but what I really needed was to talk to people in my immediate support system such as my parents and my best friends. I wasn't able to do this however, until Ali gave me the go-ahead to reveal her feelings of gender dysphoria to them.

By the time I was able to talk about these issues with those closest to me, I'd already been dealing with my own confusion, anxiety, and apprehension for several months with only Ali for support. We leaned on one another, which strengthened our bond and our trust in one another. Unfortunately, this is the first time in my life where I've felt cut off from my support system. I would not recommend this course of action to others.

We found a local support group for trans* individuals and their partners and attended our first meeting shortly before Ali was ready for me to reveal her gender transition to our support network. The trans* support group is made up of local folks who are some of the most loving, understanding, and selfless individuals I've met. Receiving this support gave us the strength to come out to friends, family, and (in my case) co-workers. While the group meets monthly, many of the people in the group have become good friends of ours and we have the opportunity to see some of them more often.

Ali started hormone therapy, including testosterone-blockers and estrogen on October 31st last year. That's an easy date to remember! She's already seeing slight physical changes such as breast development, loss of upper body strength, fat redistribution, and changes in hair thickness and growth. The emotional changes were more significant and almost immediate once she started on her hormone therapy. Her disposition changed and suddenly she was happier, easier to get along with, and generally in better spirits. I was joyous to see the positive changes in her emotions and expressions. She's never been more beautiful than when she's freely expressing herself.

Ali and I work hard to find a balance between our relationship, day jobs, volunteer work, and time spent with family and friends. Recently, we sat down to write a list of values that we'll refer to when making plans and future commitments. Both of us have cultivated a sense of trust and understanding that we could never have achieved in our relationship before her transition. We talk openly with one another and we're willing to take her transition and our relationship one day at a time.

Family members and some friends have asked me about labels and how the world will begin to see us as a couple when Ali begins to "pass." They wonder if we'll be considered a lesbian couple and then, awkwardly, they often ask about my sexual preferences.

My response is always that I've never been one to require or put much weight on labels. I see their purpose because humans love to group things into neat little categories. I find myself teaching people the meaning of pansexual in my answer to their queries. Although I understand it's not my responsibility to educate people on this subject, I'm fine doing so. Community-building and volunteerism have shaped my existence into something of a leadership role, and I'm comfortable enough with myself and my relationship with Ali to educate people and answer their questions openly, honestly, and without judgment. People are curious and I've done my research. Why not take the time to inform the people I care about, especially if they care enough to ask?

The biggest change I've seen in myself is my newfound outlook on our relationship and our lives. So many friends and family members ask what the future will bring. They worry about our future happiness and relationship dynamic. If this experience has taught me anything, it's that we have no idea what our future holds.

Living in the present in a happy relationship with my partner Ali is what I'm doing today. I hope it continues into the future. Who can say what tomorrow will bring?

The Stories We Tell

Connie North

Dear N.,

I'm sorry. I lied to you. I still cringe when I remember my duplicity. We were standing in the kitchen and I told you I had just met with a client who was contemplating transition. Playfully you asked, "Did you tell her your partner's transgender?" I froze and after what felt like an eternity declared, "No."

But I *had* told my client that you were transgender. I wanted her to know I had some experiential knowledge about trans* issues and transitioning. But I was also trying to gather some credibility to work with trans* individuals as a cis-gender psychotherapist. That is the most shameful part of my lie. I never wanted to use your story for my gain. It's like claiming to be a good white person while doing racial justice work. Ugh.

The above apology could end up concealing more than it reveals, however, if I avoid acknowledging the history associated with that fear-infused lie.

We spoke frequently about where your story ended, where mine began and what parts we shared as "ours." I aspired to honor your wishes and keep you out of harm's way. I just wasn't clear for myself that refusing to tell your story—not outing you as trans*—meant silencing my own. Unfortunately, I still struggle with clearly finding that line.

I came out as queer in what seemed like a late age for my peer group. I was 30 and had ample resources and social support. Practically shouting from the rooftops that I was a queer helped me to reclaim my authenticity after a lifetime of suppressing my own dreams in the pursuit of those others held for me. I also felt like I belonged to the community for the first time in my life and wanted to offer the future teachers who were my students a living, breathing example of an educator who was out of the closet and happier for it.

Moreover, as a writer drawn to self-inquiry, I had so much fodder with which to work. I wanted to put into words my story and share it with others as a way to connect—to remind others and myself that we are not alone.

The relative safety of being a college educated, cis-gender, white woman buffered me from the dangers trans* individuals frequently face upon revealing differences that threaten not only Euro-heteropatriarchy (doesn't that one term sum up so much?), but also the gender binary. Yet, to chalk up my yearning to live a congruent life to cis and other kinds of privilege seems to replicate the self-loathing I have worked so hard to unlearn in recent years. I would not, after all, tell a client to dismiss their dream of living more openly and honestly.

In contrast to my experience, you had taken up queerness as a sexual identity in adolescence and many people had long presumed you were queer on account of your non-normative gender expression. Indeed, in the realm of gender, the world rendered you queer from nearly the get-go. When we met, you were finally free to choose whether or not people knew you were trans* or queer. I did not want to threaten that newfound freedom.

Yet, as you know, out in the world beyond the confines of our house, your family, and close friends who knew both our stories, people responded differently to me—to both of us—once "our" story began. Most painfully, some of my closest people happily assumed I was once again straight when they found out I was dating a man. "You're finally with someone who can give you the baby you've always wanted!" went one of the projections. I did not want to go back into the closet.

You asked me if I was ready to give up being lesbian when we first started dating. I was naïve about the requirement in certain spaces to do so. Often the exclusion was so subtle I wondered if I was falsely attributing the shifts in my social scene to the change in my partner's gender—that I was playing the victim. I still sometimes have a hard time separating the fear-based thoughts spinning inside my head from the numerous messages saturating the air surrounding it.

So much silence remains about a wide swath of human variance and experience, and that silence often feels weightier than words spoken aloud.

I have long loved the concept of *borderlands*, which Gloria Anzaldúa, a Tejana queer poet and scholar, introduced me to when I was 19 years old. The idea of existing inside and outside certain spheres and identities as well as at their edge—to embrace the reality that some part of us always bleeds beyond the boxes of our own making—drew me in. Although when we began dating I tasted the bitterness of the liminal zone you had inhabited for years, I craved for an understanding from those around me that I still identified as queer—that I still fit into a queer community—despite our outer trappings when we entered a room together or the male pronouns I used when describing my partner to others.

My already strong desire for belonging ignited in flames. I desperately wanted to be seen, heard, and valued without judgment for the "I" staring back at me in the mirror.

That lie lived for one day. My killer conscience can be useful at times. I came clean about telling my client my partner was transgender and you forgave me. Just like that. Then you generously acknowledged that you would have liked to know your therapist was informed about and had intimate relationships with trans* individuals, especially in the early stages of transitioning.

We've both seemed to shift our stance on those stories over the course of our relationship. Partly out of necessity, I let go of the desire to control other people's assumptions as well as my fear of rejection. In short, I stopped expending so much energy trying to revise others' scripts of me.

With your help I've come to accept, appreciate, and love myself. You've granted me permission to submit this letter for publication, recognizing the significance for me of telling this story to a wider audience. For that, and all the other ways you have enriched my life and understanding of the human condition, I am grateful to you.

With love and affection,
Connie

Dear Dylan

MIRIAM HALL

Dear Dylan,

When I committed to you in marriage, it was a balmy summer day in southern England. We stood in my godmother's living room hand-in-hand, reciting the vows we spontaneously came up with in the days leading up to this guerrilla elopement.

Among the four vows, this one stays with me the most: "I will share all that I am and all that I have with you."

In the second week of dating seriously, in the fever period of early relationship honesty, I showed you my pain—my parents' early deaths, my molestation. And you showed me yours: knowing since you were four that you were a girl in a boy's body. Our romance suddenly made sense to me sexually: I've been bisexual since I was fourteen; of course I am attracted to someone in-between!

I said, "Sounds great! I'm all in!" You were pleased and surprised by my enthusiasm.

Even as I said that marriage vow two years after we met, I didn't understand what "all" meant. How could I? All that we are must change over time. None of us are static entities. In just the eight years I've known you, I've witnessed the variant meanings "transgender" has meant for you:

being closeted/appearing to be a heterosexual male
being a femme crossdresser
dressing genderfucked/genderqueer
wanting/not wanting/wanting hormones and/or surgery
shaving your face in shame
being out and proud…and so much more.

Sometimes you have shared things I didn't want to know about. You've also been out when I didn't want you to be out or not been out when I wanted you to be out. My sexuality as a queer woman is visibly linked to my partner, whether I like it or not. So I thought the hardest years were going to be those before you transitioned: you were hidden, I was hidden.

When you transitioned I thought all the secret crevices would be opened and revealed: no more clothes purging, no more self-hurting, no more hiding our queerness from the world. That was the biggest problem I could ever see. I could see the end, as uncertain as it was, in sight.

Like life, love doesn't hide secrets for long. When it also became clear to me that you struggled with anxiety, we thought it was a part of your trans-ness. Everything always seemed to be about trans issues in the early days, so it was easy for both of us to pin your anxiety on your identity. Of course, with that kind of thinking, it seemed like once the trans stuff was resolved, you'd be less anxious or maybe not anxious at all.

We are both very wise people. Many people asked us if we thought your transition would fix everything. Of course, we said no! Who would be that dense?

Yet, hope springs eternal, at least in me. My optimism has helped me survive. When you were sure there was no way you would ever transition, I believed you could do it. Despite your lack of faith, you made the effort and now your transition is nearly complete. To us, your complete transition means your orchiectomy is done, there'll be no more surgery. Friends and family are accepting or working on it. We both know that you will be transitioning forever, but it appears that the bulk of the hard work is behind us. Or so it seems.

If there's one thing that being married to a trans woman has taught me, it's that impermanence is real. Even basic things like gender are subject to constant shifts, both dramatic and subtle. I am Buddhist and joked for a long time that your transition is the best education a Buddhist could ever get. Yet, of course I'm also human and long to hang on to something. My lifeline has been the belief that your struggles would quell in the great sweep of transitioning.

For a few months they did. Your hormones stabilized before the orchiectomy. You had a new job where you could be out. Everything seemed to be quiet. Sometimes, you'd get sad and even depressed, but not with the same urgency. I started to get a taste of post-transition life. It was glorious but also awkward when the attention was suddenly on me after it had been on you for so many years. It's not your fault our resources went into everything related to your transition for years. It's not my fault either. We are both responsible for it.

When I put all my eggs in one basket and I give it my all, of course I hope at the end there will be respite. This fundamental confusion has bitten me in the ass before and it is getting back at me now. In the dust settling after your hormone-jolting orchiectomy, your anxiety has reared its head again. And it appears now that it was not about your transition. What is it about? Your anxiety lost its anchor. Now it is free-floating, apt to latch on to any social interaction or conversation, triggered and puffed up by strange dreams. I watched in horror, unsure of how to help.

It's not all the time, just once or twice a month for a couple days. The rest of the time you are so much more at peace than I have ever known you to be. You're happier than even your parents have ever known you to be. You can enjoy your body and your life. We can enjoy our bodies together. You smile more and are more present in the moment.

As I am learning, this is all of you. As you settle into who you really are, you are also anxious. Part of me fears your anxiety. I vacillate constantly. I accept it. I reject it. I try to fix it. I feel hopeless. I get optimistic. In all these feelings I am trying to find a way out or at least trying to find somewhere to settle down in my insecurity about your anxiety.

I am not disappointed in you. Rather, I'm disappointed in a vague, ethereal way whereby I've realized I was hoping that transitioning would fix everything in our life. I am also disappointed in my expectations. I try to find peace with this hope I had. I know that I share this with many other partners and trans folks. I know many partners who cannot find their way through mental health issues like anxiety and depression. It's a result of the transition. It's a mess.

"Transgender" is a magnet for all the intense denial and confusion society has about the identity. We internalize the negativity and assume it is all related in some way to the transition. I am not alone. We are not alone.

I am your partner. But I am also "me." Before I met you I had decided that I never wanted to marry my mother. She was a woman who, among many other things, was severely depressed and had crippling social anxiety. In my struggles I worked hard to accept and overcome my own anxiety and depression.

Yet, when faced with your issues, I balk. I know this is human. Still, it surprises me. You hold me so easily when I am upset. When you are upset it takes everything in me not to leap in and swipe around with my unexpected anger, my disappointment, my sadness, my grief.

Why didn't the transition fix your anxiety?! Why isn't this over yet?!

Through aggression and fear I aid and abet your anxiety. I secretly told you that you were wrong and should not be anxious, just as my father did to me when I was a kid. Subconsciously, I insisted it was your fault, though I was worried. It was my fault. I backed away when it appeared and shut down, even as I insisted you share all of it with me.

I married you because you are a unique blend of you-ness: musician, transgender woman who presents in a genderqueer way, compassionate, humorous and likeable, and yes, even because you are anxious. In fact, I suspected I married you because you are a bit like my mother. Since my father died while they were still married, I thought if I married someone like my mother I'd never be left alone.

If that is even partially true—which my gut says it is even as my head denies it—then there's a part of me that relies on you staying with me forever. There's a part of me that married you hoping and believing you would never leave me. While I rarely shied away from your transgender struggles, I secretly benefited from their existence. Now that those struggles are more amorphous and free-floating, I fear them and yet, I still benefit.

How?

As long as you are anxious, some part of me believes you will need me and not leave me. While you don't have to be transgender for that to happen, let's face it, it sure helps. And now that you have transitioned, what keeps you with me? If you are anxious, at least I still know you need me. This is part of what I need to face now that your transition is "done."

I feel sick to even write this and yet, those same guts say, *Yes, my dear, there's truth in there*. Some part of me—not all of me—believes this.

Again, I suspect that I am not alone. So many transgender people find strong partners to fulfill their need for someone to help them through this tumultuous process. Then, when they grow "too needy," the partners feel pain just like I do. Like me, they find it hard to admit their codependency, a secret need to be needed. Part of my codependency is focusing on your struggles to the absence of acknowledging my own. It's time to change that and it's up to me to do so.

I am only one partner married to one trans woman. I do know this: If any of your issues "take over our marriage," it is as much my doing as yours. We are two people giving our all here—you and me both, equally. That means everything is on the table which includes the shadows and secrets under the table. The less I subconsciously blame you and the more I own my issues, the more amazing "giving my all" becomes.

By amazing, I mean messy. By messy, I mean clear. Like anyone who loves someone, I want to comfort you because I want your pain to be gone forever for your sake. For our sake. Also, I want your pain gone for my sake. That's part of my all: not wanting it all. Wishing I didn't have to deal with this, wishing your issues didn't mirror mine back to me.

Is this letter about your anxiety? About your gender? About my codependency? About my anger? The answer is *none of the above* but also *all of the above* and more. Integrity is based on things falling apart. This paradox feels true to my bones right now. Bridges must bend or they will break in the wind. If our marriage is going to last the rest of our lives with both of us sharing all we can, we have to be gentle enough to get through this.

I pick up the pieces of anxiety that once wore the mask of your gender confusion. Would they exist if we stripped your identity issues from them? That's an unanswerable conundrum. I do know that when I married you, you were complete. And you are complete now.

However, I saw you then primarily as a transgender woman because I wanted and needed to do so. Now I need to see you as human and it utterly terrifies me.

Stripped more and more naked by the minute, I re-commit to this marriage every moment. The you I married does not exist nor does the me you married. Your transition has taught me this. I will keep learning long after memories of surgeries and our wedding have faded.

Love,
Miriam

Letter to My Trans Boyfriend

Anne Totero

I found my El Dorado in your skin.
Tracing your scars that you paid for just to feel a little more whole.
Interlacing my fingers in your prized beard.
As if to pull down and peel away.
Hoping to steal some of the pain.
It only took six years to be that real.
When I say "only," I mean feels like forever.
Binding what once was protecting your heart is now the noose.
Interchanging over your mouth to keep a secret,
For safety.
For identity.

Thank you:
For fielding the foolish inquiries of trans love.
For showing me twice as much mercy as you've shown yourself.
For a patience only my fingertips empathize with when I touch your wounds.
For being exactly who you are right this second.

Letter to My Trans Boyfriend

I'm sorry:
That I think you're perfect just the way you are, I should know better.
For the "oh never mind" moment when my parents ask for grandkids.
Because I can't buy you the last missing piece.
That I'm so protective of your identity.

You are my hero among sinners.
You sin differently and sin real.
You sin for the love of a true self.
For the hope that one day you can love yourself as whole as I do.

You hate that your hands run down your hips in curves.
The search for jeans that hide your birth.
"It was a mistake."
"That isn't me," you say.
"I'm not feeling this for you." You turn away.
"I'm doing this so I never break my promise to myself,"
"Tomorrow will be a better day."
And it will be, my love.
It will be.

Resilience

Goodbye Husband, Hello Wife[1]

Diane Daniel

Not long ago I volunteered to help the director of a New England nonprofit get media coverage and, we hoped, more funding for his organization that helps transgender youth. What the public responds to first and foremost, I said, are personal stories. But he told me that reporters wouldn't be able to interview the kids.

Fair enough. So I asked if he would tell his own story about transitioning from female to male, getting booted from a job because of it, and starting this organization to help other gender-questioning youth feel more empowered.

No, I was told. He didn't want the focus on him.

I was tempted to try to change his mind, but I didn't push. I figured that being a face behind a cause as sensationalized and vitriolic as transgender rights would be at least tiring, if not, life-threatening.

I will find out for myself soon enough.

I am not a transgender person, but I am happily married to one. Her name is Lina and she is a "male-to-female" transsexual. She is 47 and I am 53.

---

1 This article first appeared in the *Boston Globe* on Aug. 9, 2011. Reprinted by the author's permission.

We met at Logan Airport on Valentine's Day in 2003, when we both lived in the area (we have since moved to North Carolina for work). I had left The *Boston Globe* copy desk the year before to work as a freelance writer, and I wrote about a crazy ice-skating trip I'd taken in my column, "Where They Went," for the travel section.

After that, we dated, fell in love, lived together, and married.

The things I loved about Wessel are what I love about Lina, and, yes, in a romantic way. She is big-hearted, intelligent, emotionally mature, athletic, and adventurous. She also has great legs.

We had been together for almost two years, but married for only two months, when Wessel shared his news. He wanted to be my wife, not my husband.

He had come to the realization with a sense of clarity and joy. I, however, reacted with confusion and despair.

Had there been signs? Yes and no. I knew he had struggled with society's rigid gender lines, but so had I. I knew he sometimes liked to dress in women's clothing, but advice columnists and a host of psychologists will tell you that does not necessarily mean a man wants to be a woman. We talked about it a lot and he assured me he didn't.

Counterintuitively, perhaps, it was my love and acceptance of him that gave him the strength to become who he was on the inside: a woman.

I detached emotionally and physically. I cried every day. I wondered what else he hadn't told me. I feared something was wrong with me to attract this kind of mate. I was angry and ashamed.

Gradually, with communication and affection, I (re)opened my heart and faced my shame. Ultimately, the hardest part was the easiest. I loved him. But could I love *him* as *her*?

As it turned out, yes I could, but only after grieving my loss of him. It was a process as complicated as it sounds and one I would not have gotten through without an expert therapist.

In the trans world there's a saying that "one person's transition is everyone's transition." Spouses, family members, co-workers, neighbors—we are all affected in some way. Some of these relationships don't survive the transition, especially marriages.

My situation is rare, but not unique. In Maine, Colby College English professor and author, Jennifer Finney Boylan, and her wife and two children have remained a family since Boylan's transition, famously documented in *She's Not There: A Life in Two Genders*. Her book and the words of Wisconsin writer Helen Boyd, the country's most public "wife of a trans woman," were my lifelines. These days I know several couples in "transgender marriages."

Having been a lifelong advocate of many causes, it was now time for me to join this one, which led me to volunteer for the transgender youth group.

Unlike the gay, "we're-here-we're-queer" rallying cry, the transgender rights movement speaks in more of a whisper. People who transition, or are gender variant in some way, usually want to fit in, not stick out. That's understandable, but it's the movement's biggest obstacle.

I share our story not to advocate that couples like us stay together—because every relationship is different and people should do what is right for them—but to encourage more acceptance from wives, parents, siblings, children, friends, and colleagues.

I have heard firsthand too many heartbreaking stories of parents banishing their transgender children, wives not only leaving their husbands but breaking off all contact and fighting for sole custody of the children, adult children turning their backs on their transgender parents, and employers firing their trans workers.

I understand the impulse. I had it, until I finally felt—truly felt—my husband's anguish.

"What I fear the most," he said one day, his shoulders shaking with each sob, "is that you'll see me as a monster or some kind of a freak. That everyone will, but mostly you."

I told him I didn't, but I realized in some ways I had. Society's opinion had scrambled my own perception. Our relationship turned a corner that day.

Overall, our "gender journey" has been smooth. The love and support we have felt from nearly everyone in our lives, from Lina's family to Huck the handyman, have carried us through this.

Telling her parents was the scariest part for her. We had no clue how they would react. The first thing they said was, "You are our child and we love you." The hurt and the hard questions came later, along with tears and embraces.

At the medical diagnostics company where she works, Lina discussed the situation ahead of time with her supervisors and gave them a publication from the Human Rights Campaign about transitioning in the workplace. Not only were they supportive, they set a welcoming tone for her reentry to work as a woman.

Last November I sent an e-mail about Lina to friends, including several of my former *Globe* colleagues. After I pushed "send," I hunched over my keyboard and sobbed. I felt exposed and knew my identity would be forever changed. Within minutes, responses came in, expressing shock, admiration, and cheering us on.

I believe it was our willingness to be open, vulnerable, and honest that allowed people to see us as real people going through something rare, but nonetheless part of the human experience. It was a serious challenge for us. For my part, I am now perceived as a lesbian, which doesn't offend me, but it sure is different. (I did have a relationship with a woman in my early twenties, but I consider myself straight.) I'm partnered with a 6'1" woman with size 12 feet and a male voice that she's working on feminizing. On some days, her face looks more like a husband's than a wife's. I would rather it didn't.

I want her, or really us, to "pass," as they say in trans-speak—to go unnoticed—which admittedly belies my advocacy aspirations. It's a tricky terrain. When I am feeling content and secure, which is most of the time, things roll off my back. On darker days, when appearing different is a burden, I want to hide from the world. I want to be alone.

Writing this, I feel exposed all over again. Even though many of my friends in the Boston area know about Lina, there are others who do not. And then there are all the new people who come into our lives. Having said that, the telling gets easier with time. As I accept who we are, I don't feel the same need to explain and defend, though I am happy to answer people's questions. Nor does the issue define us. Lina and I have many interests, together and separately.

Partners, families, and friends of transgender people have a special opportunity to help foster understanding. We're on the front lines and on the side of love. To those of you who want to join me, to share your stories, step right up. I would enjoy the company.

Epilogue

Coincidentally, I'm writing this on the 4th anniversary of the day that Lina came out publicly as a woman in 2010. We hadn't even thought about the date, but her mother sweetly called to wish her daughter of four years a "happy birthday." Lina was out on an errand, so the message was relayed through me—"send him my greetings."

"You mean her?" I said with a laugh, offering my mother-in-law a light-hearted correction.

Indeed, after years into the process, I too get the pronouns wrong sometimes. Lina and I take it in stride. While I can't seem to forget the old pronouns, I can hardly remember my former husband. One day recently I asked Lina to send me a photo of the two of us in front of the first house we bought together in 2003. When I opened the file, I was shocked to see myself sitting on the porch with a man. In my mind, I'd pictured myself with Lina—even though we still displayed a wedding photo of husband and wife in our bedroom until recently. While the physical images of my mate, past and present, are a jumble, what remains constant is a feeling of love, warmth, and safety. I suppose some would call that a soul.

Over the years, I've written several articles about us for large publications, always worrying something bad would happen. It never did. A religious cousin seemingly disowned me and my car mechanic stopped flirting with me, but life has carried on otherwise. The biggest hassles have been administrative and legal—name changing, document updating and the like. But as for our daily life, I joke that we're just two middle-aged dykes. In many ways I wish that were the whole story.

In 2014, we embarked on another life change—we moved to the Netherlands to be closer to Lina's family and culture. She's Dutch and had planned to work in the U.S. for only a few years before we met. Some people assumed we were moving to a country known for its tolerance because Lina is transgender. But from what I can tell, there are several trans laws in the United States that are more generous to trans people and the Dutch are no more used to seeing or necessarily accepting trans people than Americans are.

For me, the move has brought unexpected stress—who to tell and when, if ever, about our past. While Lina's colleagues and family know the full story, I'm in the process of making new friends. I've told them I have a Dutch wife, so they've categorized me as a lesbian. Most of them haven't met Lina yet. What happens when they do? Will they figure it out? Even if they don't, do I share our past?

I'm still working through my feelings of caring what people think and balancing our privacy against wanting to be open and intimate with others, which is my usual way of forming friendships.

And then there's the advocacy component—the path to acceptance is through personal stories, just as I'd written about in the *Boston Globe* in 2010 regarding the director of the New England nonprofit who was reluctant to open up to reporters. Later, the director, Nick Teich, decided to discuss his personal transition and invited journalists to visit the awesome camp he started for gender-questioning youth. Since then, Camp Aranu'tiq has received fantastic positive exposure and expanded in amazing ways.

I realize that my tension surrounding who to tell what and when will be a lifelong challenge, but the more I examine it, the more tolerant I become of other people's differences and fears—and of my own. All of us are souls, worthy of embracing.

I'm Glad My Husband is Gay![2]

L. Daniel Mouer

"Dan does the cooking and I fix the toilet when it breaks. It's a good thing we found each other, otherwise we both would have had to go get a 'sex change'."

That's what my wife, Robin, used to tell folks. The truth is I have never thought about getting a sex change. I'm not shy about allowing my "feminine side" to show, but I am quite happy with the body in which I was born and I cannot imagine wanting to trade in my "parts" for a woman's, nor have I ever felt tempted to dress in women's clothes. The day I first asked her to think about moving in with me, she glared at me accusingly and said, "I hope you don't think I would strap on an apron and turn into Suzie Homemaker!" To that, I quickly responded that I hoped she didn't think I was offering her free range in *my* kitchen!

Rob and I have been married for 33 years. I'm sure that one of the things that attracted us to each other is that neither of us is entirely conforming to anyone's notions of gender norms.

---

2 [1] Parts of this essay first appeared in the essay, "Transitions," in *War Baby: Talking About My Generation* by L. Daniel Mouer (Createspace, 2011).

I met her in 1978 and we were married four years later. We worked together in the same profession, watched our son grow up and give us grandchildren. Twenty seven years after our first meeting, my wife confessed to me that she is and always has been a guy, and that it was her wish to alter her body, with hormones and surgery, to look more appropriately masculine. My wife wanted a "sex change." Unless you are someone who has heard something similar from your spouse, that must sound like the punch line to a very bad joke.

Many years ago Rob and I each took an online quiz that had been generated by one of the big English universities. The goal was to identify if one's brain is more "masculine" or "feminine." Well, I used to joke that Robin probably had more testosterone in her veins than I did, so I had little doubt that she would score more manly than I would on the test. I was right. Her score put her in the "very masculine" category, while I landed smack in the middle: equally masculine and feminine in the views of then-contemporary brain science.

As a child, I had felt restricted and oppressed by traditional gender norms. They never made sense to me. There were things I enjoyed doing that were "girly" things, and others that were "masculine." I was never very interested in sports, at least not until my senior year in high school, and that, alone, is enough to make your masculinity suspect when you grow up in a sports-obsessed town like Pittsburgh, Pennsylvania.

Robin has always been "one of the guys": no dresses, no make-up, never even close to being "girly." I am quite happy with our flexible and often-reversed gender roles, and I never found Robin to be less attractive for being butch. Quite the opposite in fact. I'm attracted to strong, capable, straightforward women. Similarly, I find men more likable if they also have a "softer" side: guys who aren't afraid of being emotionally vulnerable. Gender extremes, in either direction, are a turn-off for me.

I was stunned nonetheless when Robin finally sat me down and informed me that he is transgender, that he sees himself as a man and has never been comfortable when others view him as a woman. What's more, he wanted to have surgery and to take hormones to physically change his appearance from female to male. (In this paragraph, my "wife" becomes my "partner," "husband," or "spouse," and "she" becomes "he," for that is the way I now know him.) This announcement came sometime in 2004. My initial reaction was predictable. My brain screamed out, "No! No! Hell no! This cannot be real!" But, at the same time, I had come to know Robin well enough over the previous 25 years that I knew he was telling me the truth. This was not a whim, fantasy, or delusion. And at that realization, I began to catch up on my inadequate understanding of the mysterious world of gender identity.

Over the next many months, I read every book and article I could find on the subject of being transgender. I joined online support and information networks. I am a scholar by profession, and I knew I would not be able to relax with this idea until I had learned enough to consider myself a minor scholar on the subject. Of course it was not an *entirely* new subject to me. As an anthropologist I had been teaching students for years about the cultural relativism of gender norms and the ways various cultures deal with non-conforming gender behavior or with individuals and groups who blend or border-cross gender categories.

Robin and I frequently discussed the implications for our relationship, both between ourselves alone, and with a couple's counselor. I could not promise Robin I would find him attractive as a lover. I have no prejudices against homosexuality; I think of myself as being at least capable of being bisexual, but I was facing the reality of becoming half of a same-sex couple, socially as well as sexually, and that is just not how I have ever seen myself. We live in (and were married in) a state that had passed a constitutional amendment banning anything that even smells like same-sex partnership, let alone marriage.

For nearly a year I learned, listened, talked, cried, thought, felt and imagined myself living not with Robin, my wife, but with a guy with whiskers, a flat chest, and a deep voice. No matter how strange it felt, I simply kept coming back to the same answer. I know this person, I love this person, and we had come through way too many serious difficulties to allow a "sex change" to put an end to a good thing. We decided to go ahead with this transition and to tell the world: "We are now husband and husband, partners, two guys who are in love and we are married."

Rob and I are equestrians. We spend a few days a week out in the country where we board our horses and where, over the years, we have made many strong friendships. We worried the most about coming out to the barn gang. We were afraid they might not be quite as open to the changes we were about to announce as our academic friends back in the city might be.

The year was 2005. *Brokeback Mountain* had just been released and talk of gay cowboys was in the air. That day Robin and I showed up at the barn, and the first person we told was our dear friend Susan. She's a deeply religious "country girl" with good old-time values, and we were really worried this might not go too well. Robin was very direct. He explained that he feels like a man and he was going to go through the process of changing his body and his persona to reflect his proper gender. I mentioned that we would now be a same-sex couple. I was standing behind Robin and wearing a wide-brim straw cowboy hat that day. Susan seemed a little flustered. At first she just muttered that it really wasn't any of her business, but then curiosity overcame her and she asked, "But why?" I couldn't resist. I said that now that I had seen *Brokeback Mountain*, I really wanted to be a gay cowboy, and now I was going to be just that!

Susan looked at me oddly, trying to understand what I had just said, and then she started laughing. It was a nervous laugh, but she laughed. By our next trip out to the barn two or three days later, everyone knew that we were undergoing a transition. The gang had decided on their own that Robin would, from that point on, be "Rob," and to this day it remains so. We needn't have worried about losing friends, because they are, truly, good friends and good people. So Rob started on hormone treatments and we went off to San Francisco for three weeks to have his body altered. We tend to think of it now not as changing sex but more as a "gender correction."

Over the years since Rob first came out to me, I have come to know—online or in person—many dozens of transmen and transwomen. It is statistically rare for a person to be so transgender that they seek to undergo the transition across the sexes, but it isn't as rare as most people might imagine. My transgender friends are a cross-section of the North American population (with a sprinkling of Europeans and Aussies for spice). They are elders and juniors, war heroes, artists, construction workers, teachers, and engineers. Among them there are a few who have serious emotional or psychological problems that have been brought on, or aggravated by, being "trans," but most of them are as sane and levelheaded and "normal" as all the rest of the folks I know in this life.

I have become an advocate for the rights of gay, lesbian, bisexual and transgender (GLBT) people, and my passion for the cause has helped keep me active in these years of my retirement. Much of GLBT activism these days revolves around the right of same-sex marriage. This is one cause I feel I must support, if for no other reason than because my own marriage was threatened by the hateful public backlash stirred up by religious zealots and political reactionaries. However, my main focus is on doing whatever can be done to stop the emotional and physical violence that comes down on GLBT people from the time they are young children. Every year this world loses good folks to ignorant violence and to the suicide that many people choose as an alternative to persecution and social isolation.

I've become proud to think of myself as a member of the GLBT community, but it took me a while to get here. Early in this transition, when Rob and I were in San Francisco for his surgery, another friend who was married to a trans person took us one evening to an event at the large community "gay center" in the Castro District—arguably the "capital" of gay America. There, for the first time, I heard Robin and I being introduced to strangers as each other's "husband." It sounded odd, but it was also liberating: a way of chipping away at the tyranny of gender roles in personal relationships. When we were back home in Virginia, one old friend asked me if I now feel like I am gay. My response came quickly. "I don't know about me," I said, "but I'm sure glad that my husband is gay!"

Making the actual transition was nowhere near as difficult for us as I had feared it might be. Friends and family have mostly been respectful and accepting. If not, they have kept their reservations to themselves. There are personality changes that go along with transitioning. Some of those are no doubt due to hormonal effects, but others are simply the result of the trans person allowing their "true self" to emerge in ways they could not do in the past. Because Rob was never a girly-girl, those changes have been minimal for us.

For some folks the thing that kills a relationship in which one partner is transitioning is s-e-x. I admit that I preferred Rob's former body style, but we have also found ways to enjoy learning some new tricks. Folks who are very strictly heterosexual may find transitioning to be a game killer, so if you are facing a relationship with a trans person, it's good for each partner to be very clear with themselves and with each other about what lines can and cannot be crossed. It helps to keep in mind that all of us experience changes in our own sexuality, our attractions and preferences, and in what we can or are willing to offer our partners when it comes to sex. Any long-lasting relationship faces challenges from aging, injuries, and illnesses, among other things. A partner's "sex change" may not be the greatest challenge any of us face in our love lives.

I have learned that in many cases, a transgender person is often in a very big hurry to go through a full transition once they have admitted their condition to themselves and have kicked down the closet door and informed family and friends. The problem is this: The trans person has at least had clues about their gender issues since they were young, but for we partners, friends, and family, this is a revelation that takes time and patience to adapt to. I find myself cautioning trans friends to slow down and give their loved ones time to catch up to this runaway freight train. Rob was willing and able to do that. He was able to say that transitioning was extremely important to him, but so were my love, our relationship, and our sex life. So he was able to give me the time I needed not only to learn what I needed to learn, but to imagine my own changes and even look forward to them.

Now, after living nine years as the partner of another man, I think about what has been the most significant change in our relationship. From the moment we made the decision to transition, it seemed as though a huge weight had melted away from Robin's shoulders. Rob shed a lifetime of pent-up anger and frustration. There are problems, to be sure, but they are no worse than, or different from, the problems that any couple faces after thirty-three years of marriage. So far, they seem insignificant in the face of three decades of mutual trust and love.

But What About Shanna...?

Shanna Katz Kattari

A few years ago, my partner came out to everyone in his world as a queer transgender man. He was in a lucky and privileged place. Everyone he told was happy for him, asked how they could support him, and so on. His work changed a policy so he could take a different type of paid leave during his surgery rather than use his sick time. His family sent him birthday cards "to my son" and "to my nephew" as a way of showing their acceptance and love. Our friends helped us navigate some of the legal and medical moguls that awaited us, put together a meal train, and showed their support in a myriad of ways.

However, as part of his coming out process, many of my partner's friends, family, co-workers, and other folks asked these questions in various permutations:

"How is Shanna feeling?"

"What is Shanna's reaction?"

"But Shanna is a lesbian! What is she going to do when her partner is a man?"

"How is Shanna handling this whole thing?"

They all boiled down to: "But what about Shanna?"

I'd like to answer that question now.

First, it's important to know that I support my partner 100% and more if it was mathematically possible. Always have, always will. This means I was supportive of them when I met her as a butch woman, when they told me they were genderqueer, and now I continue to support him as a transgender man. The person I fell in love with is the one I share a home with, co-parent kitties with, and wake up next to everyday regardless of his name, their body, their presentation or the marker on their ID. I love this person, period.

Their gender identity, the name they prefer to be called, their body parts, the clothes they wear: None of this changes the person they have been, the partner they are or the wonderful force in my life they will continue to be. It is not that I don't see gender; gender has always played a huge role in our relationship. It is just that I will love this person regardless of what gender they present or identify as at any point in our time together.

To be honest, my partner's transition has not been a big change for us. Yes, the surgery was costly and created a pretty big change in his body. Yes, the testosterone added more facial hair than some cisgender dudes have, and he can now sing Marvin Gaye at karaoke within a deep register. However, this was not a surprise for me. It's not like I, a fierce Femme and owner of more dresses, leopard prints, and glitter than you can shake a stick at, woke up one day and told the world I was a guy, although that would have been fine too.

My fearless partner had been wearing a binder for over two years to prevent his breasts from being visible. I remember when I bought him his first Frog Bra (a specific brand known for extra strong compression) so that he wouldn't have to wear two sports bras. Later, we researched the best binders together curled up on the couch. When I met him, he was already shaving every two days. He's been "daddy" to our kitties since the day we moved in together. We're not talking a High Femme-to-Bear change overnight or anything that might be seen as a shock; this gender journey has occurred over a long period of time and has been a part of our relationship since day one.

An important note: I am not a lesbian. I may have identified as a lesbian in college and my first year of graduate school, but I have been queer-identified for over eight years. Why? Because I am attracted to a variety of people, many of whom are not feminine or even woman-identified. I have dated femmes, butches, bois, men (both cis and trans), women (both cis and trans), girls, genderqueer folks, androgynous folk and more. "Lesbian" was far too restricting for me and pansexuality didn't fit either.

The great thing about being queer is that regardless of gender, sexuality, or orientation of my partner, queer covers it, and I don't need to reexamine my attractions based on my partner's identity. Love and connection are stronger than any presentation or body parts. I love my partner deeply and have supported his transition and gender journey throughout the years we have been together.

A few years ago I mentioned to my partner that it seemed as though "genderqueer" might not be the best fitting identity for him. He's always felt more comfortable being "sir-ed" and seemed hurt and offended when someone used "ma'am" or "lady." While identities look different to people, many genderqueer folks or gender fuckers I knew were genuinely fine with either pronoun, honorific, and so on.

On the other hand, my partner would *say* he was fine with any pronoun as long as it was respectful, but he always seemed much happier when people chose gender neutral or masculine ones. In our first conversation about it, he told me genderqueer felt really good. I told him that I would support him during this period.

As time passed, we had many more conversations about gender. At one point, he said he wanted to change his name to something neutral but he didn't want hormones or surgery or pronoun changes. We discussed "new" name possibilities for him for two years before he publicly announced his transition.

Then he changed his name, started testosterone and got the gender marker on his ID changed legally. When surgery became a possibility because of a small inheritance from his Nana's passing, we talked about what a full transition would look like for him. And I reassured him that regardless of what he decided, I would be there for him in every way I could.

I hugged him and said, "How can I help?" I was like a puppy on caffeine sending him links to possible doctors for his top surgery, information on name changes, bringing home blank fingerprint cards, making him appointments, creating lists, preparing to host a fundraiser event, and more. Doing these things allowed me to show him my love and acceptance. I'm a planner, a do-er, and I got to help him plan for his transition like I did in other areas of our life.

So what about Shanna? Shanna is A-OK. In many ways my partner's transition made our lives easier. Binders are expensive and do horrible things to people's bodies when worn daily. I had to fight with my love monthly to go to our massage therapist to work on reversing some of the damage caused by binding. Explaining the concept of "transgender" in many ways is easier than trying to explain "genderqueer" to folks who don't have a background in gender. That shouldn't be the case, but it is—especially since we live in a place that has laws protecting transgender folks. People just "get" it a lot more than they ever got it when he was living outside the binary.

He was able to blend our last names together when he legally changed his first name, and now we have the blended, shared last name that we've always wanted. Also, it allowed me to support him in a way that felt equitable. I'm a queer with some major disability and chronic pain issues and my partner has been there for me, whether with an ice pack, my pain meds, or as a staunch ally at the airport when ableism rears its head.

This transition adventure allowed me to give ally-ship back to him; bringing him ice chips, giving him his testosterone shot to "make a man outta him," and gently yet firmly correcting pronouns when others slipped up. He is incredibly open and out about his trans* identity (we use the asterisk at the end of the root "trans" to designate that there are many identities that fall under the "trans*" umbrella, not just transgender or transsexual), which enables him to educate folks on what that means, as well as allowing me to be supportive of other partners going through similar journeys.

Overall, it's been good for us. We have supportive friends, family, coworkers, employers, politicians; you name it. But lest it all seem like sunshine, roses, and unicorns, there have been challenges too.

As a Femme, I am frequently viewed as a straight woman in both the mainstream world and my own queer community. I've been told at some LGBTQ events that it was nice I showed up to support them, or that I was such a caring ally, which hurt incredibly. While Femme invisibility doesn't affect me as much as when I was single and had a heck of a time picking up people, it's still frustrating to be constantly mistaken as the "privileged hetero norm" rather than a member of my community.

My partner already passed as a man about a third of the time before the transition. Now he passes probably 98% of the time. This is wonderful for him, but it has meant that I have been read as straight on a continual basis. I'm not thrilled about this, but I tell him that I'll work on being more queer in my interactions with others. He seems supportive of this decision.

Luckily for the queering of our visibility, he frequently gets read as a gay cis-gender man. When people find out we are together, I get the "oh, honey" look as people exchange glances, wondering if they should tell me that I am partnered with a gay man. Also, I might be read as an empowered dominant female who takes on more masculine roles with a more laidback, submissive male partner who takes on more feminine roles. For example, I'm super extroverted, he's super introverted. I know how to check oil, change tires, etc. while he prefers to do the laundry and clean the house. We are able to queer how people view us even when we get seen as straight by others.

The amount of money we spent on his transition is ridiculous. We simply couldn't have done it without his inheritance, thus demonstrating the sheer privilege required to be able to transition in any medical or legal capacity. Would I have rather had his health insurance cover it, so that we could have kept our savings for an emergency or down payment on our house? Totally. Would it have been better that he didn't have to take hours off work to go to the courthouse, the Social Security Administration, the DMV, not to mention the money his name change cost? Of course.

While insurance didn't cover a thing, I cannot think of a better way to spend our money than on helping the love of my life feel more comfortable in his own body. The surgery and recovery were more intense than any medical issue he had ever experienced before. While taking care of him and supporting him through his recovery was draining, luckily we have amazing friends locally who chipped in, and his mother and sister flew in to help, too. Getting all the paperwork done, especially having his passport changed before our delayed honeymoon last year, was quite an adventure and an incredible undertaking.

So, Shanna is fine but also realistic. My partner's transition didn't fix all his gender issues overnight and we both knew that. Gender breakdowns happened and still continue today. It is still frustrating to have to pay out of pocket for his testosterone, which is something he will have to take for the rest of his life.

Sometimes his passing brings hilarious comic relief, like when a doctor told us to make sure we used condoms to prevent accidental pregnancies. It took everything we had to not burst out laughing. But sometimes it's annoying, like when we are at queer events and everyone avoids us like the plague because we are seen as interlopers who don't belong.

We still have the social dances around when to come out. I've been given carte blanche to out him when I feel it needs to happen, but I don't feel that as a cis-gender person this is an acceptable solution. He should always have control over being out. It's a constant work-in-progress but one that we are both committed to sticking with throughout this journey that happens to be our life.

When we had a Queer Celebration of Love in 2011, I promised to be there for my partner through all of his gender journeys, adventures, confusion, transitions and more. I will continue to be as supportive as I can every day.

While I had biases, I planned what I think was the best "Bye, Bye, Boobies" fundraiser in the history of top surgery fundraisers. I worked tirelessly to help our friends and family remember his name and pronouns. I laughed and cried and changed his drains and rubbed vitamin E on his scars. I still stick him in the ass with a shiny silver needle.

I am there for him when gender becomes too much of a load to bear. I will be there for my partner because I love him, period.

So, what about Shanna?

Shanna's doing great! Thanks for asking.

Bella Loves Dez

Bella Giovio

My experience as a partner or spouse of a transgender person overall has been positive and it has introduced me to a very new and unexpected life.

Please, by no means, do I want you to get the feeling that I was always a closed-minded person. In actuality I have been the polar opposite. I was 10 years old when I first met a person in transition. This was 1976 in Los Angeles where my father lived and we were visiting from New Jersey. My father and his wife took me and my two sisters to get our hair done and the stylist who cut our hair was transitioning male-to-female.

I remember my father explaining to me about "Eddie" and how he was taking pills (hormones). He was very different than a typical man or woman and I noticed it, but, I didn't blink an eye. For some reason it just didn't bother me, and the same goes for a few years later when my friend told me he was gay. I was about 12 years old and at first I didn't believe him but I got over it or believed him only a few minutes after he told me. This led to more gay friends. Why? I haven't a clue. People asked why I or we—meaning my sisters and me—had so many gay male friends. We even dealt with discrimination from gay men and non-gay friends who didn't have gay friends themselves and didn't want to hang out with us. This was never said aloud but I felt it.

When I was 15 years old my best friends took me to the Ice Palace Nightclub in Manhattan. I was underage and it was a gay men's club. I danced and drank and shared the bathroom with drag queens. This was my first time in the presence of these larger-than-life women and again, I didn't blink an eye...but...when I met Dez, my now cross-dressing husband—oh, did I blink an eye! The person I thought I was, so hip and cool, wasn't so hip and cool after all.

Dez didn't tell me at first. He told me he loved me and I told him I loved him too. Then a month later he broke up with me.

Long story short, we reunited six months later and have been together ever since. That was nine years ago. He also told me he was a cross-dresser.

My first reaction was, "Are you gay?" and he said, "No, I like women!"

I probed him more and asked him if he had ever been with men and he admitted that he had when dressed as a woman, but only a few times. I thought that would bother me because I knew gay men who had sexual relationships with so-called straight men who had wives or girlfriends and it was never a good mix—lots of drama and sometimes violence. In this case though, it didn't bother me because Dez might have been around the block, but he is no cheater.

I was absolutely fine with the news that first night of knowing, but this was very different for me. I was not used to this in a straight girl/guy relationship, but I was relieved thinking that maybe this is why he broke up with me six months prior. I was cool with it. Of course I was. I thought I was the kind of person who didn't care what one liked sexually or how they identified themselves. I was cool with it.

Well, this feeling was short-lived. As I became more involved, I became more confused and even though I loved Dez very much and still do today, I really didn't want him to cross-dress. I just wanted a man, not a woman with some makeup and a bad wig—okay, she never really had a bad wig, I'm just not into wigs—but this was not a choice for me if I wanted to stay with the person I loved.

There were many days of confusion and sorrow but never anger. I felt bad for Dez just thinking he had to go through the struggle of feeling like a woman in a man's body. It hurt to know he was hurt or someone would hurt him. I just wanted to protect him.

One reason I didn't want Dez to cross-dress was because it seemed as though whenever he did, he would change and become self-absorbed and selfish and talk about hormones and transitioning.

...Okay...Transition?? What??

That blew my mind! I met him, a man—not her, a woman. I must confess that I love the penis and I've never had sex with someone else's vagina. I have one myself, which is enough for me; I don't need another.

Another reason was that, when he was a girl, he fantasized of being a straight girl, which means he wanted a *man*! Something that I am not! I had horrible thoughts that he really just wanted to be with a man and I could never help him in that department.

Also, the thought of him having surgery to change the way he looked freaked me out. I was really beside myself and stressed. I didn't like the idea and it made me nauseous at times because: *Who the hell am I to hold him back, if that is what he wanted to do?*

With that, I had to lay it on the line and let him know that if he ever really wanted to transition, I would stand by him and support him but couldn't guarantee that I would be there for him in the end as a couple. I just didn't know if I could be that cool or hip.

Dez would dress on the weekends but wear women's flats around the house each day. He wore panties and nightgowns to bed. I would buy him girlie things to let him, or her, know that I loved her whether she was male or female. Dez knew I loved him and couldn't believe I stuck around after he told me about his cross-dressing and transition fantasies. He thought that I would have left him, but I couldn't; I love Dez and he loves me.

He also knew I wasn't in favor of him going all the way or being the "girl" each time during sex. I played the role for her when he would dress and she was the "girl" and I had to take a back seat, which is fine—but, it has to be equal, to this day. I want to be the girl too, so we take turns.

I had a lot of help from my best friend of 30 plus years who is not only gay but also a psychoanalyst in New York City. He is very involved in the LGBTQ community regarding mental health. He and his husband both know about Dez's cross-dressing which is great, because they have dressed in drag many times and they share makeup and dressing tips. I have to thank him for making me feel at ease about opening up about how to fulfill Dez's sexual needs when he is a girl.

I also have to thank author Helen Boyd who wrote *My Husband Betty: Love, Sex, and Life with a Crossdresser*—for helping me understand what it means to be the partner or spouse of a crossdresser. We sat down one day and spoke for hours. I felt a real connection with her and I am so grateful to have had that time.

I have spoken to my long-time therapist about Dez, which is a great help and I think she really loves to hear about our relationship. She isn't obsessed, but I can see her eyes light up when I bring up the issue, especially the sex part—too funny! But I don't really care; she is a great source for helping me with my life.

Dez doesn't talk about transitioning any longer even though I bring it up from time to time. He plays it down by saying he was nutty then and assures me that he only said those things to see how I would react. I don't know about that.

I assume he is fine for now since I know he loves me, my friends, and my family, but time will tell if he ever changes his mind. My best friend (the psychoanalyst) has made the assumption that Dez may have just worked it all out. I hope so, but I still think it may come up again in the future; call it an intuitive feeling. And if it ever does, I will handle it then, because for now we are all doing fine.

Perhaps that is what works for me or us. Since then, Dez moved into my house seven years ago and we were married. I have two children from a previous marriage and Dez doesn't get to dress that much since my 14-year-old is always around. We find the time where she is the girl, which is fine with me.

Dez dresses every Halloween as a girl. We have a party at our house and our family doesn't seem to care, and we have another cross-dresser in our circle who does the same but presents as a man on a daily basis. So, they might know by now subconsciously.

Dez has a regular nine-to-five job but is a musician as well. He met a woman who was looking for a guitar player to create a new band. That was five years ago and she just happens to help cross-dressers dress and apply make-up. Eventually, Dez told her.

We have a small group of people who know about Dez's girly side. I think that having this small group of friends is very helpful for us. They are people we can trust and with whom we can talk about cross-dressing if we choose.

Of course, we aren't fully open to the world yet. Dez doesn't want everyone to know and, in fact, he feels somewhat ashamed after dressing. He will call himself a "weirdo" or "fruitcake" (I always loved that stupid saying by the way, fruitcake. It just cracks me up!) I just tell him, "So what? Who gives a shit? It's our world and we can do what we want in our home, so we are the 'weird' couple and you are a 'fruitcake.'" I don't really think he is a fruitcake—whatever that actually means. Please. I tell him that I give him credit for being so honest with me and his feelings and we are lucky to nurture that side.

One thing that's nice about being married to a cross-dresser is that my husband loves women. He adores them, thinks they are beautiful and prefers to be around them. All his good friends are lesbians; it's really funny that he has all girl friends and I have all guy friends. The best part is that he doesn't objectify women, so all his love for women goes all to me. I do all the objectifying to him and he *loves* it—you see, he fantasizes what it's like to be the girl and be objectified—which can be very scary for any woman if it's not done by someone they love, or at least like.

Then again, Dez and I clash at times. He can be very annoying sometimes because I am more laidback while he is a "rules and regulations" type.

He can also be the sweetest person. He is in touch with his feminine side, so he is very loving and gentle, too. My relationship with Dez has been so much better than my other long-term relationships. So, yes, my experience with my transgender spouse has been very unexpected and new—but most of all, very positive and loving.

It could be a difficult position for some people to live with the thought of your partner or spouse changing in the future. The only thing I can say is that I have set boundaries and Dez has complied and appears to be very happy. He has his rules when he is a chick—and some funny ones!—so why can't I have some too? I always felt that if I didn't, he would get lost in his girly mind and never come back. I do understand that each individual will have different degrees of cross-dressing or may transition no matter what. I just think I'm lucky for now and so we live.

The Blessings of Change

ANGELA GAIL

From Love at First Sight to Starting a Family

I met Nathan 13 years ago at a mentoring program for women in technical fields and we fell hard for each other. We were so excited that neither of us could eat or concentrate on the lectures we were attending. Three years later, we stood in a long line in the middle of the night to apply for one of the first same-sex wedding licenses in our Massachusetts community. The next week before the ceremony we took our wedding party out to a large park for photos. Nathan had gotten ready separately from me and I still remember the first moment I saw him on our wedding day. His pale pink dress was beautiful, made by his mom from an old pattern. His sister formed his long hair. I remember crying at that moment because I felt so lucky to actually get to marry him. He was a luminous marvel with brassy orange hair, freckles, and skin so light you could nearly see through it. I knew that he was made for me, that we were made for each other, and he took my breath away.

I got a Ph.D. and a started my career. A couple of years later I got pregnant and gave birth to a baby girl. Then Nathan got a Ph.D. and started his career. We learned how to navigate our family as two working moms, and Nathan, in particular, figured out how to mother a child that he didn't birth and with whom he had no genetic connection. We were both determined to be primary parents to our daughter, to share in her day-to-day care, and to feel like a family making our way through the world together. As our daughter grew out of babyhood, we found we had the family and the life we had envisioned, and it felt good.

From the start, we had planned that Nathan would carry our second child. When I met Nathan he had periods only occasionally, and when he started tracking his cycles it was clear that he rarely ovulated. So he did acupuncture for a year before he tried to get pregnant, laughing when the acupuncturist told him he was "too much of a man." His relationship with his body has always been strained and difficult and he hoped pregnancy would help him connect more with his body and love what it could do. He got pregnant when our daughter Leigh was two years old, but pregnancy was a struggle for him. He never had that glow that some pregnant people get, and near the end of the pregnancy there were complications that necessitated an early delivery. As I look back now, I see his pregnancy as a series of disappointments and unfulfilled promises.

Delivery itself was a battle, one that he fought with that same determination I have always seen in him. I remember crying to our doula late in his difficult labor because I was worried that he was headed for a Cesarean section, which I knew would be devastating to him. But he was a warrior in that delivery room, and after three days of induced labor with no pain medication he gave birth to our beautiful son with no surgery needed. For Nathan, birth was probably disproportionately important, and he was willing to suffer a great deal of pain in order to experience birth in a way he believed would be healing. After the delivery, he had to go to the operating room to repair the heavy damage his body sustained from the prolonged birth. Because I had already induced my own lactation to share in feeding, I was able to give our baby his first taste of breast milk while

Nathan was in the operating room. Once we were home, I saw the delivery as a victory and I hoped that as Nathan healed from the birth he would also find the healing in his relationship with his body that he'd hope for.

But the healing did not come. It reminds me of a story that my kids like to read about a bird couple that finds a crocodile egg in their nest. The crocodile grows and grows and eventually has to leave the nest. His bird parents love him and they encourage him to jump out of the nest and flap his wings so that he will fly. The crocodile flaps and flaps, but of course he has no wings, so it does no good. Nathan had given everything he had to feel like a whole woman but no matter how much flapping he did, no matter how he floored me with his bravery and power, he still couldn't fly.

Still, we had a brand new baby and a three-year-old, so we muddled through. I didn't think much about Nathan's difficult relationship with his body, and I never really understood why it was so strained. Sometimes, when you haven't gotten a good night of sleep in a year or so, you just let those kinds of mysteries go.

You Want to Start Doing What?

Eventually we made it to the other side of that stage of parenthood when virtually all of your energy is directed towards caring for very young kids. One evening, when our daughter was five and our son was two, Nathan and I were out on a precious date alone. We had a fun evening and we were waiting for the bus back home when he told me that he wanted to start binding.

I often walk through the world a bit unmoored. Perhaps it is my spectacularly bad memory, my tendency to detach from my surroundings and space out or even the way I simply feel puzzled by people who don't always make a lot of sense to me. Regardless of the reason, this gives me the gift of accepting the people around me as they present themselves. I'm no saint. I can be as judgmental and petty as anyone else but when something big happens, I tend to slow down, watch, and wait to see what will happen next. When Nathan told me he wanted to start binding, I was surprised. I hadn't expected those words to come out of his mouth. He wasn't a butch lesbian, even though he had recently discovered he preferred shopping in the men's department. When he started talking about binding, I just said "OK." I wondered what binding would mean and what would happen next but I wasn't afraid of the future, just curious. My response set the stage for a time that was full of wonder. A person started to come forth that I didn't know, and I just let him happen.

I could write about what is was like to support my trans partner through a grueling shift during which he doubted himself every step of the way, had to make decisions that terrified him, and coped with days that seemed to alternate between presenting new kinds of pain and new kinds of elation. Or I could write about what it was like to shepherd my kids through this change. Our daughter Leigh was five when her little brother insisted that "Mama is a man!" Leigh fiercely stood up for Nathan insisting, "Mama is a woman," and looking to me to back her up. When I couldn't, she was shocked and tried to campaign that Nathan not change anything and "stay a woman." However, once she adjusted to the idea, she became one of Nathan's most vocal supporters. But I don't want to write only about Nathan, Leigh or Ira because those are their stories, not mine. I love them all, but there's more to me than the love I have for my family.

Changes

When Nathan started to understand his gender, I was excited, confused, and exhausted at the same time. I remember feeling like I was cheating on my spouse of eight years with my new lover. I was living in an episode of *Three's Company* as I ran off to play in the sheets with Nathan, my lips on fire while pronouncing a new name, and then periodically ran back to my wife when we were around other people, stumbling over her name and pronouns. For over half my 40 years, I had identified as a lesbian. But when Nathan started questioning his gender and presenting in a more masculine way, I started questioning my own sexuality. I realized that I was, frankly, much more attracted to Nathan as a man.

I was embarrassed and confused during that period because I couldn't reconcile my attraction to Nathan the man with my attraction to the woman I had married, and my attraction to many other women, particularly ones who presented in a masculine way. Was I bisexual? Had I been this way the entire time? What would it mean for me if people stopped reading me as a lesbian and started reading me as a straight woman? I was very attached to the way that my actions in the world, like marrying and raising children with a presumed woman, identified me in the eyes of the world as a lesbian. That fit well with my internal identity, so I never needed to talk about sexual orientation. It was simply an observable fact.

I still get frustrated that I can't give the secret handshake to other queer people simply by mentioning my spouse, though at some point I let go of most of my angst around my sexual orientation. I seem to be attracted to all kinds of people. Sometimes I call myself bisexual but more often I call myself queer because this term does not confine my attraction to people aligned with the gender binary. Also, something about the term "queer" itself is delightfully disruptive. But I have to admit that my need for that disruption seems to lessen over time. Much to my own dismay, I find I like some parts of heterosexual privilege. As my relationship has become more straight, I've been seeking out opportunities to be queer that don't involve having a relationship. I want to be able to interact with queer culture on my own without using my partner's trans status as my ticket into the club. I am queer because that is my internal understanding of myself not because I spent 21 years of my life in relationships with women or because my male partner was designated female at birth.

Coming Full Circle

Today my four-year-old son, Ira, was looking at pictures. He had an old album dating back to before he was born, which feels like a million years ago. He pointed to a photo where his father with long red hair was in a doctoral robe preparing to receive his Ph.D. There were pictures of the whole family including his big sister Leigh, who was still a baby, his grandparents, and me.

He wanted to know what the pictures were about, especially the funny outfits. I explained to him about getting a degree and wearing special robes in a ceremony. Later I realized that he hadn't asked me about why his father had long hair or why he looked like a woman. For that matter, he hadn't asked about his father's female appearance in any of the photos from that album. Ira knows that his dad used to live as a woman and gave birth to him. At least for now, that doesn't seem to cause cognitive dissonance for him. Perhaps for Ira it simply falls under the category of inexplicable things adults do. I feel a bit jealous of my own son's view of Nathan—it can be so matter-of-fact and unencumbered by history.

A few weeks ago, Nathan finally had chest surgery. His recovery felt harder to me than I anticipated, partially, because my life already has so much caretaking in it that fitting in more had me running on empty batteries. But even with this difficulty, the surgery feels like a miracle. For two years now, I have been systematically erasing a part of Nathan's body, fracturing him in order to see him as he really is. When the bandages came off, I had my first glimpse of him as whole without need of any editing. He looked amazing, like part of his true self had been revealed. His breasts were like a disguise he had to wear all of the time, even though they were all wrong for him.

With his chest raw and scarred yet whole, I felt one step closer to my son's understanding of the world. With the mental weight of editing Nathan's body off, his former female figure becomes simply a piece of history, just a fact we don't necessarily have to understand.

So, yes, I still remember seeing my radiant husband the day of our wedding. In my mind, he glows and his feet never touch the ground. It is a memory I will always hold gently so as not to crush it, like the moment when my days-old daughter cried for hours on end, yet my exhausted heart suddenly burst with love for her, or the way my son's warm breath hit my skin when I held and nursed him for a half hour after he was born.

None of those memories are true pictures of the people I love now. My husband would look uncomfortable in that wedding dress, my daughter draws and sings and creates (and doesn't scream much), and my son's wiggly body hardly fits on my lap. Everyone has changed and I am hardly the same person myself.

I don't really understand how any of our pasts fit with our present and I am again unmoored and disoriented. How did my screaming baby turn into a seven-year-old girl who just performed in an opera? How did my suckling baby turn into a four-year-old who loves subway maps? How did my glowing wife turn into my handsome husband? How did I turn into a bisexual married to a man? I have no idea, but I remember that it is a gift to be able to let people be exactly who they are. Strange things that I don't understand happen all the time. I'm keeping my eyes open waiting to see the next blessing those changes bring.

Out of the Shadows

PAULA JAMES

When my husband first told me that he was going to have surgery, I was so thrilled for the both of us. I was excited for him, knowing that finally his physical sexual equipment would reflect how he had always felt on the inside. I knew how deeply important this surgery had been for him for so many years. I have always told him that I love him for who he is, not for what was (or was not) between his legs. That still remains true today. If he had never found the time or money to go through with this change, I would still love him and be by his side forever.

I was also afraid of potential complications and all the pain and suffering that he would have to go through. He was my soul mate who was going all the way to Serbia for surgery. My first thought was, *Oh, my god, he's going into a war-torn country*. But they had stopped fighting more than a decade ago. Then I wondered: *What if something went wrong and I couldn't be there to see or look after him? What happens if he dies on the table?* I knew there were always possibilities of complications, and he experienced a few of them after coming home.

I admit that I was a tad dramatic for my own good. But I was unable to go with him. Finances and running our business made traveling with him impossible. I knew communication was going to be spotty at best. So, quite naturally I worried about a lot of things. Occasionally, it also occurred to me that he might want to explore new sexual avenues opened up by the surgery and become curious about being with other women. How would I deal with that if it ever came up?

On another personal level, I also felt tremendous relief. At times, it has been hard emotionally to deal with my family and some of our friends who could not understand that my husband is a man, despite his birth sex and anatomy. I had been adopted and raised by a devout Mormon family who frowned on any kind of sexuality that wasn't heterosexual and procreative. My partner and I first met when we were young, 14 and 12, and much in love.

But because of the Mormon Church and my family's teachings, I struggled with the issue internally and felt conflicted for many years. I did not consider myself a lesbian. Nor had I ever been attracted to women. For me, he was never a woman. He was just who he was and my heart told me that he was my soul mate. Because I was so young and naïve, I struggled to understand what loving him meant for me and who I was. I felt that his surgery would finally show the world who I really was too: that I was in love with a man and not a woman, as everyone tried to argue.

When he changed his name officially, I proudly told my adoptive parents of his plans for surgery. Yet, they continued to call him by his birth name. They refused to accept him as my soul mate and continued trying to talk me out of being with him. They wanted me to marry some "nice" Mormon boy, which was the ultimate oxymoron to me. Nice Mormon boys had sexually exploited and physically abused me, whereas my partner had only been kind and loving to me. I was crushed by my adoptive family's refusal to see that he was obviously not a lesbian. They continued to call me a lesbian for many years, and I finally told them that I no longer considered them a part of my family.

We both began to see how intolerant the public was/is about gender reassignment, and I began feeling like I had to hide from people. I was willing to do whatever it took to be with him, however, so I learned how to cope with not having friends and how to form friendships based on secrets and half-truths. It has been lonely at times, but I have also seen and dealt with the harsh consequences of disclosing anything about that part of our lives. After all, people do not need to know everything.

He was concerned about my not having close friends, but just his concern at my well-being was enough to get me through lonely times. We have always been close emotionally and shared out feelings, and I knew that he too was lonely without friends. We always had each other. After a time, having close friends became less important for me. All I really needed was my partner and son. No matter what happened, he was supportive of me and took in my son as if he were his own and helped raise him. Without him, my son would have grown up to be irresponsible and selfish.

My husband's family was supportive. They knew who he was from the beginning and were not shocked by his decision to have surgery. In fact, they seemed to breathe in a big sigh of relief for him, and if I recall, their reaction was something like, "It's about time." They accepted my son and me into the family. They never made us feel like freaks as my own family had.

Initially, I was worried about being able to care for him adequately when he came back home. I was good at supporting him emotionally and helping him through his recovery. Many times I listened to him talk about his own emotional changes and what he was going through during the surgeries. I also did the usual things like changing his dressings, making sure he was eating properly, and trying to help relieve his aches and pains as best I could. His self-confidence has increased and that is the best I could have hoped for.

His confidence continued to increase in the time since the surgery. He is finally feeling more at home in his own skin. Having never gone through his experience, I will never fully understand the feelings of incompleteness that he has always felt for his entire life. But I do see the change in him emotionally, which is all the proof I need to know that he had to go through this experience to feel complete.

I love his body even more now than before, but I think that is a mental thing for me. Having never considered myself to be a lesbian or been attracted to women, I feel that I can shed any inhibitions that I may have had being with him before. He has always satisfied me, but I knew something was missing for him. I love his new penis!

My advice to other partners is to guard against taking this change as a personal affront to you as a person or a partner. His needs are not about you failing to make your partner happy. They are about your partner's body and sense of self. You are not doing anything wrong and do not need to "improve" yourself to make him happier. The best thing you can do is continue to love your partner and accept that he is doing this to feel more complete.

My husband's process has never been about me. It has always been (as it should) about him finding comfort in himself. I would have been happy to spend the rest of our lives together with him, with or without surgery, but he would have never been truly happy with himself. I feel like we are walking in the sun now.

Before, we lived our lives hiding in the shadows, afraid to even hold hands in public for fear of the discrimination that we would get from others. I mean, if my own adoptive family who was supposed to love me unconditionally created such turmoil about this, who knows what we would have suffered from strangers. It was a joy to finally be able to hold his hand in public and not feel like we have to stick to the shadows to even look at each other as lovers. We can finally enjoy the sunshine on our faces without having to deal with people's disapproving looks.

I am so blessed to have been included in his life-changing process and count myself lucky to go down this road with him. I would gladly go down this road with him again, regardless of all the discrimination and alienation from friends and family. It has been well worth it.

Dear Janet

Tasha

My wife started her transition five and half years ago and finished a year later in 2010, which was also our 10th wedding anniversary. We first met at 15, have been together since we were 17 and married at 22. So any clues about her gender issues that were present back then, I was there for it too. This meant I couldn't really blame her for not figuring anything out. She says she genuinely was a cis guy for a while and that her gender identity evolved. I like to say I fell in love with a boy, married a man and ended up with a woman. As I'm bisexual and prefer women, at first we both thought this would be "easy," but it turned out to be a pretty hellish year. I still have to come to terms with losing all the little details about the husband I'd loved, and adjust to having a wife. The process of adapting took at least a year, but at this point that period of grieving is long in the past, and I'm delighted with the spouse I have now.

Dear Janet,

Although, there were times when I thought I'd scream if I heard one more word about gender, we've had some fantastic discussions about gender and gender identity in our society. I know I have become a more nuanced and informed feminist by talking extensively with someone who is fascinated by all the myriad changes in societal reactions and treatment which occurred as you stepped over the "gender divide." It was certainly a validation of my own experiences to see the ways in which you—and we—were treated differently based purely on public perception of your gender.

It was your own gender journey that made me realize, eventually, that I am and have always been *agender*—that I lack whatever profound, innate sense of gender you and others have that drove you on this transition path. I'm still comfortable being identified as cis-sexual but not cis-gender. I also made some tentative efforts to alter my own body medically and surgically to match what I most desire after realizing that you were allowed to do so for yourself. However, I'm not willing to take the full "official transition path" to get there and typical medical professionals have so far been uncooperative.

Similarly, when you came out as a trans*, it was the impetus for me to admit both privately and professionally that I have always been bisexual, though at work I merely started referring to you as my wife with no further explanation. My coworkers' reaction was polite indifference, but it cost me some family members who couldn't cope. As far as I'm concerned, that was worth it.

But I also was confirmed in my belief over the last 15 years that it *would* drive some people away, and I don't regret waiting until I'm old enough and secure enough in my identity now to say that it's their loss. At times my coming out gets lost in the overall gender noise, though it's still been a revelation learning to live as openly and proudly non-heterosexual, even if I cannot get most people to believe/remember that I'm bisexual. Now that people generally mistake me for a lesbian, at least it's closer to accurate than before, when they assumed I was straight.

On the other hand, as I have always preferred women, I have been delighted as you became more and more gorgeously feminine. Another reason I never widely claimed the label "bisexual" was that

I was not entirely certain whether I'd enjoy being intimate with a woman, which is a bugaboo that is now thoroughly banished! It turns out gender reassignment surgery (GRS) was something we both consider just a footnote. Hence, it's amusing to note that I was utterly hysterical over things like ear piercing and laser hair removal but by the time we got to that stage I was fine with the change aspect of it.

I look back now and thank goodness that I did eventually manage to come to terms with things. I wish I'd known back then where we'd be now because it would have made the whole trip somewhat easier. I liked to say that we were going through this entire nightmarish transition path so that you could be happy, and I'd get back to the status quo (a happy, quiet life in a normal marriage). In some ways that was true, but I also had no idea what a relief the status quo would be after years of upheaval or how profoundly grateful I would be to have walked this path alongside you.

I needed the most support early on when we had no idea if it was even possible for a relationship to survive transition. Unfortunately, at that point, I found zero support anywhere with the exception of your therapist telling me she had lots of couples who did stay together. Though she added she had stopped facilitating partners' support groups because the pain was too much for her to deal with, which I [unfairly] mentally translated into "suppress all your own feelings because otherwise you'll be the reason everything falls apart."

I know it would have helped me tremendously just to know it was possible for a relationship to survive. Everyone we ran into at the time said it wasn't and we should divorce now before we both get too bitter. Since then, I have made a point of reaching out to partners online whenever I can and trying to be the support I wished I could have found. As a result, I now have a network of friendships with other trans* partners, most of whom weathered the transitioning process successfully. So, as hard as that initial period was, it's probably been a blessing both to me and to those new partners out there.

These days we are still happily married and romantically/sexually involved, and I'm eternally grateful that I stuck it out and consider myself lucky to have you in my life; I hope mentioning that publicly and frequently is a way of living the encouragement I wished I could have found.

I'm also looking back on nearly five years of being involved in the trans* community as a partner and realizing just how fantastically lucky I am to have come out of transition with my beloved wife, and how lucky we are that our marriage is not only unscathed but has actually improved.

Interestingly, I've developed a surprisingly accurate sixth sense for when a relationship will survive, which has far less to do with the realities of transition than cis people assume. I'm setting aside cases where one or the other person's sexual orientation will not be congruent with their partner's gender post-transition. That might seem like cheating to omit, but as heartbreaking as those situations are, no one is to blame and there's usually no surprise to anyone involved that the relationship cannot continue. The key factor is whether the people involved respect and love each other going into transition.

I've said many times that transition isn't actually much different than any other major relationship stressor. Now I have personal observations of dozens of couples to back this up. People break up over having kids, switching or losing jobs, moving cross-country, deaths in the immediate family and so on. Basically, if the relationship already has fault lines, one more major stressor will shatter it along them. So

I can pretty much guarantee that if one person or the other is talking with contempt about their partner, lying to/about them, bad-mouthing them behind their back, cheating on them or engaging in other myriad disrespectful and unkind behaviors and has lost sight of what they loved in the other person, then transition is far more likely to destroy the relationship. This is true on both sides. I've seen cis partners behaving like cruel jerks, and I've seen trans* people making unilateral decisions for the marriage with both sides lying about their spouses to make them look like the bad guy.

The good news is that solid loving couples with good communication have an excellent chance of survival. And more importantly, that it's not really "the trans*" that wrecked the relationship if that was the final straw, and no trans* person should accept guilt undeservedly for something they needed to do. I don't even wish that we hadn't gone through this transition, because it's bonded us in ways I never could have imagined at the start.

I love you, sweetheart, and thank you for 21 wonderful years together. I'll be OK if the next few years are less interesting, though.

Tasha

Accepting Transformation

Georgia Kolias

Back before the Internet was widely used, I posted a personal ad in a local LGBT newspaper called *The San Francisco Bay Times*. The ad read: "I Like Fun. Seeking brainy brawny girls to frolic with, etc." I had low expectations, so imagine my surprise that nineteen years later I am happily partnered with someone else who "liked fun."

As a self-identified lesbian who preferred dating butch women, I was not seeking to partner myself with a man. However, from our first phone call on the morning of January 1, 1995, there was an intellectual and emotional crackling that has always made our pairing both challenging and exciting. Back then, Willy was a butch lesbian who identified as transgender, and I was a person who articulated an interest in dating a man in a woman's body.

What I meant was that I wanted someone who would open my doors, thrill me with their chivalry, buy me pretty things, and let me be the girl. I never enjoyed dating women who wanted to be pretty. I wanted a woman who was strong. But when my strong lover decided to transition to a full-time male identity, I was faced with a choice, and I want to tell you why this lesbian chose to stay.

Willy told me about the book *Stone Butch Blues*, a female-to-male transsexual memoir-esque novel, during our first phone call. I bought it and read it by the next time we spoke. It was all on the table: now transition was within a realm of possibilities. Still, somehow it seemed very far away to me. Perhaps it was the denial that we happily float in when entering a new, sizzling relationship, but it didn't bother me. I appreciated Willy's maleness within our butch/femme context. It was just what I wanted and needed. It felt like a soothing elixir and a thrill ride at the same time to find my gender opposite and to be appreciated for my womanliness.

We butted heads on a variety of issues and spent countless hours debating on class, race, the hyphenated cultural experience, and whiteness. We learned to find each other through those lenses that we viewed the world through by arguing until we reached a common ground of understanding. Gender was often a topic we discussed, as was body image in the context of size and the pursuit of finding peace in our bodies.

As the years passed, Willy considered transitioning. To be completely honest, I was scared and resistant. I liked the gender dynamics of our relationship. I had the masculine woman I wanted.

Then again, there were aspects of our relationship that were difficult for me. Willy placed restrictions on his body: I was allowed to touch some parts but not others. There were rules that protected his soul but made mine lonely at times. And I was familiar with being a member of the queer community. I didn't know what it would mean to be the partner of a transgender man. I worried how it would affect my identity or how I would be seen in the world.

I had come out as a lesbian when I was sixteen and had never been in a relationship with a man. The heterosexuality modeled by my parents was terrifying to me. I did not want that. And yet, I knew that being perceived by others as a heteronormative couple would afford me some legal, social, and safety privileges that I didn't yet have—but I deserved those already. I resented that I could only get them if I was with a man.

What are those traditional marriage vows anyway? "For better or for worse, for richer, for poorer, in sickness and in health, to love and to cherish from this day forward until death do us part." We had all that anyway. And though it was not legally binding, Willy and I had a big wedding in 1998 at the Oakland Rose Garden followed by a reception at a Moroccan restaurant complete with a seven-course meal and belly dancers. In 2004, we rushed at the chance to get legally married when then-Mayor Gavin Newsom opened the door to same-sex marriages in San Francisco during what was dubbed, "The Winter of Love." After that marriage was voided by the courts, we became registered domestic partners before the birth of our first child in 2006. We had two more children in 2009 and 2012.

Both of us struggled through serious chronic illness, the inability to work, financial despair, and the misery of the Proposition 8 campaign when our neighbors pointed their "no gay marriage allowed" signs at our house and organized street protests in our neighborhood, yelling their hateful rhetoric at us as we drove our son to preschool. But we also have the American Dream. We own our home, we have a family, and our everyday lives are like so many people—a treadmill of drudgery, yet so sweet and lovely. My favorite moments still are family snuggle time each morning when we all pile in together and hug, goof around, sing and start our day centered on what is important: our family. I would never trade it for anything.

When I was waiting to find out if I was pregnant with our third child, Willy came to me and said, "Well, I've decided. I'm transitioning." He had been socially and professionally transitioning for some time out in the world, using male pronouns and letting people know that he identified as male. I was a hold-out though. I was still using female pronouns.

Admittedly, I was being stubborn and perhaps selfish. Even after seventeen years together, I still wasn't ready. I was resistant to being seen as heterosexual. It was ironic really, since nobody can tell I'm a lesbian when they look at me. But this had been a sore point for me over the years to feel so invisible. Willy was my lover, my queer identification card. When he became a man, I felt I would sink wholesale into obscurity, into a life that I didn't choose for myself. Coming from a traditional Greek immigrant family, I had fought long and hard for the right to be myself—a lesbian.

Also, I felt a social obligation to remain silent about my feelings of not wanting him to transition. I did not want to embarrass Willy or be an unsupportive partner, and in my darker moments, I was afraid of being seen as a secret traitor by the transgender community. I felt an uncomfortable pressure to wholeheartedly support Willy's transition no matter what my feelings were and keep my mouth shut. I've never been good at keeping my mouth shut.

Willy's decision ultimately forced my hand, as it has for many partners of transgender people. I finally had to ask myself: "Would I really break up my family and leave this person I loved if he became a man?" "Who would I become if I was with a man?" "Would he change and become someone else once he transitioned?"

My biggest fear was that he would morph into a domineering angry husband. But I kept coming back to the things I loved most about him: His passion, his loyalty, his wicked sense of humor, his intellect, his love for me and our kids. Our lives became so much better together, more than we would have ever been separately. He is meant to be mine. I knew that from the early weeks of our relationship, perhaps even from that first phone call. Imagining life without him was unthinkable.

So I told him I made a decision too. Whatever his form, I choose his essence and soul. I choose to stay. I couldn't make any promises that I would easily adjust or even know how I'd react to his changing body. But I would respect his choice and I hoped he could respect me and allow space for my feelings as I explored what this meant for me and my own identity.

Two months after his decision to physically transition, Willy underwent chest reconstruction surgery. I grieved this change in his body. Yet over time, I found an unanticipated benefit—there are no longer any restrictions on touching his chest. This area which had been banned and defensively blocked for so many years was suddenly open territory. Even though the form had changed, the new freedom allowed to me lifted my heart. And Willy was happy and more at peace than I had ever experienced him before. More than anything else, this made it easier for me to change as he changed.

Now that we are two years into this transition, I can honestly say that Willy only becomes more handsome with each passing day. When I lean into his strong arms I feel safe and loved, and I am so happy that I continue to find my home in his heart.

I can't say the journey is over. More surgeries lie ahead. I'm still getting used to people referring to Willy as my husband. As a mother, many of my friends are parents of my children's friends and they are largely heterosexual. They assume that I am too. Coming out as a lesbian used to feel pretty easy, but now my story has become more complicated. There are still awkward questions I struggle to answer. If I make a new friend, when or how or why do I tell them that I am a lesbian and that Willy is transgender? If I do, will that change how they feel about us or worse, act toward him? If he goes through so much to actualize this physical reality, what is the purpose of telling?

Yet, if I don't tell, I feel somehow incomplete in the representation of my experience because I will be perceived to have lived an easy straight life with all my queer struggles erased. It reminds me of when I had my miscarriages, which were such pivotal experiences for me. In order to feel truly connected to someone, I felt compelled to share that I had lived through that. I felt like I was not bringing my whole self to the table to have lived through something so life-changing and to keep it a secret.

I know that as the partner of a transgender person I am living my life as an ally, a tertiary participant. Still, it's my life, and in my life I am my central character. So, I seek to honor and accept my feelings whatever they are. I let them exist and I let them pass. During those moments when I still get scared, I remember the reassuring, immense love that I have been privileged to experience for nineteen years. The fear falls away.

Willy is my partner. We swim side by side through these waters. We seek to arrive at the same destination, but the strokes we choose to get there may differ. That is okay as long as we get there together.

Becoming Us

K Le Vie

I met you right after the beginning of your transition. From the unmistakable confidence of your introduction and the moment you took my hand, I understood you as butch and he. The way you lit my cigarettes, asked me to dance, and carried me to bed—I have only ever known you as man. I wasn't there when you walked through that door from female-to-male and closed it behind you.

That's not to say I knew what I was getting into when we became a couple. I've watched your baby face harden and bristle. I've listened to your voice drop two octaves—I still have the voicemails to prove it—and heard your laugh stay mysteriously the same. I've bought you four different sizes of shirts, and am still routinely startled by the breadth of your shoulders. I wish I could count the number of times in the average week I step on a wayward penis—nothing else squishes under your foot like that!

I met you right after the beginning of your transition, right before the beginning of mine. When we met, I was a queer genderqueer femme on my way to becoming the partner of a trans person. You see, in becoming the partner of a trans person, my entire self was given over to you. My own identity makes no sense without you.

For me to say I am a *lesbian* or even *queer* makes no sense without a context for my husband.

I hate that for me to come out requires outing you. Remember, when I went to that lesbian hairdresser the week before our wedding? She asked me where I met my fiancé. I told her, "Cattivo." "Really?" she said, "And he's a guy?" "He's a trans man." Lightbulb! *Then* she knew we could speak openly as queer women.

I didn't lose my queer identity to this marriage, although there are plenty of people who might argue I did. The story about crossing the border into Maryland and coming back with a "straight" marriage license does little to refute it. It's hard to complain about a piece of paper that simplifies your future while stripping you of your history.

I both respect and despise the safety that comes with walking out into the world as a straight couple. We are untouchable late at night in any part of the city, but during pride—our pride, the pride we share—we are cast sideways glances by beloved peers who feel threatened by our presence and our perceived privilege.

There are at least two different stories going on here. One is about you, and the other is about me. When we go into trans spaces, it can be difficult to know which story to tell. My presence in that space is predicated on you, and I feel expected to tell a story about you. When I married you, it was because I wanted my whole life to be a story about you—about *us*.

That might be the biggest transition of all for me: the transition from "I" to "we." I am learning how to be part of us. I started learning what "us" meant when my windfall became our windfall and let an abstract idea become an immediate reality. I sat tense and alone in that waiting room for the seemingly endless hours of your top surgery. While I felt no apprehension about saying goodbye to a pair of breasts that had never really been *yours*, I could not contain my anxiety about sending the person I loved under anesthesia with strangers and being completely helpless while it happened.

Even though I totally destroyed my sleep cycle by waking up at all hours of the night to make sure you took your medicine, I loved being the one to take care of you, and I love that you trusted *me* to go through it together. Later, when we were coming home, the tourists in the airports shot you dirty looks when they saw me struggling with all our luggage. I wanted to scream at them that they had no idea what your life was like, that it hurt you far more to see me carrying everything than it hurt me to do the carrying.

My story right now is not about being the partner of a trans person. It is about being partners with you and how challenging and rewarding that can be. It doesn't matter if I go with you to the doctor for a pap smear or a prostate exam, as long as I am there with you. It won't matter if our eventual children are biologically related to one, both or neither of us, as long as we use this partnership we're building to be the best parents we can be for them. It doesn't matter that the county clerk who filled out our paperwork began automatically with, "You're the groom, so let's start with you," as long as we have a legal link that nobody can question.

It doesn't matter what parts of our skins touch when we are finally alone together, as long as we conduct the electricity that makes us both glow. No matter where we both came from, we are here together now, and we are writing the story of us going forward.

Constricting Prescriptions: Choosing Reality Over Vocabulary

Justin Ropella

Dear Kate,

I hate to admit it, but sometimes I'm afraid. I'm afraid of what I don't know. I'm afraid of what we can't know. I'm a regimented, scheduled, organized person—you know this. I thrive when I have a roadmap and a clear view of the big picture—my destination. However, this is something that isn't really possible when it comes to your transition. There's no clear picture or pre-determined outcome here, and that scares me sometimes.

Shortly after you began the coming out conversation, you said something that has stuck with me. It's something I think about every day. I think about its truth, its inaccuracy, its implications, its weight, its meaning to my identity and to our lives. Every day, even if for just a moment, the words you said to me all those months ago cross through my consciousness.

"But you're gay!"

I've spent a lot of time deconstructing and dissecting that sentence. Ultimately, I've landed on a rather simple response to it. "So what?"

I realize our identities seem to inherently conflict with one another. When I step back and think about it with too much objectivity, it doesn't escape me that something doesn't quite align in a relationship between a pansexual transgender woman and a gay cisgender man. I think about a future in which you feel invalidated as a woman by my sexual orientation or I feel alienated from the gay community because of my heterosexual relationship. I think about a future in which I miss sexual connections with men. I think about a future in which we both constantly need to explain and defend our gender identities, sexual orientations, and our perceptions of those who simply don't understand.

I think about these things and see them reflected in the experiences of others. Sometimes it seems so intensely difficult and hopeless. But then I step out of the objectivity sphere and simply allow myself to feel what's real and relevant to us as we are.

While not all of it has gone smoothly or without stress (okay, I admit it, sometimes panic), coming out and allowing me to join you on a journey without a clear or finite destination has necessitated that I remain outside of my comfort zone of plans and checklists. You've forced me to look at my life—*our* lives—without immediately looking forward to quantify my future expectations. I couldn't ever successfully ask myself, "Will you still want to sleep with her when her body aligns fully with her gender identity?", because there's no real fact there. There's no way to know how I'll feel when something I hadn't before fathomed occurs.

Instead, I now take stock of what I know to be true as is. "Do you love her and do you want to be intimate with her?" Absolutely! "Do you have any reason to suspect that may change?" Not in the slightest.

It was no small personal challenge for me to get to a place where those were the questions that held primary real estate in my mind, which had otherwise been overrun with "what if" questions about the future. The biggest "what if" where I placed my focus was, "What if I spend my life with a woman? What does that make me? Bisexual? Pansexual? Less gay than I was before I was with her?" It's been a challenge to reconcile this with my own sense of self.

It seemed unfair to place my concerns on your already very full plate, especially early on after you came out to me. This is something I've noticed fairly regularly in both partners. It seems like the majority of partners fall into one of two camps: the people who get angry or hurt and leave or the people who become champions and pillars of unwavering support. I realize these aren't the only two responses for partners but they're certainly the two most vocal groups online.

In the beginning, I felt like if I faltered even slightly from the outlook of the latter group, it would somehow make me a member of the former by default. So I put on my most supportive face and moved forward with as much positivity as possible. Of course, that didn't stop me from looking toward the future with panic, as you eventually came to understand.

"What if" questions consumed me for a long time and I've learned something critically important over the last year. No matter how much time I spent in anxiety-ridden thought about the future, there's simply no way to know what's going to happen until the future arrives. And that's okay! We're both in new territory here. Why should that preclude us from honoring our feelings as they are or make us assume they'll change?

Sometimes this line of thought can look suspiciously similar to a sort of "get out of jail free card" mentality—as though I'm sticking around to be supportive with the knowledge that I'll leave someday.

I need you to know this couldn't be more wrong. Why should we assume that since we don't know all the outcomes, those outcomes must inevitably be negative? I don't buy that.

The thought and introspection this process has required has truly made me a better person with a stronger sense of personal identity and greater empathy for and acceptance of others. It took a good deal of time to become comfortable with the fact that I can both identify as gay and continue a relationship with you. You've given me the tools I needed to connect with a larger, freer sense of myself. Being fulfilled both emotionally and sexually with you neither suddenly makes me bisexual nor invalidates your gender identity as a woman. All it means is that we've both found the right person for us despite what expectations and assumptions we previously held about what that would look like.

Much of this process and journey can look and feel a bit bleak. In the beginning, it was easy for me to see how change like this could lead to the end of relationships. What I've learned along the way is that's only the case if you let the rigorous labels we place on ourselves make your decisions for you. I'm incredibly thankful for your help and for your support in seeing how irrelevant those labels are.

You've given me a gift that I find challenging to describe. Because of you I'm able to view an uncertain future not with fear, but with hope. Because of you I'm more able to truly experience and appreciate the present. Because of you I've learned to define my sense of self not with the labels I've prescribed for myself, but with the love and the happiness I feel in spite of those prescriptions. This is a gift that has not only allowed me to feel more grounded in myself, but also to truly treasure what we have together without reservation.

I love you, Kate, as you are, and as you will be. I look forward to seeing how the future changes and strengthens us, but more than that I appreciate the happiness and contentment we bring each other with what we have today. I both wouldn't change a thing and welcome the changes to come.

Love,
Justin

Daisy in Cement

Amber Jean Coyne

When I first met Jay I was still coming into my own skin, finally accepting my truth and fumbling trying to live authentically in that truth; to own my identity. I identify myself as a lesbian. Although, I did not always know this—a truth that I am sure resonates with many femmes. As a child, you could not keep me in pants. (Who am I kidding? You still can't keep me in pants.) I loved my long hair and soft skin. I loved painted nails and tea parties. My obsession with glitter, frills, and dainty dresses was a household oddity. My parents were never quite sure where my hyper-femininity came from, as neither of them was particularly feminine. But I loved being and feeling feminine; I always have.

Little girl
Frills glitter rhinestones
Girly girl
Knew my gender

My gender identity was consistent and persistent; an overtly feminine girl. As much as my Dad tried to push me towards more masculine interests, I was convinced that my destiny was that of a pink ordained fabulous super model princess. Like I said, I was consistent and persistent. I now know that gender identity solidifies quite a number of years before sexual orientation; a simple fact that carries quite significant social burden as the way we present gender often determines who we are supposed to like.

Junior high
Crushes attraction
Boys
Sex invading minds
Not mine

I believe now that it was my strong sense of gender identity and the social expectations woven seamlessly into my perception of what being a "girly girl" meant which prevented me from recognizing my sexual orientation. Society had given me this idea that girls like men, girls who like dresses, and glitter, and unicorns, are not the type of girls that like girls. Feminine girls like boys. End of story.

Convinced convicted
Heterosexual
Because of my gender
Identity girl
Expression girly girl

I considered my innate attraction to women as admiration. I am also a feminist, so this was a logical explanation for my fascination with women. *I just admire how beautiful she is. I admire how smart she is. It is admiration not attraction.* This worked astonishingly well.

High school single
Uninterested

College dating
Still uninterested

By my senior year of college I was still wondering why I couldn't manage to be functional in any straight relationship. I had given up entirely on the idea of marriage and the idea of falling in love the way my parents and grandparents had. I felt so distant, frigid, and endlessly guilty in relationships.

Cold heartless bitch
But a heart that can't feel
Cannot be cold
Void

In my final months of college I decided to join the cast of a fairly popular feminist play. This is when my sexual revolution happened. During rehearsals we would talk about different aspects of sexuality and gender. It was the first time I saw feminine girls like myself so nonchalantly say they were sexually fluid or queer. This was the representation that I deeply craved without knowing it. I saw a truth that intimately resonated with me. This is when I began deeply questioning my sexuality, although it would take longer for me to act on it.

23 years old
Finally see myself in another
Girly girl
Liking girls

Flash-forward a year and half later and I was falling in love for the first time with someone whom both society and I assumed was a woman. Finally, I felt true emotional intimacy, something I had yearned for without knowing it. I felt alive in Jay's arms the way I had never felt before. I was falling head over heels in the sticky heat of a Georgia summer. Stealing kisses under waterfalls, laughing at 3 a.m. over plates of hash browns, cuddling in blanket forts watching movies, and sleeping intertwined in a tiny hammock under the beautiful southern sky.

Heart finally beats
It flutters It unfolds
It escapes from
Amber

It was my love for Jay that gave me the courage to disclose my identity to the last people in my life to know, my fairly conservative family. Jay stood beside me as I bared myself to people who I knew loved me but didn't know who I truly was yet. Little did I know, this was also Jay's story.

I thought you were gonna give me grandbabies
As if I was suddenly incapable
Your lifestyle
As if what I am is a crime

Jay stood by my side when I went home for Christmas and held me as my soul broke when I was told to stay at a different home for the holiday since my "female" partner would be joining me. I painfully quarreled with the fact that not everyone was going to accept my truth. He was there as I yearned for a destiny that would be so different if my Mom was still around. She would understand.

If you assimilate me
Assume me Define me
Then you will void me
Imprison me like a wasp stuck in
Amber

After the New Year we picked up our things and road-tripped across the country together. From Georgia to Oregon we forged our way in a pick-up truck packed to the brim with boxes, topped off with two little doggies frantically panting and jumping about. The cab was crowded, but it felt empty. Silence permeated the boxes and frantic puppy shuffling like an airborne disease colonizing and killing while it spreads. I knew this silence intimately as we were lovers for years. It felt like the silence that swirled around the room every time my family used to ask me if I had a boyfriend. The silence felt like secrets to me.

Silence
Secrets
Distance
Pain

The silence tore us apart and nearly ended us. Deep down I knew what the silence was. I knew what the secret was. I had suspected Jay's secret, and known it since early October. Sometimes I could feel my body screaming inside as he walked away from conversations. His silence cut through me. *Tell me! TELL me! TELL ME!* I had prepared for the conversation in my head a thousand times. I had scripted what I was going to say. *I love you. YOU. I want to be with you. This changes nothing.*

But all of my planning did not prepare me. You can't be completely prepared for these things. When he told me, I cried. I didn't cry because I was sad. I cried because I felt guilty. Guilty that I was a part of the hurt. I was part of the misgendering. I was a part of it all. I won't pretend or romanticize the next couple of months. It was hard. Really, really hard. No book, no advice, no planning, nothing can prepare you for that whirlwind. But we survived. I stand beside Jay as a lesbian that is more in love with a man than she ever envisioned possible.

Forbidden love
Lesbian woman Straight man
We are daisy rising through cement
Resistance

Here is what I know now. I love Jay. I love the way he crinkles his face in the morning. I love his insistence on sweet tea really being a cup of sugar with a splash of tea for flavor. I love the way he says my name and talks to our dogs like they will talk right back to him. I love that he supports my odd obsession with unicorns. And I deeply love and admire his courage. Jay is the type of person that inspires you to live truth in every facet of your life. He has made me believe that I have not only the ability, but also the responsibility to chase my dreams fearlessly, even if they are misunderstood.

Our relationship evolved after Jay revealed who he truly is to me. Oddly, this dynamic profoundly challenged other people's ideas about my sexual orientation more than my own views about my sexuality. I find that when you sincerely unearth your truth, and fight for your truth, others' ideas about its legitimacy hold little weight. I am a lesbian in a relationship with a man. I am deeply in love with a man. Not just any man, my perfect antithesis: my undoing and redoing.

I want to make this perfectly clear. I am not less of a lesbian because of Jay's gender identity, nor is my partner less of a man because of my sexual orientation. Just like a heterosexual partnership doesn't change a bisexual individual into a straight person, my sexual identity isn't determined by my current relationship or my partner's gender. My sexual identity is *mine;* it is *my* truth. Frankly, no box perfectly fits how I experience my sexuality. However, lesbian is the term that most resonates with who I feel myself to be. This identity does not mean I cannot or am incapable of falling for a man and its legitimacy should not be tethered to this.

Jay has never questioned this. He has never demanded that I identify as straight for other peoples' comfort or to "legitimatize" his gender identity in the minds of people who cannot untangle the web of sexuality and gender weaved by society. He supports my identity and I support his. This acceptance forms the basis of our very queer and beautiful relationship.

How does a relationship between a lesbian woman and a transgender man work? Surprisingly well. We are able to connect in dynamically queer ways (and not just over our *admiration* for women). Jay has the lived experience of being categorized as a woman in society. He knows intimately the challenges and expectations connected to being perceived as a woman. He is able to truthfully empathize every month when my insides feel as if they are being twisted apart and ripped from my body. How many women can say that about their boyfriends and husbands?

Jay was an intimate part of my sexual exploration and I have been fortunate to be a part of his gender exploration. I stood beside Jay as he attempted to pee standing up for the first time in our tiny apartment bathroom. This is a skill he's mastered very well!

Now me, on the other hand—that's an entirely different story. I had a mishap once or twice when I tried to pee while standing. I don't think I will ever forget the night I peed on myself. Laughter rolled through our apartment as I stood in the shower crying out, "I peed on myself, I peed on myself," and Jay attempted to mop up my disappointing but hilarious puddle. We were nearly paralyzed by our ferocious snickering.

Our relationship is a little queer. Sometimes our explorations collide and we are splashing around in a sea of sexuality and gender together. I should feel embarrassed to talk about these things, but in all honesty I'm proud. I am proud to be in a relationship that embraces oddity and continually challenges others' expectations and assumptions, as well as our own. I am proud I peed on myself in front of Jay. Instead of being grossly embarrassing, it was a queer bonding experience for us. I'm proud to be the lesbian partner of a transgender man.

My Dearest Zackariah

Barb Herrera

My Dearest Zackariah,

What an adventure we have been on! From meeting at La Leche League, a breastfeeding support group, to living as man and woman 28 years later.

I didn't know you were a man in that foreign body you were stuck inside. I didn't know you hid your male self from me. Well, you *were* pretty butch. (Wasn't that your nickname as a child?) I loved that about you, and used to say you were just "this" side of being a man. I also loved stone butches, and you closely fit the bill (except you loved me making love to you).

You were pregnant when I met you. I remember thinking, "How the hell did this dyke get pregnant?" Shouldn't that have been a male clue? It was a confusing juxtaposition. Then you breastfed which was more confusing! I didn't know you were thinking, "If I'm stuck with this body, I might as well use it for good." You said you always wanted a child. You did great things for him with those hated breasts of yours. I remember you saying that you wish that you could put them on a shelf and use them when you needed them.

When we split up for a few years, I didn't know what you were doing with your life gender-wise. As it turns out, you continued to live a non-traditional female life working as a mechanic, construction worker, and deputy sheriff. When we reunited you were the same "Sarah" I had always loved.

Remember when we were getting back together and spent that night in the hotel in downtown San Diego and you wore a dildo? How I asked bluntly, "You don't want to be a *man*, do you?" You said "no," but the way I asked you didn't invite disclosure, did it? I'm sorry for that! I wish I had been more understanding and accepting for you to disclose your true identity.

I often wonder what I would have done had you said, "Yes." Would I have continued our reunion? Or would I have ended it? I honestly don't know what I would have done. I like to think I would have been fine with your disclosure, but I can't be sure. Certainly, I wasn't so gracious when it finally came out.

The discussion opened up when we watched a special on Chaz Bono. I don't remember the exact words you used but you told me that you were a man, not a woman. Initially, I was very excited for you! I was happy because you were going to live a more authentic life. At that moment, I didn't think about what it would mean to me; I was just delighted for you.

We even had some great sex in the beginning. Remember that? Then you realized I was getting drunk to have that great sex and you wondered what was up. I recalled how I had to get drunk to have sex with men and the realization smacked me in the head *hard*. I had to face the issue that I was now living with—and having sex with—a man. And I fell apart.

I've identified as a lesbian since I was 18 years old. Even in my heterosexual marriage, I still felt I was lesbian. This new wrinkle threw a wrench in my identity. I didn't know what to do with the information.

As we talked, I accepted the trans part of you, albeit grudgingly. I could not accept that you wanted to cut your breasts off and was most assuredly against you having bottom surgery. In fact, I used the term "mutilating" several times. At first, you said you didn't want bottom surgery because you didn't want to lose your orgasm. (You hadn't done much research at that time.) I was upset about the thought of bottom surgery that I know I told you more than a few times it was a deal-breaker.

When you were going to have your breasts removed, I was very sad. Even if they had always been a nuisance to you, especially when wearing clothes, they had been such an important part of our lives—nursing the babies and having lovely sex. I knew how much you hated them, but to have them cut off? I mourned the inevitability of your breasts being gone.

The last night before your double mastectomy was a tearful time. You were so loving and let me take pictures of your breasts and nuzzle them, saying good-bye. The next day, when I was taken in and shown your breasts as they lay on a tray, I was traumatized by seeing them lifeless and disconnected from the man I loved. I can still see them in my head; I wish I'd never gone back to see them. I never look at those pictures. Blech.

As upset as I was about your breasts, it was nothing compared to the thought of you having bottom surgery. When you started talking about it, I couldn't speak without going into near hysteria and crying. The thought of losing your beautiful vulva and lovely, deep vagina was more than a little distressing. It was definitely the lesbian in me coming out. How scared you must have been to bring this up with me. I'm so sorry for that. I didn't know how to cope. While the mourning period about your breasts was fairly short, my mourning about your vulva has been longer and deeper.

Initially, I didn't understand *why* you wanted a penis and wanted such an odd makeover. At first, you said you couldn't explain it and I told you that you *had* to figure out an explanation for me. It seemed like your mind was obsessed with having a penis. *Why did you want one?*

You told me that every time you peed, you thought about what you didn't have, and that peeing in a public men's restroom without a penis was dangerous. I hadn't thought of that. You always seemed so strong and sure of yourself as a woman who was never afraid of anything. You'd been a deputy sheriff for goodness sake. So hearing you talk about being raped was bizarre and frightening. But then I thought if you were talking about it, it must be real a real fear.

Then I began to understand why you wanted a penis. It wasn't superficial penis envy but a matter of life and death in some circles. I'm still confused sometimes. I've never found penises particularly pretty, but I'll get used to it, again. I mean, it won't be the first time I've had sex with a man with a penis.

Until now, I've thought of myself as a lesbian in a relationship with a man, but then I heard someone advising another lesbian who's in a trans relationship about the way she identified the couple. Sidestepping identity labels altogether, she used simple descriptors like "happy" and "contented" as an alternative way to understand her relationship. I've found this new way of explaining our relationship helpful and now believe I am bisexual. I want to honor your masculinity with my own identification. Some people think there's no reason to identify at all, but it's a serious part of who I am and feels right to me. Bisexual. That's what I am.

You've said you want me to find another woman with whom I could have a relationship. You were glad when I joined up with the bisexual community, hoping I would find a woman to satisfy my lesbian self. But I don't want anyone else. You think I say that now because you still have woman parts and that once they're gone, I will miss them and need someone to fulfill that part of me. I don't think so. Even though we are theoretically polyamorous, I don't want anyone but you.

I don't want anyone but you! Do you hear me?!

I will learn to work with your new penis. I will learn to pleasure you with it. It will be a whole new experience for me, but I'm up for it. I love *you* and want to please *you*.

In the year that's passed since you first brought this up, I am doing better, well over a year after first talking about it. I'm able to hear about the actual surgery, something that's also taken a long time to do. I know you are worried that I will freak out and leave you once you have a penis. While I am sure I will need a period of adjustment, I will not leave you. I promise.

Where is our life going? What will it be like when your transition is complete? You have several surgeries ahead, medical tattooing, and an erectile implant to put in, so the transition is still ongoing. However, what will our life be like when your transition isn't the focus of your world? Since we don't spend lots of time talking about it, I don't think *our* lives will change that much. Sex will be the most different aspect of our lives, but it's nothing we can't work through.

Am I still scared? Yes, somewhat, though it's more about not wanting to disappoint you. I want to make you happy with your new body and new life. You will be the happiest you've ever been and I want to join you in that.

I love you Zack with everything I am and have. This isn't the life I asked for or expected, but it's the life we've both been dealt with and we can handle it. And we can do better than that! We can thrive with joy and love through anything! I know it. As sure as I am alive,

I am with you forever. Don't ever doubt that. You are the love of my life, with penis or not.

Love,
Your Partner

Update: August 2014

Now, you are on the other side of your gender confirmation surgery. You no longer have a vagina, vulva, or clitoris—instead, you have a penis and scrotum. You're still in the first month of healing. I am not having the hard time with your phallus like I thought I would a year ago. We're still many months away from having intercourse, but I look forward to learning about your new appendage, getting to know the "new" you.

I know you are thrilled to have the surgery behind you; I am so glad you're happy. Our lives will be different now, but we will be the same inside and I love that about us. I love you very much. I hope you can feel it even as your body changes. My love for you stays the same and grows as time passes.

A Letter to My Husband

Marci Peters

The Golden Hinoki Cyprus is now over thirty feet tall. Thirty-one years ago, you had planted it as a backdrop for our wedding along with the bright blue lobelia that matched the colors in my wedding dress. Amazingly, a hundred and fifty of our relatives and friends had gathered to witness this event on the three acre farm in Oregon that was part of our personal contract: to maintain our joint values of living a semi-rural lifestyle and continue raising the three sons I brought into the relationship in a healthy environment.

It was a grand party which continued into the wee hours as we escaped for a one-night stay at the Lodge on Mount Hood clearly visible from our house. Your parents were relieved that you had finally found someone to marry and mine were still annoyed I had divorced a guy who seemed to be perfect in every way. I was now coupled with a much younger man who I met at a workplace designed to support adolescent kids having difficulty transitioning into adulthood. Your mother was the only one to live long enough to tell about your other life.

It was only the beginning of my being forced into changing my identity as an educated, white, Anglo-Saxon, cis-gendered woman with the privileges that accompany that status. If you married the "right man" this status was almost as good as the males of that group.

For the first decade of our marriage, we were consumed by the effort to get those boys out into a world where they could find happiness and fulfillment. We had little financial support but were mutually committed to do all we could to support them as they matured. Primarily due to your ability to connect with them and provide the essentials necessary, they are all more than we could have dreamed. My belief was that you would be the great stepfather for them.

As that phase of our relationship changed into one where we began looking at our own future, you left the teaching position you held when we married and transitioned into a full-fledged landscape contractor. I was a school counselor with an investment to maintain an externally "perfect" heterosexual marriage at that point in time. In that decade, I had time to pay attention to some rather odd aspects of our relationship.

You had never been the type who was overtly appreciative of my feminine characteristics. You didn't seem to react positively to new clothes I bought, especially underwear. Any pressure I put on you to be more sexually aggressive caused you to pull further away from me. This enraged me, as I believed you were spurning my femininity. We had many arguments on the subject that created serious tension in our marriage. In order to feel sexually appealing, did I need to end it?

That decade was very difficult for other reasons as well. I found the location of your "closet" and confronted you about all the lovely women's clothing that I had never before seen. After much pressure, you admitted that you loved to dress in them. In fact, you were spending quite a bit of time wearing them around the house, now that the boys were independent.

As an added stressor, my mother was dying of lung cancer. I was forced to leave my job for three months and travel to the opposite side of the country to care for her. During that time, we were still in the process of negotiating whether you really needed to be dressing *en femme*. In reality, you did need to and did it a lot when I wasn't around. By the time I returned, your female identity was out, never to return to the closet again.

About 15 years into our marriage, I did go to a therapist. I brought you in on it. I knew there was something in our relationship that was causing dissonance. I didn't understand the relationship between your wanting to present as a woman and our intimacy issues. The therapist didn't either. After not seeing her for some time and then returning, her first comment was, "Is your husband still hiding his dirty little secret?"

That did it. I knew enough about gender identity to know it wasn't dirty and didn't need to be a secret.

I left her office knowing she had some issues of her own. Finally, we were lucky enough to find a lovely older woman who invited people with gender issues in her home. You went to see her first. When it was my turn, her basic message was that your gender identity had solidified and would unlikely change over time.

Things began to clarify for me. You needed to be out where you could talk with other men who loved to dress as women. You were reluctant to do this alone. I needed to decide if I was going to fight your needs or support them.

It was a gut-wrenching time. My self-concept as a female was crumbling. I wanted to scream, hit, and get rid of this problem. Somehow, over time, I accepted that I didn't want to lose you. We shared too much to just end it all. So I needed to give up my identity as the traditional, all-American wife, and consider other ways of being.

Wait a minute, could I give up being heterosexual?

We are blessed to be living in an area that began embracing its LGBT community over a decade ago. We decided to attend La Femme International, an annual extravaganza produced by the owners of Darcelle XV's Showplace in Portland, Oregon. You wore a fabulous two-piece 1930s' style gown.

At the time, you were still creating a wardrobe mostly purchased at thrift stores with an occasional splendid piece acquired surreptitiously from friends. On the way out, we passed a large woman. We were 15 feet ahead of her when I said to you, "You have got to go back and talk with her. She will know what's available in the area." That was a literal turning point in our lives. We did go back to meet Diana, at that time a two-decade member of the Northwest Gender Alliance (NWGA), who graciously enfolded us into our first experiences with the part of the trans* community generally referred to as "cross dressers."

You became a member of the group, rapidly becoming more "out there," and I was embraced by the wives of several of these men. They were wonderful women who loved their husbands and were willing to accept their husbands' needs. A few did it publicly, but most of them did not. Many members of the NWGA were divorced, their marriages not having survived the shock of disclosure/transitioning.

Over the next several years we dealt with the loss of your father, my father, and your mother. I retired from my full-time job, finding it too stressful to deal with the demands of work, our family losses, and personal changes. When I was gone to deal with these situations, you wanted to be more public about who you are. Imagine my consternation when you decided to appear as Linda at our local political group to enlighten them about your alternative identity while I was away. There it was out in the open for all the folks in our small town to discuss.

I am not sure how I adjusted to that. Perhaps it was the love of our good friends, who either accepted your choice or at least chose to continue to care for us despite the obvious anomaly. I know I have always wanted to be a person who lived honestly and openly in the light. This was part of being honest about who I am.

Before her death, your mother embraced Linda as the daughter she never had. She was a rare woman about whom much more could be written. Because Gay Pride in Portland is always on Father's Day, it became necessary to tell the children, now in their thirties, why we couldn't celebrate Father's Day with them. They loved you and it was no longer possible to keep the information from them.

Risking the loss of our children's love was a very hard step in this becoming public. Each of them reacted differently; one not wanting to know, one embracing the reality, and one knowing but not wanting to deal with it. As their mother, I can only respect each of their decisions. Fortunately, we can still gather as a family without major trauma since Linda doesn't showed up, only their stepdad. The spouses and granddaughters all know that Grandpa likes to dress in women's clothes and the kids, being in their teens, mostly just scratch their heads and wonder how this could be. Not much different than my reaction off and on.

Now that your brother and his wife are in on the "secret," pretty much every one in our personal lives knows about our lifestyle.

It is different with your employees. I can understand that it would not be a good thing at this point to announce or act on your clothing preferences while out doing landscaping. Since you are getting close to retiring and closing the corporation, I suspect things will be different in the future. I do find it sad that you need to compartmentalize that part of your life, and look forward to a future where this kind of duplicity will be unnecessary.

You have definitely decided that you are not interested in changing your male genitalia, and I have been able to make the transition to spending a lot of my public life with Linda. I cannot see myself as lesbian and I know this because one of my dearest friends wanted me to be her partner—an offer which I had to decline. I am heterosexual.

I still cherish the things we do as husband and wife, presenting as male and female. I suppose others who see us together as females wonder what our relationship is like. I guess it's not any different from what everyone wonders about everyone else. And I love that we are closer physically than ever before. I marvel at the realization that I, who was raised for three and a half years by my mother because my father was away at war, really enjoy the delights of female companionship and the joys of male sexuality all in one person.

Your political activities in support of LGBTQ issues are now taking a lot of our time. Granted, many people wonder what I am doing at gay events but nowadays I can fall into the "straight ally" category. I am so happy that marriage equality has become the reality in our state and many others. It was so much fun to celebrate with our friends who have recently wed and will be doing so in the future. What a joy to meet a couple who have been together for 31 years who now get to be legally married just like us.

Our life now demands that we spend more time supporting the youth who are coming into the world that is starting to accept gender variance. Being able to "chaperone" an Alternative Prom was so much fun. The kids were having a great time being who they were.

I've become more aware that I have been gender non-conforming all my life, always pushing the envelope to become successful in traditionally male roles. I finally gave up and became a school counselor after starting as a high school math teacher at the age of 20 and almost becoming an Episcopal priest. I believe what I was looking for spiritually I found with you, a whole human being with whom to share a common commitment to changing our world's inclusivity.

We are entering our "golden years." The times that Linda will be my spouse will probably increase. I am not fighting today like I did for so many years. I am better at saying that I need a male partner for certain things, although I look forward to a future where gender roles are fluid enough that what we happen to be wearing makes no difference to anyone.

Pieces of Us

Jocelyn Ferraro

"To commit to love is fundamentally to commit to a life beyond dualism."
-Bell Hooks, Feminism is for Everybody: Passionate Politics

"This one I shall call Chad! Yes, Chadly The Chin Hair." I declared as I playfully tugged at a stray hair protruding from Mitch's chin. It was late at night and we had both become overtired and silly, holding each other in the lamplight. Exploring his body—locating the intruding hairs sprouting from his chest, face, and shoulders—was a new, exciting habit. I welcomed them in their naming ritual and Mitch would obligingly submit to this process with a smile and a nod. His mustache hairs would be called *Michaels*, shoulder hairs were *Stanleys*, chest hairs were *Charles*.

This was around October, three months into Mitch's transition, and I knew he was becoming impatient with how slow the testosterone was taking. All I could do was make him laugh and document the process with pictures as evidence to prove that, *yes, there have been changes*. Subtle, but they were there.

At the time, Mitch was working at a BBQ restaurant and I was in my senior year of college earning my English degree. I was deep in Russian literature attempting to balance my studies and my relationship—a relationship that needed a lot more of my attention than I had to spare. But I gave so willingly because of my love for Mitch.

When he first told me he was thinking of transitioning, we were lying together in bed, restless and putting off inevitable sleep. It was around December and it was a cold night, so we had to snuggle together and turn up the heated blanket to get cozy. I could tell Mitch was struggling to try to tell me something and it wasn't just the chill that was bothering him.

Through tears he blurted out what had been on his mind for some time now. He wanted to become a man.

We were both scared and daunted; saying it out loud made it all the more real. I selfishly hoped this would be a fleeting desire and that Mitch would change his mind. I was comfortable being in a lesbian relationship. I felt pride in my identity and it took me years to get this far. Walking down the street holding my partner's hand was a special experience for me as a femme lesbian because it instantly outed me and I was suddenly visible to the world. I was terrified at the prospect of losing that.

Four months after Mitch began his social transition, we made a trip to Fenway Health Center for him to get his first shot. It was the 18th of July, making the day significant because it was Mitch's birthday. Sort of a re-birthing. He had the prescription in June but decided to wait and give the moment a symbolic meaning.

I think the time also helped to mentally prepare himself for the shot because he was terrified of needles. His brother and I were there for moral support, holding his hand. The nurse was much better than

I had expected. She was quite friendly, allowing us to be there for him and easing Mitch's nervousness in a way that only a practiced nurse knows how. I guess I had expected to be Mitch's warrior in street clothes, quick to correct every incorrect pronoun or inappropriate comment. To my relief, I did not need to be defensive.

The nurse administered the shot without hesitation and I watched in awe, knowing that this would soon be me. We couldn't afford to come all the way out there and pay a nurse to do this every two weeks, so we would have to do it at home.

The first time I gave Mitch a shot I was so nervous, though I've never told him that. I put on a calm demeanor to prepare the necessary paraphernalia; I laid out the syringe, alcohol wipes, Band-Aid, and the comically tiny bottle labeled "testosterone." I could tell Mitch was a nervous wreck so I'd bought a bottle of Jack to try to calm him down. "Shots and Shots!" He laughed uneasily as he eyed the items on the table.

That first shot was the worst. Every part of you tends to resist the urge to stab a piece of sharp metal into your partner. But I knew he really needed this for his survival. In my mind, the memory went something like the scene from *Pulp Fiction* when John Travolta plunges the adrenaline into Uma Thurman. It was that intense. But it got better from then on; it got easier.

I take comfort in knowing that if the roles had been reversed, Mitch would absolutely bend over backwards to care for me in the same ways. Yet, all this love and attention I was pouring into Mitch left me in great need for my own self-care.

I felt a lot of guilt about wanting my own support for this relationship. I couldn't talk to just anybody because I didn't want to stop and educate someone on trans* issues before I talked about my own. People sometimes just didn't get it even though they had good intentions.

I also had the idea that my needs had to come second while I supported his, even though I knew this could lead to a lot of resentment and frustration. I finally reached out and found my own support group of people who date trans* folks. Talking to them was a huge relief and made me feel less alone. They understand the sting of being pegged as straight by casual acquaintances. They know the invisible work that goes into assisting a partner through transition. I'm now quite close to all of them.

It's so refreshing to have someone in my life that I can talk with about my relationship and who I know will totally get it. I realize how lucky I am to be in a major city with a large network of queers. There are Facebook groups and online discussion boards also for folks who live too far away. I had no idea these resources even existed at first. Connecting to other partners gave me an outlet to express my frustrations in solidarity with other folks, while also celebrating our journeys.

I've been thinking of a way to end this piece for a while now, so I turned to someone who knows about writing: my partner Mitch. He asked me why finding an ending was so difficult and I thought about it. I think to end this would mean that it's time for me to release this from myself, and that's what scares me. I guess I've always thought of this as Mitch's story, his transition, his struggle. Yet I was the one by his side for the whole ride, I went through a huge transition along with him, and I can control my own narrative—at least in this piece.

Mitch's transition changed both of us in positive ways; it brought us together physically and emotionally. He became a more healthy and positive person who is able to achieve his goals now. I came to realize that the label of my former identity was too limiting and I now identify as queer, which is quite empowering in itself.

Right now Mitch is sleeping in the other room and I'm finishing this up along with my wedding vows opened on a separate Internet browser tab. I've realized that life is full of transitions from one state of being to the next and I feel confident knowing that we can do this together as a team.

Worlds Collide

D.

Dear E,

You have changed my life in so many ways. You gave me a different perspective on life that I may have never gotten if I hadn't met you. Where do I start? Where is the beginning of our story?

I suppose it began when I fell in love with you. Me, the straight girl who knew very little personally about oppression and being part of a minority. You, the masculine, amazing, protective person who just happened to be in a female body. We became close friends, and I was very attached to you. I didn't realize I was in love with you until I was head over heels.

The funny thing is, falling in love with you never made me question my sexuality. I was who I was, and the object of my affection didn't change that. However, everyone else seemed to be incredibly confused. "So, you're gay," they'd say. I'd furrow my brow. "No, I don't think so—not that there's anything wrong with that!"

They thought I was in denial. I gave up trying to explain to anyone, but my closest friends. I wanted to be understood, if even by just a few people. In the bigger picture it didn't matter. I just wanted to be with you forever. Like I told you in the beginning: "Even if we end up in a shack on the beach, I don't care, as long as we're together." Love is a beautiful, intoxicating thing.

In 2006 we married at the base of the Eiffel Tower. It was one of the best days of my life. Me in a simple cream dress, you in a tuxedo. Gender identity or expression was not on our radar at that time. We were just *us*. We said, "I do." It rained that day, and you know what they say about rain on your wedding day.

Being in public in Southern California and being seen as a lesbian was an interesting experience for me. You were more reluctant than I to show public displays of affection; perhaps you were more experienced in censoring yourself than I was. I remember every time I said "my partner" to a stranger or a new acquaintance, I could practically see the wheels turning in their head. "Huh," their eyes would say. "I hadn't pegged you for a lesbian." It bothered me only because I was misunderstood, not because I felt being a lesbian was a negative thing to be.

Of course, I didn't explain it to people. It just was something that was.

At the time, I was a therapist just branching out into private practice. In order to market myself, I advertised on Craigslist. One of the first respondents changed my life. He was seeking a therapist for support during his gender transition. I didn't know much about this topic but I was willing to learn the specific duties of a therapist when helping someone who is transgender.

Why this person was "changing" genders was of no question to me; it just made sense. I simply had letters after my name that would make doctors and surgeons listen to me when I told them this was the right choice for him. He already knew this, and because he knew, I knew.

Many of the things he told me made me think of you. Some of the things he said sounded very similar to the things you had told me about your personal experiences. I came home to you one day and said, "Do you think you might be transgender?" The answer was a resounding "NO!" I left it alone. After all, it was *your* gender identity.

I got more into the field of gender work and continued to see an increasing number of transgender clients. In 2007, I went to the Gender Odyssey Conference in Seattle. You came with me, and it was there you had your "Aha!" moment. "This *is* me, this *has been* me, everything makes sense." You told your closest friends and family members and the ball started slowly rolling. I think at that point you knew who you were, you just didn't know quite what you were going to do about it yet.

Proposition 8 came in 2008, and we marched and fought for equality so that all people who loved each other could marry. It was my first experience with discrimination and it's hard to describe the feeling of betrayal knowing my own family would be voting against my civil rights. I am thankful for your family; ever supportive, ever true.

We pursued the path to parenthood as we always knew we would; it was one of the things that brought us together. I became pregnant with our first child in 2009. We had long talks about what name you'd like him to call you. As someone others regarded as "female," we knew most people wouldn't understand if you wanted to be called "Daddy." I assured you I didn't care, they didn't have to understand. If you wanted to be Daddy, that was what our son would call you. You finally landed on "Papi," and so Papi you were.

We were so excited and happily prepared for our little one. We didn't think too much about the structure of our family, how it came to be or about the sperm donor. But it seemed that other people did.

I remember cringing when people would reference us as "two mommies." It simply didn't fit. I was the mommy. It was a role I had always wanted—that I coveted—and it suited me perfectly. You were not a mommy. You and I both knew it; we knew you were the daddy. I'm sure being misunderstood bonded us in some ways we might otherwise not have known. The worst cringes came when someone would reference the sperm donor as "the dad."

Our son joined us and we reveled in our roles as parents. We celebrated Mother's Day for me and Father's Day for you. People close to us were onboard and did the same. Our son adored you and would whisper "P-P-Papi."

Around the time he turned one, your realization and true identity that had remained dormant came to life. You said, "I want to teach my son to be true to himself. How can I do that if I don't do it for myself?" With that, your transition was underway.

You came out (again) to close friends and family. You pursued assistance with medical transition and started testosterone at the end of 2011. You came out to most everyone; I did my share of "coming out" as well and explaining your journey to others.

Of course there was fear that as a gender therapist, people would think I had made it some sort of goal to change you or to convince you to transition. The only way I can best explain it is that the part of me that could overlook gender and fall in love with you is exactly the part that makes me a good gender therapist, but one didn't cause the other.

You had your own fears. As a self-employed person whose business came largely from word-of-mouth referrals, you were worried this transition would negatively affect your income and you wouldn't be able to support our family. You became exhausted with having long conversations about your transition and eventually changed your email signature; a lot of people in your business world found out about your transition that way! The response was better than expected (it almost always is), and you had your most prolific and successful year yet.

During your transition I underwent one of my own, too. I was now able to say "my husband" and reference my child's father, which I hadn't been able to do. I felt a sense of relief, which I have to admit I feel guilty about. In my work there's a bit of a stigma that comes with someone seeking a "heteronormative" lifestyle. All I can say is that it seemed to fit better, like putting on slippers after wearing shoes that are too tight. Really, it was just a matter of feeling understood.

As your hormones were all underway, so were mine: I became pregnant with our second child. We easily transitioned to using "Daddy" and I don't think our son remembers it any other way.

You had top surgery on my birthday when I was hugely pregnant with our daughter. I was scared about helping you up the stairs in the place we were staying alone near the surgery location. Like everything else, it all worked out, and it was better than expected. I never mourned the loss of your previous chest as I have heard other partners do. Your male chest fits you and it's the type of body I am attracted to.

It's been an amazing parallel process to walk with you through your transition as I walk with so many children, teens, and adults through the same. To say I'm immersed in the world of gender is putting it mildly—and I wouldn't have it any other way.

Just this year you marched with me in the Trans* Pride March. I was proud to see you wearing your "Trans* And Proud" button. When we attended the rally with transgender speakers that kicked off Pride, I was practically high on the knowledge that I was surrounded by like-minded people. As they raised the flag and I stared at it against the bright blue sky, I thought: "This is my church. This is my religion." I could burst with my feelings of love for this community, and the feeling that I would forever fight for civil rights.

Now that you have transitioned and we are settled in our busy, full life. I would say the hardest parts are definitely behind us: coming out, changing your name on all your documents, etc. You seem to have achieved a healthy balance in regards to disclosure. You don't tell everyone but you're not worried if anyone knows. If the topic comes up, you've given me carte blanche to tell new friends or neighbors. There's no shame for either of us. We have two happy, healthy kids who adore you. We'll tell them someday when they start asking questions. We'll tell them about your history, your transition, and your journey to be seen as who you truly are. We'll tell them someone gave us a great gift to let us have them, but that they only have one dad. You saved your childhood Christmas ornaments, saying when the kids ask about them you'll say, "Remember? That was from when I was a lady!"

You are one of the most amazing people I've ever met. You've gone through your transition like you do most everything: with passion, persistence, humor, and strength. You've made it your own and I am so proud of you. I am grateful that because of you I am a part of a community that is bigger than me.

Love,
D

My Husband's a Woman Now

Leslie Hilburn Fabian

It's been more than three years since my husband ceased to exist. I lost him not through the usual forms of losing a mate—death or divorce—but through his transition from male to female.[1]

Saying that I lost him is inaccurate, of course, since we've remained together and are nearing our twenty-fourth wedding anniversary; but I no longer have a man. We are happy now, and our combined family of six grown kids and their partners have all accepted the radical change in their father/stepfather.

The past five years have been anything but smooth sailing! It's been more like a rocky, jolting journey through an ocean of uncertainty, pain, distress, and challenge, infused (thank God!) with our great love, support, and appreciation for one another. We are fully committed to our marriage and continue the process of creating a new equilibrium in maintaining our loving relationship.

I now have the happiest mate anyone could hope for, though I assure the reader that I place my own satisfaction in very high regard,

1 I use both male and female pronouns when referring to my spouse, having written about my husband's transition from male to female, David to Deborah, both before and after the transition.

as well. In fact, my concern for maintaining my own happy life impelled me to tell David for a good two and a half years, "I don't know what this transition will mean for us as a couple. I cannot guarantee that I'll stay with you as your wife."

Blessedly, my mate told me for at least a year into transitioning, "I will stop this immediately if it means losing you." While I recognized this as the profound gift that it was, I also realized that halting the process would likely lead to even greater misery than before. I countered that there was no way I'd support him doing that; I was finished being partnered with a miserable man.

Needless to say, this new configuration was not what I'd envisioned for our life together in this second marriage of ours. However, at 65, I've lived long enough and have endured *more* than enough to understand that life rarely conforms to the mold any of us creates for it. Since the transition began in 2009, I've known that I might not remain in our marriage.

Despite this awareness, I encouraged my mate to transition and supported him completely in taking the only steps that would lead to his fulfillment and happiness after six decades of pushing it down. Obviously, this was one of the most challenging and paradoxical experiences of my life.

In the preface of my book, *My Husband's a Woman Now: A Shared Journey of Transition and Love*,[2] I explain my compulsion to share my story:

> When my husband David was in transition to become a woman, I needed a vessel to contain the churning within me. Filling a daily journal page or two, as I'd done for decades, fell short of my overwhelming need to express myself and work through the process. I was the supportive, heterosexual wife of a male transsexual, transitioning to female. I had no guidelines.

2 Leslie Fabian Hilburn, *My Husband's a Woman Now: A Shared Journey of Transition and Love* (Virtual Bookworm, 2014).

I'd begun writing about a year into the transition, knowing how helpful and clarifying this process was for me. My writing continued for three years, providing focus and dedication, as I stumbled and jolted through the turbulence in our lives.

Deborah had been present throughout our twenty-year marriage, but only on a part-time basis. We'd enjoy an evening together *en femme* or go away for a weekend. This had worked for me; I'd gotten my husband back! Finally, after years of observing his devastation upon returning to his very masculine self, I'd realized that my spouse would never feel complete or comfortable or happy as a man. I could no longer watch my beloved suffer.

> Eventually, there was no denying David's transsexuality. He began to verbalize this awareness in 2009, though he lacked the belief that some action might result. However, I'd lived with his pain for two decades. By the fall of that year, I was unwilling to watch him try one more antidepressant, hoping for relief from a near-constant malaise.

As he spoke again of a new therapist and a new drug to alleviate his depression, I surprised us both by suggesting an alternative, which we knew to be an elixir for those who self-identify as transgender. "I just don't think it's another antidepressant you need, Sweetie," I said. "I think it's time to talk to an endocrinologist and investigate female hormones."

Ultimately, we pursued this route together, as we discovered how to proceed with creating the happiness and the "rightness" that David so badly needed. This immense alteration to our lives is chronicled in my book, including a year of my journal entries following Deborah's coming-out. Perhaps the best way to sum-up what occurred leading up to the transition is to include the letter I sent to relatives and friends at that time which is also in my book:

October, 2011

Our Dear Family and Friends,

This letter will come as a shock to many of you, as you have been unaware of the hidden life that David has lived since early childhood. When we met in 1987, David was cross-dressed and temporarily using the name "Deborah." Throughout our twenty-year marriage, David's cross-dressing has been an important and enjoyable part of our lives. We have an amazing community of transgender friends and couples.

Two years ago, it became apparent that cross-dressing was not the limit to David's transgenderism. We both realized that he is transsexual; that he truly feels like and wants to live as a woman. He began taking female hormones in fall 2009, and has since experienced the greatest happiness and satisfaction of his life.

This month Deborah will emerge full-time. The life of David is over; Deborah Rae Fabian, M.D., has taken his place. Though there will be no surgeries at this time, David has assumed the feminine gender role and, hereafter, will be legally known as Deborah (or Debby or Deb). She is currently revealing her new identity to the medical staff and patients.

All of our children have been told of the transition and their reactions vary. Each seems to be finding, or working toward, acceptance of their father/step-father in her new form. One of our greatest concerns is that some of you may drop out of our lives. We are hopeful that this won't happen, as you mean a great deal to us.

Please consider that this choice means the end to six decades of depression and longing in David. It will in no way alter the kindness, brilliance, warmth, and loving nature of this individual. In fact, these qualities are enhanced as Deborah's sadness falls away. We hope that you can be happy for her.

I am, for obvious reasons, having a transition of my own. While I've encouraged David to follow his soul's desires and I fully support this enormous change, I am experiencing a great sadness. The fact is—I am losing my husband. At the same time, I am comforted and supported in my grief by the same dear, incredible individual to whom I've been married for two decades. This is the paradox with which I am dealing.

Once you begin to absorb the meaning of our announcement, many obvious questions will arise. The answer to your first question is: *yes, we are staying together*. The love that we share, the commitment to our marriage and each other, transcend the form that we take. Nevertheless, in my desire to be completely honest with my mate, I have stated that I don't know what will happen with us in the future. We hope that we'll someday be two little old ladies growing old together, but only time will tell.

Of course, it's too soon to know how we, as a couple, will fit into society as our new form is presented to the world. Naturally, we are concerned about the reactions of the medical staff and Deborah's patients, as their rejection of Dr. Fabian's new gender would affect the status of our livelihood. It seems absurd to us that anyone would allow this transition to alter their appreciation of Deborah's surgical skills, but we are not so naïve as to think that there will be no negative responses.

The same concern applies to our family and friends. We love you and hope that your love for us will allow you to accept this situation.

With love and appreciation from us both,

Leslie

Naturally, as with any life altering experience, we learned a great deal throughout this journey. The lessons are enumerated in my book, including their details. For the sake of brevity I simply list them here in the hope that they may be of assistance in your own life.

1. Learning to live with contradiction and the unknown is essential.
2. It is crucial *never* to say "never."
3. The solid foundation in our relationship can help us endure almost anything.
4. A basic personality will remain the same, despite transitioning.
5. Being true to myself means many things.
6. Taking care of myself was, is, and always will be crucial.
7. Vulnerability, though risky, can build connection to others.
8. Feeling happy and optimistic does not negate the need to be practical, realistic, and mindful of the need for alternative plans and options.
9. It's important to notice when my thoughts and opinions are coming from my ego, rather than from my loving heart and a strong sense of self.
10. We must be prepared to take legal action.
11. Holding resentment does not serve me.

To others in my shoes I would say: Please be true to yourself first. As you know, your mate's transition will irrevocably change your life. I encourage you to find your own path to happiness and fulfillment, whether you stay or go. Consider that your partner has lived a lifetime of pain and distress and has finally found the courage to be true to him/herself. I wish you courage, compassion, acceptance, and love.

No Big Deal

Blair Braverman

Dear Quince,

Remember on one of our first dates—we weren't even dating, really—when you invited me to pick up a horse, which your cowboy friend had just driven 500 miles to drop off for you? We were late, as usual. The cowboy was waiting for us at McDonald's. He let the horse out to stretch its legs, and I always pictured it tied to the base of the golden arches, neon in the prairie night.

The horse didn't have a name, maybe because you're skeptical of names. We were at grad school in a small city and we'd driven out of town through rolling cornfields to the farm where the horse lived. You taught me how to ride, though the height made me nervous. Sometimes you'd jog down the road and the horse and I would follow. Bareback—you wouldn't let me use your saddle until I'd first learned to feel the horse's movements through my legs. After a while I started calling the horse "Untitled," which was perfect, you said, for a writer's horse.

Now I remember those moments as when we first fell in love, though I couldn't let myself see that at the time. I was in a crumbling relationship with a man far away and I was determined not to cheat on him. So I made up excuses: You and I were *just friends*, blah, blah, the usual. I was so desperate to keep spending time with you—to allow myself to keep spending time with you—that I used your transness as an excuse: *obviously* we're just friends, because he's trans and I'm straight.

Looking back on that excuse, I can't get mad at myself. I'm embarrassed to write it down, sure—in the three years we've been together, I've sharpened (though not perfected) my understanding of trans* issues, not to mention my own sexuality. Now, the stories I told myself seem so naïve.

So what happened? I broke up with my boyfriend. You and I kept riding Untitled. Soon we rode him together with you sitting politely behind me; soon you sat closer to me with your hands resting on my hips. I don't remember if I was still lying to myself. With your hands on me, it was hard to think at all.

By the time we acknowledged our feelings, they were too strong to ignore. As for my original excuse, well, I didn't know what was in your pants until the day that I took them off and found out. At which point frankly, I could have cared less about the shapes of our bodies. All I wanted was your skin.

I didn't think about becoming a "trans* partner." I thought about becoming *your* partner, and the complexities that come from two people folding their lives together: Should we move to your home in Wisconsin? If we did move, what would we do for work? Where should we go over the holidays? Why *shouldn't* the dog be allowed to sit on the couch with me?

We talked about your gender, but no more than we talked about mine. Once I really thought about it, trans*-ness seemed fairly dull. When I watch those talk shows where trans* people are asked invasive questions, I feel like the joke's on the host. If only they knew what an uninteresting thing they were investigating and how dumb they looked to be so engrossed in it. A woman with a penis! A man with a vagina! Someone who *isn't a man or a woman!* OMG...Yawn.

The first time I mentioned to you how boring trans*-ness seemed to me, I was nervous you'd be offended. You just laughed and said, "Thank God."

What's not boring is the perspective you've developed over the course of your experience, your insight into gender and the ways gender dynamics play out, your forgiveness of well-intentioned mistakes, your comfort with and sense of humor about human bodies, your keen eye for bullshit.

When I *do* think about your body, I feel defensive of it, because it's precious to me and I know it may be misunderstood or sensationalized. But your body isn't mine, and it's not up to me to decide what is and isn't a violation. I try not to defend you when you don't want defending.

It wasn't until recently that I read work by another trans* partner, the wife of a trans* man, and I was surprised by what I read. She wrote of their fears for the man's safety, how every time he's in a public bathroom for more than a few minutes she begins to worry that he's being attacked. That fear had never occurred to me. If you're gone in a bathroom for a long time, I begin to worry that you're constipated.

Maybe that's the privilege of living in a rural community, but even when traveling, I don't worry for your safety. In yet another example of how our relationship, though queer, is pretty damn gender-normative, I figured that if either one of us is ever in danger, you'll be the one to defend us while I run away and call 911. Whether or not this conviction is true, I'm grateful for it.

Of all the things straight cisgender people learn about dating trans* people, the one story we rarely hear is that it's not that hard. Or that it's boring. Or simply: No Big Deal. Maybe because people whose relationships with trans* folks are NBD don't feel a need to tell the story. Either way, most of the narratives I encounter by trans* partners are about being changed.

I've been changed by you but not because you're trans*. Your health struggles for example, have had a much greater impact on our day-to-day lives and have challenged my compassion and my ideas of dis/ability. Your curiosity and contrariness have modeled for me new ways of understanding the world. Your love has supported me through journeys, both geographic and internal, which I might not have completed alone.

Recently we watched a video of Laverne Cox's powerful speech at the 2014 Creating Change conference. We were especially struck by one line: "Loving trans people is a revolutionary act." On a societal level that's true, but true between you and me? We looked at each other and shrugged. My love for you isn't revolutionary. It's inevitable.

Yours,
Blair

Epilogue

HELEN BOYD

I have long awaited a collection like this and I'm pleased to read an anthology that tries to represent many kinds of people and experiences. No book could ever cover all of them, but this one offers a lot of variance of trans relationships. It has a hell of a lot of try.

We cisgender fetishizing crap allies, we I'm-gonna-make-it-all-about-me scene stealers, we trans and non-trans partners of trans people—well wow, are we full of love. We bring an equal amount of try, so much try, even when we fail. We subsume our orientations, possible futures, sometimes our own genders. We drop friends, family, public identities. We do a lot of Trans 101 with strangers and coworkers and friends.

Oh, wow, do we try.

You trans people all know we love you, right?

So many of us take transition or our love for a trans person to re-become ourselves, to make ourselves over into someone we are but wanted to be more of, the lovers we aspire to being—expansive, inclusive, capable, compassionate, smart. We try to kiss your wounds away—the trauma of living in a trans body, when it is that, the surgery scars, the tender nipples of second puberty.

We name your goddamn hairs.

We suck clits like penises and lick penises like clits—love them before, during, and after the changes hormones bring. We don't touch breasts or find the right bras for new ones; try not to notice erections even if we love them, rub our faces against shaved legs once the facial stubble has been lasered away.

We are all Chryssie Hynde. We use our arms, legs, style, sidestep, fingers, imagination, to love you, but heavy on sidestep and imagination.

We love your budding nipples and your bilateral mastectomy scars. We love your reports about how different your skin feels/desire is/orgasm happens. We try to sympathize with the pain of binding and the weird, burnt popcorn smell of laser hair removal. We want to know if the hormones are bringing the results you want, if the acne is making you nuts, if actually having thighs makes your skinny jeans fit better or worse. We help you shop as sizes change, shapes change, confidence changes.

We are also sometimes tired of not knowing which parts are okay to touch, to love, to kiss, to fuck. We want to caress you gently without making you feel less like a man; we want your long, strong fingers inside us but won't ask you to cut your nails because we know that manicure is a visual reminder of your femininity.

We try, we hug, we scream. We do whatever contortions are necessary to deal with your insistent or absent libido.

And we do it all in a wilderness with little support from our own closest friends. Sometimes, when I speak to partners, I remind them that *we are out there* and we may not have an academic professor to find us all, but we exist. We are raising children and packing lunches and going back to school ourselves and sighing at our in-laws or at Oprah getting it wrong again. We are sex blogging and arguing with doctors and following the arguments about Proposition 8 and DSM V.

No wonder some of us forget who we are, forget our self-care; no wonder we occasionally rant and sob and grow some giant-size anger.

Where we find ourselves is often between that infamous rock and hard place: if our partner's transition makes us look like half a lesbian or gay couple, we have to deal with homophobia; but if our partner's transition makes us look like half of a straight couple, we often lose the support of the lesbian or gay community we've belonged to and found safety in for many years of our lives.

Because we transition into trans partners, no one really knows anything about us. We don't become lesbians when our wives become women, and we don't become straight when our guys become men. That joke, as Morrissey so famous quipped, isn't funny anymore. We end up in a place where we have our own histories, our own orientations, hidden from public view, especially if our trans love isn't out as trans. Some of us opt to identify as bisexual to explain, perhaps, why we're married to women while nursing a crush on Mark Ruffalo. I swear my taste in men got bigger and hairier as my partner transitioned. We find stories to explain why we're lesbians and why we're sad about Leslie Feinberg's death—or why, indeed, we even know who Leslie Feinberg was. In straight and gay communities, an awful lot of people think you're only ever one or other; we have some common ground with bisexual people in that we're largely invisible and must, must, be repressed/oversexed/self-hating/whatever crappy things people think about bisexual people these days. Yet some of us don't like *bisexual* because it's binary. So a lot of us, you'll find, wind up under the big bad queer umbrella, so we don't have to explain a lifetime of dating women but being married to a man; we don't have to explain becoming non-monogamous because we miss certain kinds of sex or desires or even ways of being desired. We don't want to feel like jerks for missing the bodies or parts or sex acts that we love. But we also don't want to be judged for loving your trans bodies because they're trans.

We are always standing on the edge of the forest, machetes in hand, hacking our own paths.

We can't complain to people we know because we know so many of those around us want us to fail or cry or be pathetic and pitiable or even to condemn the trans. If you give in a little, if you complain about the transition to a good friend, then all of a sudden the whole reason you're unhappy is because your partner is trans. That happens with therapists, too, way too often.

In trans community, when we're allowed to partake, the complaining we do or the gentle mocking or the loving critiques or not so loving critiques—*please stop dressing like a 19 year old, dear, because you're 35*—are often viewed as transphobic. If we are not on board and behind every single decision the trans person makes, we're out. Suspect. If we ask the trans person to slow down so we can catch our breath or save up some money or come out to someone else who needs to know, we are, again, judged unwilling or transphobic. We can't refer to our former boyfriend as a boyfriend even though he was because she is our girlfriend now and has only ever been so and don't you forget it, and that's even when your own trans person is perfectly okay with hearing you talk about what a cute guy/hot butch you once were. We don't seek to offend but we do need room to deal with transition our own way. We're going to screw up pronouns and new names and you know what? So do trans people, sometimes. Our intentions matter.

Despite feeling like outsiders in so many other communities we once belonged in, we often feel liminal even within trans community. We know that. We own our cisgender privilege, if we are cis. We know more than anyone else what it means to have it.

And that's when we're even allowed in. So many lesbian women and their trans guys get shut out of queer women's events; so many straight women and their trans female partners are never let in. Gay men flirt with my wife as if she's a guy in a dress, and sometimes straight women do, too. Queer women fetishize trans guys as if they're prizes and yet refer to our trans husbands with female pronouns when they're not around. We end up defending your gender identities and yet all the while try not to speak for you.

We need more support from the trans community, and we need for the rest of the LGBTQ+ community to realize we're here and we're queer and get used to it, already. Sometimes we look straight but we're not. Sometimes we are straight and don't know how to do this. Sometimes we need someone to say, "Hey, you look nice," and sometimes we need people to understand that transition is like some crazy combination of marriage (name change), medical crisis (hormones, surgery) and divorce (social ostracism, pity). It's a lot to deal with at once, and often, when the trans person is busy dealing with all of the emotions and fears and new discoveries, we are picking up an awful lot of slack emotionally and even just logistically. But you get to be brave and living your own truth, or whatever condescending stuff it is that non trans people say about transition these days. You are noble, and suffering, while we're often assumed to be codependent or desperate.

We get asked all the offensive, obnoxious questions they know not to ask you by now.

And we worry. So many of us are women and so many of us are feminists and so many of us know exactly what sexism and discrimination and threats of violence feel like, and despite knowing that you love to flirt/don't flirt/don't like men/kinda do like men, we want you to be safe and to come home without anyone having done anything mean or for anyone to have said anything stupid.

But we know better. And because we're in love with you, we know sometimes how long it takes for you to realize some micro-aggression that happened last week is really what's been troubling you.

So we just keep trying to love you, to let you know we know, to let you know we're angry, too, and sad and frustrated at how slow the world is to know transness exists and to take it seriously and to stop making you feel humored as if your gender is a delusion.

But we know you love us, too. You love us for and despite our own traumas, medical crises, possible futures, and difficult paths. You love us despite the crying and the screaming and the digging in of heels. You wait. You, too, are full of try for us. You try to keep us with you, and many, many, too many of you nearly break when you have to let us go when the going gets too rough. You know what trans is; you know what we're in store for when we don't, yet. And you try to shield us from our own insecurities and fears. You try to make us laugh, hold our hands, tell us you know, god do you know, how hard it is.

My own wife was just deciding to transition when I was at a concert in Connecticut. So when Rufus started to sing, "You walk alone in the valley of life, In the shadow of love, Under the trees of happiness…" I could feel my eyes fill. He went on: "You walk alone like a baby unborn, Like a father unknown, Like a pocket penniless…" so that by the time he got to

Does anybody know how scary
This is for you and is for me
Does anybody know?

I was weeping sheets of tears, just standing there, in this tiny, enthusiastic, stunning little group of fans, not knowing really where I was anymore.

All I can do, he says, *is write a song for you.*

So here are our songs, for you, the Natashas and Bettys and Mitches and Michaels. Nobody knows but us, really, how scary it can be.

It is less scary because of love. May Blair Braverman's reality become our own futures; maybe she's right that loving a trans person isn't revolutionary, maybe, instead, just maybe, love is always, or can always be, a revolution for the person expressing it and the one receiving it, and that has nothing whatsoever to do with the trans. Maybe that's just love.

Mostly we'd all just like a little more credit for the help we do give, forgiveness for the ways we screw up, and recognition that we're here and love you and are often dealing with a whole lot of the same stigma that you are. We want to be part of your story because we are part of your story, but we also have our own stories that need to be told.

In the meantime, we could use more chocolate.

Contributor Bios

Ann Bloomfield is a native of northwest Ohio and resides in Tempe, Arizona with her wife and two sons. She has a master's degree in business administration and is currently working on a master's degree in counseling to work with adolescents and young adults.

Blair Braverman is a nonfiction writer currently based in northern Wisconsin. Her journalism and essays have appeared in *Orion*, *The Best Women's Travel Writing*, *Waging Nonviolence*, and elsewhere. Her awards include an Iowa Arts Fellowship and a residency fellowship at Blue Mountain Center. When she's not racing sled dogs, she's working on a book about the Norwegian Arctic, forthcoming from Ecco/HarperCollins (2015).

Michelle Bressette is a 47-year-old queer, cis-gendered woman and liberation theologian with an Bachelor of Arts from the University of North Carolina, Chapel Hill. Currently, she is pursuing a Master of Arts in Pastoral and Spiritual Care at Iliff School of Theology in Denver, Colorado with a focus on social justice. She works in hospice and specializes in yoga instruction, Thai massage therapy, and is a patient navigator. She loves to play outdoors in all seasons, particularly with her partner of two years and their 14-year-old son.

Andrea Briechle lives in Germany, where she grew up in a middle class, liberal Catholic, academic family. She decided to fly out to study

Medieval History and to find a place to build her own nest. Recently, at the age of 33, Andrea fell in love with a non-binary trans* person shortly before their process of "transition" started to became a serious matter.

Elspeth H. Brown is a white, middle-aged, queer, non-trans historian who lives in Toronto, Canada with her partner and son. She teaches history at the University of Toronto.

Kathe Burkhart is an interdisciplinary artist and writer. Her visual art has been widely exhibited nationally and internationally. She is the author of four books of fiction: *Dudes* (Participant Press, 2014), *Between the Lines* (Hachette, Litteratures, 2006), *Deux Poids, Deux Mesures (The Double Standard)* (Hachette Litteratures, Paris, 2002; Participant Press, 2005), and *From Under the 8 Ball* (LINE, 1985). Her work appears in the anthologies *Wreckage of Reason 2* (Spuyten Duyvil Press, 2014), *The Unbearables Big Book of Sex* (Autonomedia, 2011), and a forthcoming collection on new narrative writing from Nightboat Books (2016). Periodical publications include *Esopus*, *Women and Performance*, *Cultural Politics*, *Purple Fiction*, *FlashArt*, *High Performance*, *Red Tape*, *Brooklyn Review*, *Mirage Periodical* and *East Village Eye* among others.

Melissa Contreras is a patron of the arts, United States Marine Corps veteran, aneurysm survivor, connoisseur of kitsch, amateur aerialist, and Hoosier transplant to San Francisco.

Loree Cook-Daniels is currently in her 50s and resides in Milwaukee, Wisconsin with her partn er michael munson, where they jointly staff the trans*/SOFFA organization FORGE. She has two pieces in this book, one to each of her life-partners. The first ("Body Parts") was written when her partner Marcelle Cook-Daniels transitioned female-to-male in 1994, and describes her awakening to her own gender stereotyping and prejudices. This essay represents one of the key steps that led her to becoming a transgender advocate. The second piece, "Creating," celebrates the life she and michael have built together since Marcelle's 2000 suicide. Loree has bachelor degrees in women studies and history, a Master's in Conflict Management, and a Certificate in Trauma Counseling. The son they all helped raise, Kai Cook-Daniels, is now living on his own.

Amber Jean Coyne is working on a Masters of Public Health focusing on LGBTQ+ health equity with a minor in queer studies. She received her Bachelor of Science in Molecular Cell Biology from Sonoma State University in 2012 graduating *summa cum laude*. Amber is a writer and theater enthusiast, performing in such plays as *The Vagina Monologues* and *The Glass Menagerie*. She is previously published in *Language, Violence & Resistance* (2014) by The Alter Collective and Queer Studies at Oregon State University.

Konnor T. Crewe is a 50-year-old trans* man who resides in the greater Boston, Massachusetts area. He has a Bachelor of Arts in Linguistics from Southern Illinois University at Carbondale, and is the editor of *Late Transition: Older Trans Men Speak Out*, forthcoming from Transgress Press (2016). Konnor met his long-term partner online.

Diane Daniel is a longtime editor and writer for newspapers and magazines. She lives in Veldhoven, the Netherlands.

Briyana Davis is a Brooklyn-based twenty-something focusing her energy on loving her communities through the arts, education, and organizing. A performer and writer since she was a little black girl living in south Jersey, she is passionate about musical theatre, mangoes, and memoirs. Briyana holds a Bachelor of Arts in Sociology from Princeton University, where she researched LGBTQ activism in Brazil and the Slutwalk Movement. You can read of her words on Twitter and Tumblr @black and bendy.

Kaylin De is a native of Houston, Texas where she fondly grew up. At the age of 21, she relocated to the East Coast in an effort to spend more time with her extended family. Being raised by northern parents in the South, she believes she's from the best of both worlds. Her career path includes working as a special education teacher and writing coach in Pennsylvania. She has earned degrees in liberal arts and secondary education from Temple University

Vanessa Espino is a 29-year-old playwright and theatre collaborator living with her boyfriend in Santa Clarita, California. She received her undergraduate degree from California State University at Fullerton with an emphasis in Playwright and the Theatre Arts. She was a KCACTF Regional finalist in 2012 for her original play *Odilia* and has had original works produced in Orange County since 2011. She is also the author of *Butterfly Truth*, a blog on Tumblr chronicling her current relationship.

Leslie Hilburn Fabian is an author and licensed independent clinical social worker in Massachusetts, though she's recently moved with her spouse to Louisiana. She holds a master's degree from Boston College and continues to write, volunteer, and travel extensively. Her book, *My Husband's a Woman Now: A Shared Journey of Transition and Love*, chronicles her early life with David, the two years leading up to transition, and the first year following Deborah's coming-out. Visit Leslie at *www.lesliefab.com*.

Jocelyn Ferraro lives in Somerville, Massachusetts with her husband Mitch Kellaway. She works at an elementary school and enjoys teaching young children. This is her first published piece of writing.

Angela Gail is a 43-year-old white, cis-gender woman. She identifies both as queer and bisexual. Angela lives in the Boston area, is married and has two children, and her family is Jewish. She has been a professor of mathematics for 10 years. Angela also volunteers with Girls Rock Campaign Boston in their summer camp and other programs. She writes a blog with her husband at http://firsttimesecondtime.com.

Bella Giovio is a 49-year-old straight woman living in northern New Jersey where she works part-time with special needs children and runs her own online vintage clothing store. She resides with Dez, her husband and stepfather to her two daughters. Dez is also a crossdresser in private, which only a handful of people know (she refers to him and herself here with pseudonyms).

Leah Goldberg is a 28-year-old Jewish queer female. She is from Massachusetts and in a monogamous relationship. Leah contributed to this anthology because she thinks it's important to see yourself reflected in the world, but reflections of your own experience are not always easy to find. The more we share our stories, the easier it will be for all of us.

Jaime M. Grant is a lesbian feminist writer/activist, high femme dyke, sex activist, (clean and sober) mother of two living in Washington, D.C. in a multigenerational, multiracial queer village of gender outlaws and thinker/activists. Dr. Grant founded the Global Trans Research and Advocacy Project in 2012, spearheaded and founded a queer feminist addiction recovery group in the nineties, and served as principal investigator for the National Gay and Lesbian Task Force's reports on aging, Outing Age 2010, and transgender discrimination, *Injustice at Every Turn* (2011). Grant's writings appear in Leslea Newman's *The Femme Mystique* and Rachel Epstein's *Who's Your Daddy?* Her most recent work on white anti-racist activism, *Emptying the White Knapsack*, was published by the Praxis Center.

Miriam Hall is a 37-year-old cis-gender female born in Appleton, Wisconsin and currently lives in Madison. She is married and a contemplative arts teacher. She thinks letters reveal intimacies and depth of knowing one another that don't come across in essays. The more she writes about her marriage, the more she discovers and understand, and she realizes how much more there is to learn.

Laura Harrington is a Euro-American southern Femme who lives in Seattle, Washington with strong Kentucky roots. She is married with two children and one grandchild. Laura has a master degree in public administration and has worked with the University of Washington for eight years.

Barbara Herrera is a Hispanic Anglo licensed midwife who lives in San Diego, California with her partner, four kids and two grandbabies.

Jessica Lynn Johnson is a white cis-gender female originally from St. Louis, Missouri but now lives in Los Angeles, California. She has a Bachelor of Fine Arts in Theatre Performance and has been an actor in television, film, and stage for a decade. Being a straight, cis-gender, Christian woman who fell in love with a transgender man not once, but twice, is a story she needs to tell.

Georgia Kolias is a Greek American femme lesbian writer who seeks to cultivate the intersections of food, fertility, and culture through the written word. She is currently shopping her novel *The Feasting Virgin*, featuring a quirky Greek American foodie who struggles to reconcile her religious beliefs with her emerging sexuality. She holds a Master of Fine Arts and Master of Arts in Creative Writing from San Francisco State University and blogs for the *Huffington Post*. Her work has also appeared in the *Advocate.com*, *The Manifest-Station*, *Role Reboot*, and *When*

Women Waken. Her interview series, *Fotini: Illuminating the Greek LGBTQ Community*, can be found on her blog. She lives with Willy Wilkinson, her partner of 20 years, and their three children in Oakland, California. You can find her at www.georgiakolias.com, Twitter (@georgiakolias), and Facebook.

Shanna Katz Kattari is a 28-year-old partnered white agnostic Jewish queer cisgender disabled English-speaking fat Femme. She was born and raised in the lovely state of Colorado and she traveled and lived throughout the U.S. and Germany while working as a board certified sexologist, sexuality educator, and author. Shanna has a bachelor degree in sociology and a master's degree in human sexuality education. She enjoys combining the discussions of identity along with sexuality. Currently, Shanna lives in Denver with her partner and three cats where she is working on a doctorate in social work and focusing on power, privilege, and oppression for LGBTQIA people and people with disabilities.

Lacey Losh is a 30-year-old married cisgender female from Lincoln, Nebraska. She currently works at the University of Nebraska-Lincoln in the Print and Copy Services Department. She is also a volunteer community organizer with Common Root Mutual Aid Center.

K. Ann MacNeil comes from tenements, roller skates that fit over sneakers, and sauce simmering on Sundays. She is an old-school, queer femme with a soft spot for pretty butches, grown tomboys, and genderqueer FTM's. She has taught at a public school for grades 6-12 in Washington Heights for 21 years with their first dual language (Spanish/English) kindergarten opened in fall 2014.

Tasha Martin is a Sicilian who lives in northern Connecticut. Tasha has been a professional editor for over 15 years.

Jennifer Miracle is a trainer and professional speaker with a vast background in student affairs. She is an alumna of Central Michigan University with bachelor degree in recreation, parks and leisure and master's degree in educational leadership. Jennifer landed her dream job as the Director of the Lesbian, Gay, Bisexual, and Transgender Resource Center at the University of Georgia, Athens (UGA) in 2008. While at UGA, she was reconnected with her soul mate, Ethan, whom she married October 4, 2014. Jennifer and Ethan reside in the Detroit area with their three cats—Sassy, Lilly, and Kitten.

L. Daniel Mouer, Ph. D. is a retired professor of anthropology, a photographer, printmaker, writer, and winemaker. Dan and his partner, Rob, enjoy their life together in Virginia surrounded by family, including two teen granddaughters, their sweet pooch Bubba and equine pals, Tinker and Gunsmoke. Dan is active in various online support groups for transgender folks and their significant others, and his creative works can be found on Flickr, Tumblr, Facebook, and Blogger.

Connie North is a 38-year-old, white, queer, cisgender woman who lives in Madison, Wisconsin with her partner and their three cats. Connie is a recovering academic currently working as an individual and relational psychotherapist. She is also an insight meditation community member, and her hobbies include writing, biking, and hiking.

Shawnee Parens has been living in Madison, Wisconsin for the last 20 years. She is married with two sons who are hurtling into young adulthood.

Marci Peters was born in Syracuse, New York and comes from a working class background. She currently lives in Oregon where she is married with three grown sons and three granddaughters. Marci is retired from working as a school teacher and counselor.

Dr. Mignonne Pollard owns M. Pollard & Associates, a company that consults with nonprofit organizations on issues of volunteer management and facilitating diversity. She facilitates workshops that address several areas: developing intercultural competence, gender equity, cross-cultural communication, creating multicultural curricula, and supporting bilingual learners. Currently, she works with foster care parents and youth on issues that involve LGBTQI youth. She holds a Doctorate of Education from Harvard University Graduate School of Education, a Master's degree in Urban Affairs and Policy Analysis from New School University and a Bachelor of Arts in Spanish/Latin American Studies from Flagler College.

Marcelle Richards is 31 years old and has a Korean, French, and mixed European ancestry. She identifies as genderfluid and lives in Madison, Wisconsin. Her career path has included journalism and shamanic healing.

Justin Ropella is a 31-year-old cis-gender white male who now identifies as queer. He has a Bachelor of Arts in English from Metropolitan State University in St. Paul, Minnesota and is currently a blogger at the *Huffington Post* and *The Good Men Project.*

S.J. Sindu is a 27-year-old Sri Lankan Tamil, Hindu raised atheist writer who focuses on traditionally silenced voices—the immigrant, the poor, the queer, the female-bodied, the non-Christian and people of color. Sindu is a doctoral student at Florida State University and has published in *Brevity*, *Water~Stone Review*, *Harpur Palate*, *The MacGuffin*, *Sinister Wisdom*, and elsewhere. Sindu identifies as queer and genderqueer and prefers gender neutral pronouns. They live a single writer life in Florida with their cat. Find out more at: www.sjsindu.com.

Sofia Rose Smith is a mixed race, queer, femme of color poet from Los Angeles. She has worked intimately in queer and trans communities of color as a counselor, organizer and healer. She is 30 years old and marrying her love this summer. See more of Sofia's work at: sofiarosesmith.com.

D. is a licensed psychotherapist living in Southern California. She is married with two awesome children.

Anne Totero is a 26-year-old white, Italian-American from Madison, Wisconsin. She has a Master of Science in Marriage and Family Therapy. Currently, she works as a crisis worker at Dane County Crisis Unit during the day and an outpatient psychotherapist in the evenings. Anne is in a long-term committed partnership.

Audrey Silver, 33, enjoys spending her time with her beautiful wife and three spirited tiny dogs. Being from Upper Michigan originally, she now calls Minnesota home. She is grateful every day for the chance to love and be loved, and while to some her family may seem unusual, she never sees it as anything but perfect.

K Le Vie is a queer, genderqueer writer, and gender villain who chooses Pittsburgh, Pennsylvania as hir home. Ze is an active founding member of the gender performance troupe, Hot Metal Hardware, where ze experiments with drag and burlesque. During the day, ze is a speech language pathologist working in special education. Ze is a member of a broad and supportive family of origin and choice. K sees gender as a playground and likes the swing set best.

Amanda W. lives with her best friend and partner of eight years, Gina. They enjoy traveling, camping, and working in the entertainment field. Their next adventure is their wedding in summer 2015.

Moe Wendt identifies as a trans* man. He was born in 1952 in Los Angeles, grew up in a white, middle class suburb of Sacramento, California. He lived for 25 years in Sonoma County, California where he founded and operated an independent bookstore. He is proud of having birthed, nursed, and nurtured four wonderful human beings. He has been married for 25 years to Chelsea Rose Wendt who began her transition male to female three years before his own. Moe now lives on Salt Spring Island, British Columbia where he is developing an 11 acre permaculture farm with his youngest son.

Jeffrey Zweig, II is a 28-year-old male, freelance filmmaker, and professional truck driver from Austin, Texas. He has a Bachelor of Science in Radio/TV/Film from Indiana State University.

Appendix

Additional resources

BOOKS

Anderson-Minshall, Diane and Jacob. *Queerly Beloved: A Love Story Across Genders*. Valley Falls, NY: Bold Strokes Books, 2014.

Boyd, Helen. *She's Not the Man I Married: My Life with a Transgender Husband*. Emeryville, California: Seal Press, 2007.

_____. *My Husband Betty: Love, Sex, and Life with a Crossdresser*. Berkeley, California: Seal Press, 2003.

Boylan, Jennifer Finney. *Stuck in the Middle With You: A Memoir of Parenting in Three Genders*. New York: Broadway Books, 2013.

_____. *She's Not There: A Life in Two Genders*. New York: Broadway Books, 2003 (2013).

Fabian, Leslie Hilburn. *My Husband's a Woman Now: A Shared Journey of Transition and Love*. College Station, Texas: Virtual Bookworm, 2014.

Diamond, Morty, ed. *Trans/Love: Radical Sex, Love & Relationships Beyond the Binary*. San Francisco: Manic D Press, 2011.

Online Sources

en|Gender – Helen Boyd
http://www.myhusbandbetty.com

Gender Odyssey
http://www.genderodyssey.org/

GLAAD 's Tips for Allies of Transgender People
http://www.glaad.org/transgender/allies

Heartland Trans* Wellness Group: Significant Others, Family, Friends, and Allies Resources
http://transwellness.org/resources/support-and-community-resources/soffa/

HRC Resources for People With Transgender Family Members
http://www.hrc.org/resources/entry/resources-for-people-with-transgender-family-members

Kinsey Institute: Trans* 101 For Significant Others, Partners, Friends, Family and Allies (SOPFFA) of Trans* People
http://www.kinseyinstitute.org/resources/pdf/Trans101forSOFFAs_v4.pdf

PFLAG: Welcoming Our Transgender Family and Friends
http://community.pflag.org/Document.Doc?id=202

Philadelphia Trans-Health Conference
http://www.trans-health.org/

Resources for Partners of Trans* People
http://journeyintomanhood.tumblr.com/post/54801294358/resources-for-partners-of-trans-people

Transgender Law Center
http://transgenderlawcenter.org

Trans Ohio - Partners & SOFFA
http://www.transohio.org/wordpress/?page_id=456

Trans Partner Network
http://www.transpartnernetwork.com

TransPartners Project
http://www.elspethbrown.org/page/transpartners-project

Trans People of Color Coalition (TPOCC)
http://www.transpoc.org

Acknowledgements

This anthology began with the vision of Laura and Joe (read Laura's piece, "Personal is Political" in this collection) who saw the important need for a book honoring the voices and journeys of the partners, spouses, and significant others of trans people. Their efforts to collect partners' stories many years ago laid the early foundation for this project. We are grateful for their efforts and support in bringing this book to fruition.

We would also like to thank Mitch Kellaway of Transgress Press for his devotion and guidance in bringing this project to fruition. His contributions were invaluable.

Previously Published

Diane Daniel, "Goodbye Husband, Hello Wife." *Boston Globe*. August 9, 2011.

Georgia Kolias, "Accepting My Partner's Gender Transformation." *Advocate*.com. July 18, 2014.

Isabella Abrahams, "A Femme's Chrysalis." Edited by Trystan T. Cotten, *Hung Jury: Testimonies of Genital Surgery by Transsexual Men*. Oakland, CA: Transgress Press, 2012.

Justin Ropella, "How My Partner's Transition Gave Me Schlubby Ape-Man Complex." *Huffington Post: Gay Voices*. April 15, 2014.

L. Dan Mouer, Ph. D., "I'm Glad My Husband Is Gay!" *War Baby: Talking About My Generation*. Create Space, 2011.

Leslie Hilburn Fabian, "David Is No More—Deborah Has Taken His Place." *My Husband's a Woman Now: A Shared Journey of Transition and Love*. College Station, Texas: Virtual Bookworm, 2014.

Previously Published

Paula James, "Out of the Shadows." Edited by Trystan T. Cotten, *Hung Jury: Testimonies of Genital Surgery by Transsexual Men*. Oakland, CA: Transgress Press 2012.

About The Editors

Jordon Johnson, M.A., M.S.W., is a doctoral candidate in the Department of American Studies at the University of New Mexico. His dissertation focuses on the Transgender Movement in New Mexico with an emphasis on dominant narrative, ruralism, and organizational development.

Becky Garrison is a 2012 recipient of the Knight Grant for Reporting on Religion and American Public Life for her coverage of trans clergy. For more information about Garrison's work, log on to: *www.beckygarrison.com*.

About Transgress Press

Transgress Press is an Oakland based indie publisher focusing on trans, queer and feminist writing that pushes the boundaries of conventional ideas. Founded by trans scholar and activist, Trystan Theosophus Cotten, Transgress mixes art and social entrepreneurialism with a passion for social justice to create a powerful mouthpiece of social change for marginalized voices.

Made in the USA
Middletown, DE
21 July 2015